OUTSIDE THE BOX

A Statistical Journey through the History of Football

DUNCAN ALEXANDER

CENTURY

1 3 5 7 9 10 8 6 4 2

Century
20 Vauxhall Bridge Road
London SW1V 2SA

Century is part of the Penguin Random House group of companies
whose addresses can be found at global.penguinrandomhouse.com.

First published in Great Britain by Century in 2017

www.penguin.co.uk

A CIP catalogue record for this book is available from the British Library.

ISBN 9781780895611

Typeset in 12/14.75 pt Dante MT Std by Jouve (UK), Milton Keynes
Printed and bound in Great Britain by Clays Ltd, St Ives Plc

Penguin Random House is committed to a sustainable
future for our business, our readers and our planet. This book is
made from Forest Stewardship Council® certified paper.

To Big H and John

Contents

Contents

Introduction

When the Premier League launched* in August 1992 no one was thinking of the 1966 World Cup. If you'd mentioned England in August 1992 most people would have had sudden, upsetting memories of Graham Taylor's team and their performance at the Euros earlier in the summer when it had quickly become apparent that Keith Curle and Andy Sinton were not the new Bobby Moore and Alan Ball.

You might ask: what is the significance of all this thrilling but diverting Euro '92 chat? Well, August 1992 was 26 years after England's first and possibly only tournament win. We are now 25 years on from 1992, so images of Brian Deane and Alan Shearer and Preki are almost as old to everyone in Brexit Britain as Geoff Hurst and Jack Charlton were in the world of John Major's cones hotline.

Essentially, a lot of time has passed since the Premier League came into being and yet in many ways it doesn't seem that way. Created as a sort of hermetically sealed entity, albeit one that sanctioned relegation of its members to the Football League, the Premier League has now enjoyed 25 seasons of thrills, excitement and, naturally, a certain amount of tedium

---

* The first goal of the Premier League came from a long throw, so launch feels like the correct terminology here.

in what generally seems like an ever-developing rollercoaster of sports content.

'The Premier League era' is a phrase that enrages many football supporters, as they infer that this means everything that happened before 1992 is worthless preamble, when it clearly isn't. Towards the end of 2016–17, Cristiano Ronaldo homed in on another record, this time Jimmy Greaves's total of 366 league goals in the top European leagues. For 1992-deniers, this was a huge blow because it showed that, where data is available and relevant, people have precisely no qualms about referring to a (wonderful) goalscorer from a different era.

Nevertheless, there is beauty in neatness, and 25 years of the Premier League is an apt point at which to pause and examine the quarter-century history of the competition. 1992 was a watershed year in the game, with the introduction of the back-pass rule shaping the modern game more significantly than any new league or organisation ever could. Not even Pep Guardiola would bother looking for goalkeepers with exceptional footballing (in the literal sense) ability if the last line of defence could still just pick the ball up.

If you work with numbers then you're naturally going to gravitate towards competitions and eras for which the most data exists, and 1992 onwards is, like it or not, that point in English league football. It's not an easy process either. For instance, the only reason that there now exists assists data for every player in Premier League history is because, a few years ago, a devout colleague of mine hunted down and ordered VHS end-of-season reviews for every top-flight club between 1992 and 1999 and filled in the gaps. Every single Swindon Town defeat, every terrible 1–0 Oldham win, all were dutifully added, later becoming part of the public discourse, as they should. When Cesc Fàbregas reached 100 assists in the Premier League in 2016–17, it could only be wholly appreciated because of that meticulous work watching all those grainy club videos with their relentless and terrible guitar solo interludes.

Ultimately, football is nothing without history and the blessed context it provides, and in *Outside the Box* I have tried to weave my way through different parts of the game's story, using numbers as the main but never the only ingredient. One fan's stat is another fan's fact is another fan's myth. What every fan wants is information, be that on the last time their team did something worthwhile, or what their team might be doing to find the player who will alter the club's fortunes. From the famous to the forgotten, from Upson to Downing, from Pelé to Mal Donaghy, this book goes deep into the folds of the game.

A Brief History of Data

'The problems are solved, not by giving new information but by arranging what we have known since long'

— Ludwig Wittgenstein

The collection of data from human competition is not a recent creation. In the fiercely competitive world of the medieval tournament, an ambitious knight's reputation grew from his ability roaming in the ferocious world of the melee and the subsequent ransoms he collected after capturing a (hopefully) wealthy opponent. But without people recording this data, how was a competitor to reliably demonstrate his success and skill? It should not be a surprise then that people in the 12th century did not differ much in their approach from those in the 19th or 21st, and opted to write things down. In the 1170s, Young King Henry's clerk Wigain recorded that William Marshal and another knight in Henry's household, Roger de Gaugi, captured 103 opposition knights in a 10-month period, truly the Messi and Neymar of medieval north-west Europe.

The rediscovery of a copy of *L'Histoire de Guillaume le Maréchal* in the late 19th century at around the time the Football League was formed in England was neat timing because this dusty but hugely important medieval document massively increased both our knowledge and understanding of tournaments precisely because it contained facts and figures, albeit written in verse, about Marshal's stellar career. As Victorians devoured this 600-year-old information, a new association football competition was taking shape, for which more data was being recorded than ever before, data that is still being referred to and used (almost) every day in the 2010s.

The essential point is that we know a bit more about the glamorous tournament circuit in northern France in the 1170s than we do about football in the early part of the 19th century for one reason alone: we have more data. Football was wildly popular in England for much of the second millennium, with regular mentions of it by people from Shakespeare to Pepys, and yet a fog hangs over the actual competitors and their achievements. It's possible that the game was so frenetic and violent that even video footage of these seething rudimentary matches would be impossible to interpret and yet the fact remains that someone in 1723 (to pick a year at random) was the best player in the country, or the top scorer, or the best at shattering shins. Or all three. We'll never be able to identify them but that shouldn't stop us saluting their hypothetical roughhouse achievement.

It was the Victorians who not only codified football but also started to reliably record what happened and even begin some early interpretational work. A recent paper by Simon Eaves, of Manchester Metropolitan University, identified numerous instances in the 19th century of sporting events being recorded and used for analytical purposes, from tennis in the 1880s and 1890s ('In Wright & Ditson's *Lawn Tennis Guide* (1891) an "analysis of the strokes" for the 1890 [American] Singles Championship game was presented which included an assessment of the strokes returned in and out of court, passing shots by the opponent, double faults, aces, and total strokes played') to rugby in the 1900s ('The analysis is extremely comprehensive, listing game time, pitch location and ideographic symbols, to provide the reader with an indication of key match events such as scrums, lineouts, stoppages, fouls, penalties, tries and various types of kick'). Dr Eaves concludes that this analysis, compiled by 'mere' sports reporters, was unlikely to have been 'their first attempt given the complexity of the system and the fact that this must have been a "real" time analysis'.

Even more interesting, given that it is easy to understand how rugby and particularly tennis analysis was collected live, even though it would have taken a lot of skill to record accurately, is a mention of some football notations from a December 1907 issue of *La Vie Sportive du Nord et du Pas-de-Calais*, specifically diagrams that showed 'passing sequences leading to goals in the association football match between Paris and Nord'. Goal-move graphics, to use their slightly functional 21st-century name, are still popular on the internet, especially among platforms who do not have broadcast rights to show clips of matches, yet here they are being used in a publication 30 years before the first game was ever shown on television.

Dr Eaves also uncovers a wonderful quote from *The St Louis Star*'s David Barrett in 1910, about football and how 'all that the average soccer fan pays attention to in the game is the number of goals scored and who scores them. He pays no attention whatsoever to the other fine points of the game.' Barrett then proceeded to invent his own notational data collection system so he could tally players' game actions, predating Charles Reep by nearly half a century, Opta by almost 90 years and the US soccer blogging community (responsible for rebooting Barrett's ethos if not his collection methods) by a century.

One factor that links all these data recording exercises is that they will have been done via the classic method of combining eyesight and handwriting. Without computers and video, both the scale and complexity were obviously reduced. If you study one of the contemporary league tables from the Football League in 1888–89 the main thing you notice is that it is a handwritten monster (how the weekly compiler must have loathed trying to fit Wolverhampton Wanderers into a small horizontal box. He also on numerous occasions writes West Brom and then adds Albion at a jaunty angle at the end, as if there were numerous other sporting franchises operating out of West Bromwich in the late 19th century).

Slavish devotion to alphabetical ordering put Accrington top and Wolves, sorry, Wolverhampton Wanderers, at the bottom, which isn't an ideal way to view a league table, something tacitly acknowledged by the compiler, who has added the teams' positions on the left- and right-hand side as well as writing out the table in positional order in the bottom margin. As an exercise in precise spidery calligraphy it's a marvel, but as an at-a-glance information source it's not ideal.

Reliability and accuracy, then, cannot be guaranteed from data collected from this era. With no way of re-watching goals for more than half of the game's codified history, the number of errors that must have slipped through the net is disturbing. An average Premier League season will see around 1,000 goals and roughly 50 will have needed considerable study and may have required reassigning or adjusting in some way. To think that this is the case in homogenous modern stadiums, where players are obliged to wear kit that easily identifies them, leads you to suspect that the proportion in the 1880s,

1890s and early decades of the 20th century must have been much higher. This was barely given a thought when Jamie Vardy's Premier League record of scoring in 11 consecutive matches was compared unfavourably with Jimmy Dunne's feats in the 1930s. With anecdotal evidence that early data collectors could be influenced by favouritism and even by their employer (most were employed by the home team), it casts a partial if not total shadow over much of the data we have from the game's early period.

★

The next leap forward, or upwards at least, came in the 1950s with the flinty arrival of Charles Reep into the data collection world. Reep, an RAF wing commander (and a man who had an innate need to command wingers), began recording football numbers in March 1950 after being disillusioned by the opening 45 minutes of a game at Swindon, an unusual outcome from a relatively common experience. He concentrated on the somewhat amorphous term 'attacking moves', something he calculated that a team would have around 300 of per game (obviously not all these Reepian moves led to a shot, even in the 1950s).

Just a year later, Reep's combination of data collection and the rudimentary analysis he layered on top led to him snaring a part-time job at Brentford, truly a club friendly towards the Non-Proper Football Man community, and the Bees' subsequent recovery in the league bathed Reep in a favourable light, one that allowed him to continue his research throughout the remainder of the decade.

The brutal essence of Reep's work was that direct football was far more effective than longer chains of passes, in terms of number of goals scored, a conclusion he drew from data collected from fewer than 600 matches over a period of more than a decade (just two Premier League seasons contain 760 games, and Reep's selection method, a mixture of World Cups, international friendlies and league games, brings a vast element of cherry picking into the equation straight away).

Reep's Damascene moment in Wiltshire, and his subsequent work with Brentford, observing lower league players whose skill levels were naturally lower than the stars of the day and thus less suited to 'Continental' passing patterns, was inevitably also a factor in his zealous backing for direct football. Reep seemed to not just dislike progressive football but to be actively disgusted by it, a kind of Mary Whitehouse figure, but for through balls.

This loathing of footballing artistry seeps out in the headlines on some of Reep's published articles from the era, such as 'This Pattern-Weaving Talk Is All Bunk' from 1961, which would be an excellent segment on *Monday Night Football*, and in a 1962 piece given the superbly English headline 'Are We Getting Too Clever?'. Using the vagaries of our pal the internet I managed to find a man on the south coast who had a copy of *World Sports* magazine (April 1962) and, after purchasing it (for substantially more than the 2 shillings cover price) and reading it, I feel that Reep's analysis in it deserves a closer look.

The piece starts with Reep explaining how the study is of England's performances in the 1960–61 and 1961–62 seasons and that, although he attended only four matches in each of the two seasons, he saw the goals from the other matches on television. A gigantic data table on the second page confirms this with 'full' data for eight England games and goal summaries for some other matches.

Reep notes that of the 48 goals England scored in the

two-year period, 12 of them came from moves of three or more passes (the hated 'indirect play'), neatly proving his principle that only one in four goals comes from unnecessarily complicated construction methods. He also notes, with dismay, that England have become less direct in 1961–62, something that is clearly a concern to Reep with a World Cup in Chile looming. He does state that ' "association with" does not mean "reason for" ', a sort of early sixties version of 'correlation does not imply causation' but in the closing section of the piece proceeds to veer wildly from this stated stance.

First, Reep posits the idea that 'there is no indication that skill in passing the ball has much, if any, bearing on winning matches' despite having no passing data other than his 'passing move' numbers. We can't look into his accuracy on this for 1961 or 1962 but we can do for the 1966 World Cup (see Chapter Six for more details on exactly how). Of the 40 goals in Reep's study of the 1958 World Cup (there were 126 goals in total and we have no idea from the article which matches Reep included, which could, of course, have skewed the outcome in many ways), just eight (20 per cent) came from moves of more than three passes, with the maximum number of passes in a move that resulted in a goal being just eight.

In the (complete) Opta data for the 1966 World Cup, the proportion of goals coming from moves of four or more passes is a reasonably similar (to Reep's incomplete 1958 data) 22 per cent, but there are eight goals coming from moves of six or more passes, with Helmut Haller's goal for West Germany against Uruguay taking the intricacy crown with 13. Reep's thoughts on that particular goal remain unknown but the fundamental flaw in his thinking remains: the majority of goals (penalties, rebounds, free-kicks, scrappy play) will come from small passing chains or no passing chains at all, but that does not make them more productive than an intricate approach. The best teams control games by retaining possession and destabilise their opponents by moving the ball in unpredictable ways. Smashing a team repeatedly with aerial assaults may have been tantalisingly attractive to an RAF man, but the wing commander was mistaken.

Similarly, a glance at the (Opta) pass completion data for 1966 shows that winners England had the third best pass completion rate in the opposition half. In 1970, winners Brazil had the best pass completion rate in the opposition half. In 1974 winners West Germany had the best pass completion rate in the opposition half. In 1975 there was the incident with the pigeon. You get the idea. It's not that there weren't elements of insight in what Reep was putting forward, it's just that with a small dataset and a big chip on his shoulder, he kept ending up firmly in the wrong place. In other words, all this direct football talk is just bunk.

Reep ends 'Are We Getting Too Clever?' with a series of scattergun broadsides such as: *'Reflection upon the significance of all this must cause one to question many tactics now widely praised as "good football". One might ask the following questions: Is the "building up" of attacks by "thoughtful", "cultured" football in the "Continental" style, with use of "link men" a fundamentally unsound ideology?'* and *'Have British observers been deceived for years by too readily accepting the assurances that "Continental style" football is superior to the English direct style (as it was before 1953) and therefore has to be imitated? Statistics prove the answer to all these questions is definitely YES.'*

Reep's repeated use of inverted commas around 'cultured' and 'Continental', as well as his reference to England's superiority-destroying evisceration by Hungary in 1953, an event that seems to have left the wing commander with deep mental scars, points to a man who shaped the data he collected around an existing belief, rather than seeing what the underlying trends were really pointing to. Sadly, English football did slowly succumb to Reep's bleak world view and 1966, of course, remains the international team's only major honour. Brexit means Brexit, and World Cup exit means World Cup exit. You can point to occasional successes for direct football in the decades that followed (Watford under Graham Taylor, Cambridge under John Beck) but it's no substitute for the artistry that led the likes of Brazil to the greatest honours in the game.

Is it unfair to dissect someone's well-intentioned article from more than half a century ago? Possibly, but it illustrates something that Opta has always strived to avoid, that is, drawing stark, binary conclusions from datasets (particularly ones as limited and restricted as Charles Reep's). Reep claimed that his data proved something, a position no modern analyst would dare to occupy. Reep can be applauded for his pioneering data collection but not much else.

★

It took until the mid-1990s for a new way of collecting football data to emerge, specifically 1996, when Opta was founded. At this stage Opta worked much like Reep, with paper and pencils, but crucially this was the heyday of VHS and, with all Premier League games being filmed, a complete dataset, albeit one that took four or five hours to compile, was available for every match. By 2002, team and player data was available live and by the middle of the decade every single game analysed contained around 2,000 pieces of information collected on custom-built computer software, including x,y & z coordinates and timestamps for every on-the-ball event. Big data for football had arrived.

Opta initially worked mainly with the print and broadcast media but by the mid-2000s there were a handful of football clubs who saw the potential in receiving regular information on their own players and/or their opponents. This complemented or competed with reports from other data collectors such as Prozone, and by the end of the decade other companies were even offering the speed and distance data in a live format. Increased revenue and competition in some of Europe's top leagues such as the Premier League and Bundesliga meant that clubs were looking for any advantage they could find, and starting to employ their own data analysts and researchers.

This was football's *Moneyball* moment, and yet, really, it wasn't. Michael Lewis's 2003 book about sabermetrics, Billy Beane and the Oakland A's had, as the decade progressed, slowly turned more conservative sports on to the potential of using data to enhance both their own players' performance and to unearth hidden diamonds at other teams. These principles apply equally to football as they do to baseball but, as people discovered fairly quickly, the fact that football is an invasion sport (i.e., not turn by turn) and extremely low scoring as well, means that even identifying the metrics that value players best is difficult, never mind applying them to the real world where form, personality and psychology all play a part in the heady mix.

Certain other sports have generally agreed benchmarks and key performance indicators but, even in 2017, football is still searching for any kind of 'holy grail' that 'solves' the game, and it is unlikely it will ever be found. Instead, clubs are increasingly seeing the benefit in another overused phrase, marginal gains, many of which are delivered by careful applications of data and statistical modelling.

To this end, in 2012, OptaPro was created. It is a dedicated channel and resource for professional sports organisations, at its heart powered by the biggest sporting database in the world, and which aims to help teams scout their opponents and recruit new talent in a more effective way. Unsurprisingly, compared to the elements of Opta that fans are exposed to in the media, this is a secretive world, where competitive advantage and innovation are kept close to the chest, although events such as the OptaPro Forum, held every February and attended by football clubs from across the globe, are important for innovation and the development of ideas.

The head of OptaPro is Ben Mackriell, who has previously worked at Burnley, Norwich, Reading, Fulham and Everton. Initially introduced to the world of microanalysis as a Welsh youth hockey international in his teens, Mackriell's life and career has coincided with the rise of performance analysis in UK sport. A sports science degree at Liverpool John Moores University led to his first role at Everton in their analysis department, a key development in David Moyes's transformation of the club in the 2000s.

I asked him about the biggest barriers he has faced in his career in an emerging but often wildly misunderstood area of the sport. 'The issue has always been the deeply embedded culture that exists within the game, where decisions around assessing or changing performance are made through "gut feel" and "instinct". Due to the fact the game overall has progressed so rapidly and successfully over the last 20 years, the result has often meant a lack of progression in coaching processes and scouting because "it's always been done this way". All of this means that the huge influx of people with backgrounds like mine, who have come into the game in the last ten years, has received significant resistance to changing this culture as I believe often it's seen as a threat to the roles of these "football lifers", but this simply isn't the case.'

No matter what career you embark on, gaining the trust of people above you and learning from them is the key to progression. Mackriell agrees. 'The challenge was more for people like me to be willing to learn about the game from the people who really know it. The best piece of advice I was ever given was by a coach at the start of my career: "Forget everything you think you know about the game and learn from people who do." By taking this approach, analysts are able to learn about the tactical side of the game and look at the game in the way coaches and scouts do, which means you can have the football conversations with them, which, in turn, creates buy-in to your more data-driven ideas.'

At the 2017 OptaPro Forum, Dennis Lock, director of analytics at the Miami Dolphins, delivered a speech in which the key message was that 'simple and clever is better than complicated and brilliant', stemming from the fact that one of the biggest disconnects preventing the successful application of analytics in sport is the overly complicated, possibly nerdy approach of the analyst clashing with the dressing-room culture the coach has to dominate.

This is something that Ben Mackriell has experienced and tried to fix. 'The biggest impact in football data and analytics is the culture of innovation that has allowed us to contextualise data in a way that actually means something to coaches and players and can impact performance and change it,' he says. 'In the professional game this took a long time but, through years of the growing analyst community working with coaches, we've figured out ways to use data to reflect a coaching message or support tactical analysis. This has now created a new wave of metrics like Expected Goals, which describes the quality of chances in a game, something coaches talk about and assess themselves in every game. In the professional sector, it is the culture change that was shaped by analysts who understood the tactical side of the game that has had the most significant impact on football data.'

The development and impact of something like Expected Goals is interesting here as it closes the circle between the old-fashioned football men, the data analysts and even the looming spectre of Wing Commander Charles Reep. How many times has a co-commentator or pundit said something along the lines of 'he has to score there', essentially applying their own chance-quality method to a random player? What was Reep's lifelong mission if not to maximise a team's scoring opportunities through an admittedly flawed dogma? Technology has brought us to a point where the pundit doesn't have to rely on his subjective judgement, and Reep, were he alive, would not be restricted to a limited dataset from 500 or so games. Now there is a database of more than a million shots, each with a calculated probability of scoring, based on the performance of every single player to have taken one from that exact position on the pitch.

There's no turning back now. Contrary to those newspaper articles that dredge up disgruntled former managers to complain about groupthink transfer policies, data and analytics are now deeply embedded in the ecosystem of most football clubs in Europe, from the Champions League red giants to the relative dwarfs in the second tiers and lower, something Mackriell knows from working with them every day of the year (for analysts, unlike players, the summer, for understandable reasons, can be even busier than the actual season). 'In the last three to five years I've seen a huge surge in the amount that clubs at all levels of the game are using data across the whole club. Clubs rightly keep their internal processes very private but I'm not sure people realise the level of depth and detail that coaches and scouts go into using data to analyse team and player performance. The first real data analytics that was done in clubs focused around assessing physical performance and this is still probably the most universal use of data because it's a more mature area of data analysis than the use of technical data. However, now, tactically focused analytics is being done at every professional football club in some form. Whether that's using data to analyse the style of play of their next opposition, identifying scouting targets by using statistical profiling to assess a player's fit for their team or assessing the development of academy players – data is now used extensively throughout a club to support decision-making.'

And, although football is unlikely to ever be 'solved' by numbers, the spirit of the Oakland A's is still present. 'Probably the most interesting misconception is that this type of work can only be done by the cash-rich, elite, Champions League-type clubs with the resources to spend on this type of work,' says Mackriell. 'However, in the spirit of *Moneyball*, it is actually some of the smaller clubs in the bottom half of top divisions or even second-tier teams that are doing the most advanced data-driven work to try and make smarter decisions. It is pretty easy to identify the clubs who are taking this type of approach as they are often the ones that are perceived to consistently outperform their resources.'

★

What does the future hold for data in sport? As we've seen, people from other epochs were equally committed to the concept of collecting and using sporting numbers as those in the 21st century, the only real difference is the advancement in technology, which is something that should continue in the coming years. Something like Expected Goals is derived solely from the data Opta collects but there is huge potential in combining different datasets to create entirely new metrics, something that Perform, Opta's parent group, is investing in heavily at the moment.

Ben Mackriell agrees that constant innovation and development is the key to the sector's continued growth. 'The hot topic in the professional analytics community is the ability to better assess aspects of the game such as defensive structure or off-the-ball movement. These conversations tend to centre around the need for the continued advancement of player-tracking data in combination with technical data to allow us to assess these key aspects of performance and the ability to statistically recognise the shape of a team or the tactics they are trying to employ. Also, one of the biggest questions asked by scouts and directors of football is how can we quantify the difference between leagues and the relative performance of a player in one league to the league they play in. The ability to assess this could have a huge impact on scouting and recruitment.'

There was minor excitement in 2016 when *Football Manager* added data analysts as a staff role in the popular computer game, although the lack of clarity on what they actually did in the game hinted at how their real-life tasks remain shrouded in mystery. Nevertheless, it did show how the sector has changed over the past decade, from a niche curiosity to an essential part of the structure of a modern football club. The three pillars of the industry are ideas, technology and data collection and, as long as all three are equally nurtured and developed, then the importance of sports data in the 21st century will only grow further.

Premier League season No. 1: 1992–93

Is it called the Premiership? NOT YET

Champions: Manchester United

Relegated: Nottingham Forest, Middlesbrough, Crystal Palace

Top scorer: Teddy Sheringham (22)

Most assists: Éric Cantona (16)

Biggest win: Blackburn 7–1 Norwich/Sheffield United 6–0 Tottenham

Overview

Here we go, here we go, here we go, here we go, this is it. Those were the basic but undeniably accurate lyrics to Sky's Super Sunday coverage, which launched (the first human mentioned by presenter Richard Keys was fictional criminal Robin Hood) along with the new competition in August 1992. Luton and Notts County, relegated along with West Ham at the end of 1991–92, remain the only clubs to receive Premier League prize money (£1.5 million in the form of parachute payments, a new phrase but one that would become more familiar as time progressed) without ever appearing in the competition.

The new competition looked much like the old one, though, with Manchester United, who had come so close to ending their long title wait the season before, battling with Aston Villa and surprise package Norwich City for the first Premier League crown (and the new trophy did have a detachable crown, ushering in an era of players wearing said crown on their heads during the title celebrations). This was still a campaign without squad numbers and it was the first season in which the new back-pass rule was enforced, which seemed to hamper some teams more than others, with Liverpool conceding 55 goals, their most in a league campaign since 1964–65.

England's slow emergence from continental exile was highlighted by the fact that it didn't have a single quarter-finalist in European competition, something that wouldn't happen again until 2014–15, but no one really minded as the entertainment on the domestic front was ramping up. Manchester United took only one point from their opening three games and didn't reach top spot until January. An abysmal March, when they took only six points from five games, handed the initiative to former manager Ron Atkinson at Aston Villa but seven successive wins in April and May, including the magnificent dawning of Fergie-time against Sheffield Wednesday, ensured that their time not being champions of England was ended at 26 years.

The biggest surprise was Nottingham Forest finishing bottom of the league. Since landing the title in 1978, Brian Clough's team had finished lower than ninth only once (12th in 1981–82) and had finished eighth in the two seasons preceding 1992–93. An opening weekend win against Liverpool via a goal from Teddy Sheringham looked promising, but the striker moved to Tottenham a week later and Forest proceeded to lose six games in a row and sink to the foot of the table. They briefly

escaped the relegation zone at the end of February but two
wins from their final 14 matches condemned the two-time
European champions to the second tier and Clough to retirement at the age of only 58. Alex Ferguson won eight Premier
League titles after he was 58.

Three Things We May Have Just Learnt About 1992–93

Positively negative

East Anglia has never been a boiling hotbed of association
football but both Ipswich and Norwich have flirted with
excitement at different times; Ipswich's league title in the
1960s and 1981 UEFA Cup success being notable examples.
Norwich's peak is harder to pinpoint but the period between
1992 and 1994 is a good candidate (with honourable mentions
for their League Cup wins in 1962 and 1985). In the Premier
League's first season the Canaries battled with Manchester
United and Aston Villa for the title, under manager Mike
'Ian's dad' Walker and led, up front, by a wholly positive Chris
Sutton. A third-place finish was enough to qualify the Norfolk side for the UEFA Cup in 1993–94 (when they became the
first English team to beat Bayern Munich at the Olympic Stadium in European competition) but the notable fact about
that third place is that they did it with a negative goal difference (minus 4 as it happens), the best top-flight finish by a
team who scored fewer than they let in (OK, Burnley came
third with minus 2 in 1898–99 but this was the goal average
era, and it was 1899). Sixteen of Norwich's 21 wins were by a
single goal margin, while they lost by three or more goals on
five occasions, including 7–1 and 5–1 batterings at Blackburn

and Tottenham respectively. Only two teams have since finished in the top five with a negative goal difference, West Ham (fifth in 1999 on minus 7) and Everton (fourth in 2005 on minus 1). Like your mum and/or your life coach told you, sometimes even negatives can be positives.

Visitors

The modern Premier League is awash with representatives from the global game but in 1992–93 overseas players were still a rare treat, with only 52 from countries other than the UK and Ireland. Some, like Robbie Earle (Jamaica) and Ruel Fox (Montserrat), would have been seen as English at the time, only later playing for countries they qualified for through ancestry. Earle and Peter Schmeichel (Denmark) were the only 'foreigners' to play in all 42 games in 1992–93, while Éric Cantona (France, 15) scored more than twice as many goals as any other foreign player. The country represented the most was, in a manner that reeks of the early 1990s, Norway, with eight players (name them*), while Oldham's Dutchman Orpheo Keizerweerd remains, in my opinion, the most obscure player to play in the Premier League in its history.

Fables of the Reconstruction

'Who scored the first ever Premier League goal?' has been used in pub quizzes so often that there really should be a drinking establishment called 'The Brian Deane'. But Deane's goal, from a long throw, goal origin fans, was just one of 15 he scored in that first season, as many as more storied contemporaries such as Éric Cantona, Mark Hughes and Ian Wright, and the publicity around his Premier League–opening strike possibly went a long way to earning him his third and final England cap, against Spain in September 1992. Deane also ended his varied career with a pair of appearances in the Champions League, thanks to a brief spell at Benfica in 1998.

Verdict

It was billed as a 'whole new ball game' but the main trends of the 1992–93 season were continuations of those seen at the end of the First Division era, notably the rise of Manchester United under Alex Ferguson. The first live game shown on Sky Sports was Nottingham Forest v Liverpool and the two clubs, so powerful in the 1970s and 1980s, both fell off their perches as the Premier League era gathered pace. Norwich and Villa showed that there were still opportunities for unfancied teams but 1993–94 would see the continued improvement of monied Blackburn and resurgent Newcastle as the new reality started to make itself known.

* *The eight Norwegians were: Gunnar Halle, Erik Thorstvedt, Erland Johnsen, Stig Inge Bjørnebye, Frank Strandli, Pål Lydersen, Kåre Ingebrigtsen and Henning Berg.*

Premier League season No. 2: 1993–94

Is it called the Premiership? RED ALERT: IT HAS JUST BEEN RENAMED THE PREMIERSHIP

Champions: Manchester United

Relegated: Swindon Town, Oldham Athletic, Sheffield United

Top scorer: Andy Cole (34)

Most assists: Andy Cole (13)

Biggest win: Newcastle United 7–1 Swindon Town

Overview

After a tentative birth into a new world in 1992–93, this was the season when the fledgling competition took more confident steps to differentiate itself from what had gone before. Teams were now obliged to wear squad numbers (mavericks Arsenal and Sheffield Wednesday had worn them in the 1993 League and FA Cup finals a few months earlier) and the league was now called the FA Carling Premiership. After their nervy progress to a first title in more than a quarter of a century the previous season, Manchester United had no hesitation in adding a second Premier League title 12 months later, as well as the FA Cup, to become only the sixth team to do the double. This was the muscular, super-charged United midfield of Paul Ince and new signing Roy Keane in the centre, with Kanchelskis, Sharpe and Giggs providing pace and direct threat from wide positions. Alex Ferguson may have gone on to build superior teams later in his career, but this one remains one of his most cherished.

The 1993–94 season also marked the installation of the first of (so far) 52 managers in the Premier League from outside of the British Isles, in the form of Ossie Ardiles at Tottenham. It would be another three years before he was succeeded by the second and third overseas bosses: Ruud Gullit at Chelsea and, possibly surprisingly given he is still here, Arsène Wenger at Arsenal. It is difficult to recall just how unusual it was to see someone manage a top-flight side for whom English was not their first language, and coverage of Ardiles during his 17 months at Spurs was always on the uncomfortable side of enthusiastic. 'See how the foreigner doesn't try to defend! LOL.' (NB, no one knew what LOL meant in 1994.)

In Newcastle's first season back in the top flight they scored 82 goals, a total they have never since matched at the highest level. They came closer to the title in later campaigns, but the relentless, semi-naive nature of the team in this season, under Kevin Keegan, has rarely been emulated in English football, with Brendan Rodgers's Liverpool side in 2013–14 perhaps the nearest replica. Wimbledon's excellent form at the end of the season led to Joe Kinnear picking up the final two manager-of-the-month awards, but his team's 3–2 defeat at Everton on the final day, after being 2–0 up, got the Toffees out of a fix and kept them up. Elsewhere in the relegation battle, Southampton became the first team in the Premier League era to lose more games than any other club and not go down (something since emulated by West Ham in 2006–07 and Wolves in 2010–11), while Swindon were, well, Swindon (see below).

Three Things We May Have Just Learnt About 1993–94

Swindon Down

Swindon's elevation to the top flight came after their 'fake' promotion in 1990, when illegal payment sanctions meant they were relegated two divisions (later commuted to one demotion). Their performances under Glenn Hoddle in 1992–93 (with the manager luxuriating in his latter-day role as a genuine sweeper) saw them win the play-offs for a second time in three years, and this time they were up. Sadly for Wiltshire football fans, Hoddle decamped to struggling Chelsea (five Premier League games at Stamford Bridge in 1992–93 had attracted fewer than 15,000 fans) that summer. Taking the reins at the ramshackle County Ground was amiable Scot John Gorman, described by Stan Collymore as a 'cone man' when Gorman assisted Hoddle in the England set-up. Four games into their first, and so far only, top-flight campaign, Town had conceded 14 goals, including five against both Liverpool and Southampton. By 22 August they propped up the entire division and would do for the rest of the season (97.4 per cent of their Premier League existence was in the relegation zone, an all-time record, unsurprisingly), yet the Robins had conceded 'only' 43 goals by the halfway stage of the season, so the century still looked unlikely. But it was a bleak early winter, mid-winter, late winter and spring in Wiltshire, with Gorman's hapless team letting in 26 goals between

15 January and 12 March, before ending the season with a 5–0 home loss to Leeds to clock up the hundred. Club stalwart Shaun Taylor was the only player to be on the pitch as all 100 goals went in, and his side became the first to let in 100-plus goals since Ipswich in 1963–64. Still, at least Swindon hadn't been league champions two years earlier like the Suffolk side.

Andy Cole, Andy Cole, Andy Andrew Cole

Never a cultivator of the media, Andy Cole's record in the Premier League has frequently been overlooked in favour of Alan Shearer's (actually, mainly just Alan Shearer's), Thierry Henry's and Wayne Rooney's. But Cole's performances at Newcastle before he moved to Manchester United (and won virtually every honour possible) were exceptional. The 1993–94 season was Cole's first real crack at the top flight (after one Division One appearance for Arsenal), and he did not disappoint. Not only was he the division's top scorer with 34 goals (none of them a penalty) but he also led the assists chart with 13 (never again would he reach double figures in a Premier League campaign), thanks to his captivating partnership with Peter Beardsley. Only one other player in Premier League history has scored and created the most goals in a season, Jimmy Floyd Hasselbaink in 1998–99, and he was only a joint leader in both categories. Cole's 1993–94 season, therefore, has a strong argument for being the most devastating contribution by a centre-forward in the competition's 25-year history. Outstanding.

No fun Gunners

At Arsenal, the George Graham era was unknowingly winding its way towards a sorry, illegal payment-based end, although his team did follow up their haul of two domestic trophies in 1993 with the European Cup Winners' Cup in 1994. In the Premier League Arsenal secured a fourth-place finish, an improvement on a dour 10th the previous season. Even so, the 1993–94 Gunners were the lowest-scoring team in the top nine, and although Ian Wright and Kevin Campbell chipped in with a healthy 23 and 15 goals respectively, only four other players scored in the league for Arsenal. Paul Merson scored seven, Alan Smith three, and Ray Parlour and Steve Bould contributed one each. That spread of six scorers in an entire season remains the smallest, most meagre, spread at any club in the Premier League era. Boring, boring.

Verdict

The 1993–94 season has a certain early-era charm that 1992–93 probably doesn't. Swindon's epochal demise, the arrival of Keegan's renaissance Newcastle, the pace and power of Manchester United and, not least, squad numbers (in the last Premier League season not to see at least one team wear a kit made by Nike). A classic of the genre, 1993–94 should be cherished like a fine wine. (NB, no one knew what fine wine was in 1994.)

Premier League season No. 3: 1994–95

Is it still called the Premiership? OBVIOUSLY

Champions: Blackburn Rovers

Relegated: Ipswich Town, Leicester City, Norwich City, Crystal Palace

Top scorer: Alan Shearer (34)

Most assists: Matthew Le Tissier (15)

Biggest win: Manchester United 9–0 Ipswich Town

Overview

SAS: Bravo for the 2–0. Blackburn's title win under Kenny Dalglish rated only 6/10 on the romance scale (if we consider Leicester in 2015–16 to be a solid 10) owing to the funds pumped in by club owner and metallurgy icon Jack Walker. But while this wasn't largesse on an Abramovich/Sheikh Mansour scale (even the source of Walker's wealth, the long-neglected British steel industry, seems quaint), it was enough to shake up the top of English football. Described by the *Independent* as 'the most unpopular man in English football' on Blackburn's arrival in the newly formed Premier League in 1992, some of

Walker's abundant coin was shipped to Southampton for striker Alan Shearer ahead of 1992–93 and he proceeded to score 47 goals in 61 games in Rovers' first two seasons back in the top tier. But 1994–95 was his masterpiece: the only Premier League season in which Shearer featured in every league game for either of his clubs; the England man scored 34 goals in 42 appearances, as well as supplying 13 assists.

Shearer had been joined in the summer of 1994 by Chris Sutton, who had signed for a new British record of £5 million (which would possibly get you a right-back in the Championship in 2017), and his partnership with Shearer was the driving force behind Rovers' successful title tilt. Between them the pair scored 49 of Blackburn's 78 goals (63 per cent) while also supplying 23 assists (they assisted each other 13 times alone), forming possibly the greatest strike partnership in Premier League history, and certainly the one most associated with a Hereford-based military special forces unit.

Even so, had Manchester United managed to beat West Ham on the final day, instead of dominating the match but drawing 1–1, they would have recorded a third successive title, which would have been a good thing, but also, possibly, a bad thing as their failure was a large reason why Alex Ferguson ditched big-name stars such as Mark Hughes, Andrei Kanchelskis and Paul Ince (although the suspended Éric Cantona was spared), and pressed a glowing red button marked 'the class of '92'.

Three Things We May Have Just Learnt About 1994–95

22 and out

It's a marathon not a sprint, but it used to be more of a marathon. The 1994–95 Premier League season was the last to feature 22 teams, the four teams going down being replaced by two as the league sliced four games off each team's chunky itinerary. The current run of 22 seasons with fewer than 40 games per team is the longest such run since the pre-First World War era, with 42 games a season having been an absolute between 1919–20 and 1986–87, before a clumsy campaign with 21 teams in 1987–88 (meaning someone had a week off every matchday; infuriating for as-yet non-existent fantasy football players) and a 20-team division between 1988 and 1991. Fitness maniacs may salute the reduction in games on biomechanical grounds, but from a statistical point of view, the first three Premier League seasons containing more games than the subsequent 22 is the equivalent of going over the edges when colouring in. Messy.

Toffee grapple

Everton's season ended in triumph with an FA Cup win against Manchester United (who became the eighth team to finish second in the league and the FA Cup in the same season, which Everton had done themselves in 1986 and something only Arsenal in 2001 and Manchester City in 2013 have done since) but it started in utter disarray. Notorious for flirting with relegation in the 1990s, the Toffees started 1994–95 by failing to win any of their opening 12 league games, meaning that the previous season's saviour, Mike Walker, was ditched and replaced by Joe Royle. The genial Royle lost only six of his 28 league games and led the team to safety, and that cup glory. Everton remain one of only two teams in Premier League history to win none of their opening 12 games and not go down, alongside Derby in 2000–01 (not that Derby team, the other one). After riding out their terrible start, the season ended with Paul Rideout's winner at Wembley.

Classy Ferguson destroys Tractor Boys

So Manchester United came second and second, but they came first when it came to scoring nine goals against Ipswich. Town were a bad team (their total of 93 goals conceded is the second worst in Premier League history after Swindon's delightfully neat 100 a season earlier), but on 4 March 1995 no one expected United to eviscerate their visitors from Suffolk. It was the first time a team had scored nine in the top flight since Liverpool had inflicted the same scoreline on Crystal Palace in 1989, and only Tottenham (9–1 v Wigan in 2009) have done so since. As you'd imagine, teams scoring nine or more goals is very much a pre-war escapade (see table), with the highest number of goals in a top-flight game (14) occurring twice: Villa 12–2 Accrington in 1892 and Tottenham 10–4 Everton in 1958.

Teams scoring 9+ goals in a top-flight game

Era	Times
19th century	15
1900s before WWII	21
1946–1992	8
PL era	2

Verdict

The glory went to steely Blackburn but the longer-term beneficiaries were Manchester United, who used their disappointment to break up their version one champions and meld the side who would go on to win the treble four years later. The sight of four teams going down made for exciting viewing. Norwich, title hopefuls in 1993, were gone just 48 months later, and Crystal Palace could count themselves particularly unlucky to go down with 45 points, just two years after being relegated with a top-flight joint record of 49. Just as there had been in 1993–94, there were 1,195 goals, a seasonal total we are unlikely to see again, in the current format at least.

2.

25 Years of Solitude – the Forgotten Men and Deeds of the Premier League

'As soon as someone is identified as an unsung hero,
he no longer is' – George Carlin

Your Ryan Giggs-es, your Frank Lampards, even your Shay Givens. They'll never have to convince people that they were Premier League footballers. Even Mark Draper features on numerous editions of *Premier League Years*. But 3,835 people have featured in the competition's history since that epochal afternoon in August 1992. Not all of them have performed deeds that echo down the ages, but there are plenty who deserve at least a footnote. Here, then, are just a few. To all that have taken part, we salute you.

Lee Norfolk

There can't be many places the Premier League hasn't reached. North Korea, perhaps. Canvey Island, maybe. Even though the world is generally accepted to be a big place, England's top flight has been witnessed or read about in almost every nook and/or cranny. But just who has travelled the farthest to play in it? That, it seems, would be Lee Norfolk, a player from the New Zealand city of Dunedin, officially the urban area with more than 100,000 people that is farthest from the UK. Confusingly, Norfolk travelled more than 19,000 kilometres only to end up in the wrong county, with all three of his Premier League appearances coming for Ipswich Town, of Suffolk, in 1994–95. His mammoth journey was worthwhile, at least, with two wins and an assist for Lee Chapman's only league goal in his long-forgotten spell at Portman Road. Fans of county-specific endgames will be pleased to learn that Norfolk did indeed reach Norfolk with a stint at everyone's favourite Hanseatic trading post, King's Lynn, in 1998.

Stewart Castledine

Castledine played only 52 league games in his entire career, exactly half of which came in the Premier League. He was one of those fringe players at Wimbledon in their Premier League years, along with the likes of Walid Badir and Duncan Jupp, so why and how has he made it into this chapter? Well, Castledine's 26 appearances in the top flight were spread delightfully thinly across six seasons and he remains the only player in Premier League history to play in more than five campaigns yet never appear 10 or more times in a single season. The footballing equivalent of the Christmas-themed gravy jug that comes out once a year.

Jens Lehmann

Many of the players in this section are relatively obscure but there are plenty of stars who deserve their inclusion thanks to some sort of left-field achievement and Jens Lehmann, the goalkeeper who played in every minute of Arsenal's unbeaten league season in 2003–04, is a fine example. Three bookings in his first three Premier League campaigns at Arsenal did not offer a hint of what was to come in 2006–07, the season in which the Gunners moved to the Emirates Stadium, a relocation that possibly drove their German goalkeeper to madness. For in that season Lehmann managed to accumulate eight bookings, the most by a goalkeeper in a single campaign. The finest was probably the fifth, which came against Wigan at Arsenal's new stadium. Pushing time-wasting to a new artistic high, Lehmann threw the ball against the advertising hoardings and it bounced back into the, by Premier League standards, large area behind the goal. The yellow card meant that the German missed the League Cup final, although this was the era in which Arsène Wenger's slavish commitment to fielding young players meant it was unlikely he would have featured. Lehmann ended his volatile Premier League career with 12 yellows in 148 games, which is unlikely to impress Lee Cattermole, but is the highest cards per game rate by a goalkeeper who has made more than 100 appearances.

Craig Forrest

While we're looking at goalkeepers and discipline, let's not ignore one of the great pleasures of the game, namely custodians being sent off. The decision to allow substitute goalkeepers a spot on the bench, made in the early 1990s, reduced the chances and joy of seeing an outfield player don the gloves, but it does at least allow spectators to see which outfield player the manager deems least important as he quickly makes a substitution after his goalkeeper is shown red. The leaves were still on the trees when Ipswich's Craig Forrest was sent off against Sheffield United in September 1992, in one of the first official mix-ups caused by the new back-pass rule. And without wishing to labour the medieval arboreal theme, the man brought down by Forrest was Adrian Littlejohn, while the referee was Ron Groves. Leave it.

Francis Benali

A strong advocate of the moustache long before it became a charity device, Benali played for Southampton for 16 years, a reliable and spiritually ever-present full-back throughout the 1990s. His inclusion here is because he was the first Premier League player to succumb, like the oceans, to the strange forces unleashed by our lunar neighbour. The answer to the age-old question 'do more players get sent off when there's a full moon?' is 'yes', and Benali's red at the aptly named White Hart Lane in February 1993 makes him the competition's lunatic pioneer.

Chris Freestone

'Hi, Chris. I hear you played in the Premier League?'

'That's right. I played for Middlesbrough in the mid-90s. Not for long, though.'

'Still, you played alongside Juninho, right?'

'Yep, and I scored and assisted on my debut against Sheffield Wednesday.'

'That seems like it should be pretty rare?'

'It is. I'm one of only 14 players to have done that.'

'So what happened next?'

'I made only one more start, got an assist at Old Trafford as a sub, ended my top-flight career with just six appearances.'

'You played at King's Lynn I see. Was Lee Norfolk still there?'

'No, he'd left, but people still spoke about it. Norfolk in Norfolk you see.'

'I'd heard that, yeah. Still, there can't be many players to play fewer than seven Premier League games and have a goal and multiple assists to their name?'

'I'm the only one.'

'That is something. That is definitely something. Bye, Chris.'

'Bye.'

Branko Strupar

They say you need a centre-forward to be a maid in the living room, a cook in the kitchen and selfish in the penalty box, but even the most focused forward will occasionally look up and spot a team-mate in a better position. Even Djibril Cissé assisted two goals in the Premier League. So special mention must go then to Derby County's Branko Strupar, who scored 15 goals over three seasons at Pride Park but did not set up a team-mate for a goal in any of his 36 appearances. He remains the highest-scoring Premier League player never to assist a goal, and a bastion of single-mindedness.

Alan Kimble

For every yin there is a yang, and for every Branko Strupar there is an Alan Kimble. You should already be ahead of me here, but to confirm, Kimble is the Premier League player who assisted the most goals without ever troubling the back of the net himself. Kimble created 24 goals for Wimbledon over seven seasons from his berth at full-back, a touch of artistry in the mechanical, aggressive heart of the Dons.

Unhappy birthday

Everyone wants a card on their birthday (although many adults will instead fret about the additional amount of recycling introduced to the weekly rotation), but no Premier League player wants a red card (clue: not a birthday card) on their special day. To date, only three players have been sent off on their birthday: Les Ferdinand in 1993, Gerry Taggart in 1997 and Dwight Gayle in 2015. Taggart and Gayle were both given their orders in matches against West Ham, official birthday disruptors of the English Premier League.

Tomáš Řepka

There are some players whose game is subtly aggressive, and there are some players who look like they would slide tackle a shipping container. Tomáš Řepka fits into the latter category and, with a reputed 20 red cards in his career, was no stranger to the early trudge and the premature bath. Řepka's Premier

League career was spent at West Ham and he marked his September 2001 debut with a red against Middlesbrough at the Riverside. A week later (this being the glorious era when suspensions didn't begin in the next game, but rather after a somewhat elongated review period) he managed a calm 90 minutes against Newcastle as West Ham collected their first three points of the season. Chalk his debut transgression up to nerves, perhaps. Řepka then missed a 5–0 defeat at Everton, a result that must have at least guaranteed his return to the starting XI for the trip to Blackburn. Unfortunately, Řepka's second away appearance brought a second red card after he tripped Corrado Grabbi; by full-time his new team had lost 7–1. Two reds in three games marks the most dismal start to a Premier League career by any player. After the match at Ewood Park his crushed manager, Glenn Roeder, complained that 'our squad is at least four or five people short'. Seeing Řepka showered and changed by 4.30 every week can't have helped.

Neil Finn

Youngsters who fill certain positions are more likely to get an early chance than others. Rookie striker: get him on, see what he can do. Willowy midfielder: let him learn the game alongside the veteran captain. Teenage goalkeeper: whoa, back away. If he makes a mistake we're ruined, he's ruined, everything's ruined. The point, essentially, is that goalkeepers usually have to wait to get their chance. But not always. The youngest goalkeeper to feature in the Premier League made just one appearance for West Ham, on New Year's Day 1996 at Maine Road. Neil Finn, who had turned 17 only three days earlier, had four seasons condensed into one day and never featured again for the Hammers. He can at least be comforted that his particular age-related milestone is unlikely to be challenged in the near future.

Colin Cramb

A single Premier League appearance for Southampton in December 1993 is enough to ensure that Cramb has the unique claim of being the only player to feature in all four divisions of league football in both England and Scotland. Cramb's brief brush with the Premier League is also a reminder of a distant time when most clubs in England had young Scots on their books. Only one season between 1992–93 and 2005–06 didn't include a Scottish teenager in the top flight south of the border, but there hasn't been a single one since Grant Hanley in 2011–12.

Peter Atherton

It's all very well celebrating players who had the tiniest of brushes with the Premier League but what about rewarding stalwarts who, for some reason or other, have slipped into the dark recesses of the mind. A good example would be Peter Atherton, a consistent presence for Coventry and then Sheffield Wednesday in the 1990s, and the man who made more appearances in the competition in that decade than any other player. As empires fell (hi, Liverpool) and dynasties rose (hi, Manchester United) and managers brought in durum wheat as a source of complex carbohydrates (hi, Arsène Wenger),

Atherton was a steady presence, clocking in his 36.9 appearances each season. He outlasted Britpop; he will be with us for ever.

Ruben Loftus-Cheek

In January 2017 Ruben Loftus-Cheek made his second Premier League appearance for current Chelsea manager Antonio Conte. He came on as a substitute against Leicester City.

In October 2016 Ruben Loftus-Cheek made his first appearance for new Chelsea manager Antonio Conte. He came on as a substitute against Leicester City.

In May 2016 Ruben Loftus-Cheek made his final appearance for interim Chelsea manager Guus Hiddink. He came on as a substitute against Leicester City.

Radhi Jaïdi

'Actually,' you smile wanly, 'it was a really good game. I've genuinely seen many matches with plenty of goals that were of a lot lower standard than this.' Inside you're fuming, you've just expended time and/or money to watch a 0–0 and everything in the world is wrong. If only there was a player who guaranteed there would never be a goalless draw. In fact there is, or at least was, in the form of Tunisian defender Radhi Jaïdi, who played in the Premier League 61 times without experiencing a game devoid of goals, despite playing under Alex McLeish at Birmingham for some of those games. Truly, a mystical force for good (goals).

Philippe Clement

There have been some certifiable big guns born on 22 March, from Emperor Go-Horikawa, the 86th emperor of Japan, to William Shatner, but it remains a relatively barren landscape in Premier League terms, the only date in the calendar to have just a single player born on it (even 29 February has four). That player, Philippe Clement, is also fairly unremarkable, a journeyman Belgian who made 12 appearances for Coventry City in the 1998–99 season. I really have nothing to add here.

Efan Ekoku

I was speaking to my uncle Ben on Saturday and said that many people don't know who the first Premier League player to score four goals in a single game was. He took the glass of champagne out of my hand and said: 'You mean Efan Ekoku in September 1993, don't you?' I told him that he had made a very good point and promptly went home.

Sadio Mané

Whether Sadio Mané has a particular love for beaches or the ocean is unrecorded but his goalscoring certainly seems to be affected by the lunar forces of the tide. So far in his Premier League career, 29 of Mané's 34 Premier League goals have come within two nautical miles of the English coast. It helps that he has played for Southampton and Liverpool, of course, but this array of goals also includes a decent amount scored at places other than St Mary's and Anfield. No man is an island but some men are clearly inspired by the psychogeographical limits of landmasses.

Aruna Dindane

A lot of players have scored hat-tricks in the Premier League, a few players have scored lots of hat-tricks in the Premier League (Luis Suárez with six in 110 games certainly stands out), but who is the most obscure Premier League man to have claimed a hat-trick? The player with the fewest number of games (16) to have one is Fredi Bobic, but perhaps more interesting is the player with the second lowest number of games and a hat-trick, Aruna Dindane with 19. That total of appearances is in fact a cruel footnote as the Ivorian, whose hat-trick came in his fifth game for Portsmouth, was dropped, permanently, before his 20th match as it would have triggered a £4 million payment to French club Lens, which Pompey, thrashing about in administration at the time, absolutely could not afford. Dindane was done.

Robbie Blake

Do you support a football team whose name begins with B? I think you might as there are lots of them. In the Premier League alone there have been eight (Barnsley, Birmingham, Blackburn, Blackpool, Bolton, Bournemouth, Bradford and Burnley), but 'who has played for the most B clubs?' is the question that is causing a sensation up and down the country. The answer is Robbie Blake, who appeared for Bradford,

Burnley, Birmingham and Bolton in a top-flight career that spanned exactly 100 games. Breadth.

Victor Wanyama

If you name your child Victor you'd better hope that if he becomes a Premier League footballer then he wins more matches than he doesn't. So far there have been four players called Victor to appear in the modern-day English top flight and only one has a win percentage higher than 50 per cent, Victor Wanyama. Victor Moses, the surprising break-out hero of Chelsea's title win in 2016–17, could break through the threshold soon but for Anichebe and Obinna, the future looks bleak.

Joe Hart

'Joe Hart!?' you splutter. 'Charles Joseph John Hart? What on earth is going on here, Alexander?' Look, Joe Hart isn't an obscure player but hear me out. A few years back, goalkeeper hipsters were all about glovesmen who scored. But then your Tim Howards and your Asmir Begovićs made it a common event and the obscurantist lost interest. Now, the only way to signal your achingly cool interest in the men who try to stop goals being scored is by knowing how many throw-ins the 'keepers have taken. It's all very well scoring goals, or winning penalties (see also: Paul Robinson) but the former implies you have possession and the latter can take place only when your team has the ball in the opposition's penalty area. Taking a throw-in, by contrast, requires the goalkeeper to move to the side of the pitch and to restart the match. As a statement, it's a huge one. Anyway, the goalkeeper to have taken the most throw-ins in the Premier League in the past 10 seasons is Joe Hart, with four, one ahead of Pepe Reina and Chris Kirkland. Three of Hart's total came in Manchester City's epochal home game with QPR in May 2012 and, given the context of that match, that makes a lot of sense. Goalkeepers taking throw-ins: look out for it in a stadium near you soon.

Nicolas Anelka

Nicolas Anelka, a player who was probably underrated and overrated at different points of his surprisingly long Premier League career (364 games, only two fewer than Roy Keane), is, aptly, the player with the most games and a win rate of exactly 50 per cent. Was Super Nic going to turn up, or Nicolas Sulker? You didn't know and neither, it seems, did he.

Brian Deane

No, not for that goal, but rather for the nine he scored between April 1995 and November 1998 for Leeds and Middlesbrough. In that period, Deane scored in eight successive appearances on a Sunday, in the sort of sustained period of Sabbath-based form designed to enrage Christian fundamentalists and garden centre operators. Deane's run finally came to an end in December 1998, on the same day Hugo Chávez was elected President of Venezuela.

Premier League season No. 4: 1995–96

Is it still called the Premiership? SURE THING

Champions: Manchester United

Relegated: Bolton Wanderers, Queens Park Rangers, Manchester City

Top scorer: Alan Shearer (31)

Most assists: Steve McManaman (15)

Biggest win: Blackburn 7–0 Nottingham Forest

Overview

'But it really has got to me. I've voiced it live, not in front of the press or anywhere. I'm not even going to the press conference. But the battle is still on and Man United have not won this yet.'

Those words, the lesser heard conclusion to Kevin Keegan's famous explosion on Sky television in 1996 (and 'Man United' is such a delightfully Keeganish and mid-90s abbreviation of the full thing), were the beginning of the endgame in a classic early Premier League campaign. It was one in which Newcastle's first league title since 1927 looked a certainty, before they were reeled in by a Manchester United team boosted by the return of Éric Cantona from his kung-fu-trawler suspension, and who were able to grind out a series of narrow wins. Between the start of March and 17 April, Manchester United scored only 10 goals in eight games, but picked up 19 points. Thirteen wins from their final 15 games enabled Ferguson's team of emerging talents, despite the infamous grey kit (Wo Di L4), to demolish Newcastle's 12-point lead and claim a third league title in four years. Their monotonous but effective stalking of 'The Entertainers' was a big reason behind the antipathy United faced throughout the rest of their years of dominance, while Ferguson's successful psychological ear-flicking of Keegan set the tone for future battles with Arsène Wenger and Rafa Benítez.

Defending champions Blackburn were not quite Leicester 2016–17 but they put up a fairly sorry show in the Premier League (seventh) and took one point from their first five Champions League matches (in what would be the last Champions League campaign not to see Manchester United involved until 2014–15). Even so, they still had the muscle to dole out the odd beating and their 7–0 destruction of Nottingham Forest in November was the biggest win by any side in 1995–96, especially impressive as Forest had not lost any of their previous 25 Premier League games, a run surpassed by only three teams in the competition's history.

At the bottom, it's traditional to say it was a closely fought battle, but this time it really was. For the first, and so far only, time in Premier League history, two teams stayed up on goal difference (the same had happened in 1987–88, although the team who went down, Chelsea, did so in a short-lived, violent and possibly ill-advised relegation play-off). In 1996 it was Manchester City who were relegated, on 38 points, with Southampton and Coventry surviving on the same number. Alan Ball's City team famously spent the final few minutes of their 2–2 draw with Liverpool on the final day wasting time, thinking that the point would keep them in the top flight, only to realise Coventry and Southampton had closed the trapdoor shut and weighted it down with bricks. Given they had taken two points from their opening 11 games, City's demotion on goal difference was a form of (extremely) minor victory. Two years later City sunk meekly into the third tier, as Pep Guardiola won a league and cup double in Barcelona's midfield.

Three Things We May Have Just Learnt About 1995–96

Chicken and beans

Alan Shearer scored three times in Blackburn's demolition of Forest (see above), the second of five Premier League hat-tricks that season, which remains a competition record. Fifteen of his 31 goals that season, therefore, came in just five games and it was the third successive season that he had scored 30-plus goals in league competition. Six other players have scored 30 or more in a Premier League campaign, but no one more than once. By the end of 1995–96, Shearer had scored 112 Premier League goals in 138 appearances for the Lancashire side, and topped that off by ending the season as the top scorer at Euro '96. A pre-season move to Newcastle for £15 million was the romantic option for the Geordie striker but, despite plundering 148 Premier League goals for the Magpies, Shearer could not add another medal to his solitary Premier League title with Rovers.

Spice of life

Think of Liverpool in the mid-1990s and certain images spring to mind. The Spice Boys, Robbie Fowler's astute left leg, David James's issues with fifth-generation games consoles and the white suits on FA Cup final day in 1996 all appear. Roy Evans's team outscored Keegan's Entertainers in the league that year and, perhaps more impressively, did so by using only 19 players in the entire campaign, the only instance in the competition's history of a team using fewer than 20 men. James, Fowler and Steve McManaman played in all 38, with 15 players in total playing at least 20 games. So next time you hear anyone suggesting this Liverpool team were too delicate to compete, hold up 19 fingers. (NB, you'll need an additional person to help you.)

Snatch

If red cards were a relative rarity at the dawning of the Premier League era (there were only 33 shown in the whole of the opening season), a great man emerged in 1995–96 to take the discipline game to a new level. Vinnie Jones, a popular menace since the late 1980s, became the first player to receive three red cards in a season (he also scored three goals and collected three yellow cards in 1995–96, neatly), all of which came in the space of 108 days between September and Boxing Day.

Verdict

In August 1995, the *Independent's* Premiership preview pre-dicted that Manchester United, shorn of star players sold and suspended, would finish fifth, and the paper was not alone. United's eventual title win, ("You can't win anything with kids said Alan Hansen), therefore, remains one of Alex Fergu-son's best at the club, although it will always be framed by Newcastle and Kevin Keegan's corresponding meltdowns in the spring. Even so, after Blackburn the previous season, it set the narrative template for some time to come: Ferguson ver-sus determined challenger. Dalglish had gone, Keegan was soon to follow; somewhere in Japan, Arsène Wenger's phone (a limited edition Nokia 8110) began to ring.

Premier League season No. 5: 1996–97

Is it still called the Premiership? YES

Champions: Manchester United

Relegated: Nottingham Forest, Middlesbrough, Sunderland

Top scorer: Alan Shearer (25)

Most assists: Éric Cantona (12)

Biggest win: Everton 7–1 Southampton / Newcastle 7–1 Tottenham

Overview

Manchester United's fourth title in five years – and yet it was supposed to be so different. Newcastle had signed Alan Shearer for a world-record £15 million and were finally ready to unseat Alex Ferguson's men. Liverpool were recovering from the Graeme Souness era and could now field Robbie Fowler and Stan Collymore, along with an emerging talent called Michael Owen, while in September Arsenal became only the third team in the Premier League to appoint a foreign boss (after Tottenham with Ardiles and Chelsea with Gullit) in the form of Arsène Wenger.

United hit what seemed like a nadir in October with successive defeats to Newcastle and Southampton, 5–0 and 6–3 respectively, a dark moment that was followed by a loss to Gullit's Chelsea, which left the champions in sixth and seemingly facing an end to their dominance. No such luck for the challengers; within three months Kevin Keegan had resigned at St James' Park and Liverpool's title bid went sour with just four wins in their last 12 games (including a 4–3 win against Newcastle; no, not that one, the other one). Roy Evans's Reds had been in the top three since November but slipped out on the final day, and this in an era in which finishing fourth meant . . . largely nothing.

Mopping up like a shadowy dictator were Ferguson's United, who remain the only team to concede five or more goals twice in a Premier League title-winning season (United did the same thing once in 99–00 and 12–13, while Chelsea and Leicester did it in 14–15 and 15–16 respectively). Their final points total of 75 would have been enough to get them only third place in 2003–04 and, based on three points for a win, is the lowest title-winning total since Derby's in 1975. But there were no asterisks when Ferguson retired; 13 title wins is 13 title wins.

Three Things We May Have Just Learnt About 1996–97

Neal and pray

Nestled in between the soon-to-retire Éric Cantona in first place and the likes of Gianfranco Zola and Dennis Bergkamp beneath him, the second most creative player in the Premier League in 1996–97 was Wimbledon's Neal Ardley. He played in all eight of Wimbledon's Premier League campaigns, yet 11 of the 24 assists he recorded came in one effervescent season, one in which Wimbledon not only came eighth in the league but also reached the semi-finals of both the FA Cup and the Coca-Cola Cup. Ardley's season in the sunshine has largely vanished from memory but his reputation in south-west London endures as the manager who led AFC Wimbledon to promotion from the fourth to the third tier in 2016, finally putting the reformed club back in the same division as their spin-off rivals MK Dons.

Managers of the month. Of the year? Less so

The Premier League manager of the month is a variable beast. Note, for instance, that Stuart Pearce has won it three times, as many as three-time title winner José Mourinho. Arsène Wenger, on the other hand, who has also won the Premier League three times, has been manager of the month 15 times. What is a little unusual about 1996–97, though, is that two of the award winners post-Christmas were teams who were relegated in May. Temporary Nottingham Forest manager Pearce was the choice in January, thanks to three wins from four games (this all less than a year after his penalty of redemption against Spain in Euro '96, of course), but redemption for the two-time European Cup winners was short-lived, with Forest scoring only eight times in their final 14 games, by which point Pearce had handed the reins to Dave Bassett. The March award went to Middlesbrough's Bryan Robson, who had started the year by making his final league appearance (a whole 90 minutes against Arsenal, 375 days after his previous outing), thanks to four wins from six, but possibly also thanks to Boro's enterprising play from the likes of Juninho and Fabrizio Ravanelli, who led the club to the final of both cup competitions. Ultimately, a season that promised so much ended in relegation owing to the three-point deduction the club suffered after failing to fulfil their fixture at Blackburn in December along with the Knowledge that they had just played the youth team in that game at Ewood Park they'd have stayed up.

Grey/white

Leeds began the Premier League era as league champions and briefly shook things up in the early 2000s with a heady mixture of youth and financial recklessness, but sandwiched in between was some dour old fare, with former Arsenal manager George Graham almost wholly responsible. In 1996–97 Leeds bent the space/time continuum by scoring 28 times in 38 games yet still comfortably avoiding relegation. It was the lowest goal total by a top-flight side who didn't go down since Bolton in 1898, although the Trotters had to play only 30 games. Overall Leeds' games in 96–97 produced an average of 1.74 goals, with Liverpool in 1970–71 (1.57) the only team to post a lower figure.

Verdict

The most even of the 25 Premier League seasons, 1996–97's champions recorded what remains the lowest points score of the three-points-for-a-win era, while the three teams who were relegated all finished with at least 90 points in the second tier in 1997–98 (all three would have bounced back had Charlton not overcome Sunderland in what people like to think of as the greatest play-off final of all-time). But this evenness, lauded in theory by many supporters, led only to one of the more forgettable campaigns. There's the rub.

Premier League season No. 6: 1997–98

Is it still called the Premiership? YES

Champions: Arsenal

Relegated: Crystal Palace, Barnsley, Bolton

Top scorer: Dion Dublin, Michael Owen, Chris Sutton (18)

Most assists: David Beckham (13)

Biggest win: Manchester United 7–0 Barnsley

Overview

The season the lights went out. Not at Arsenal, who recorded their first league title since 1991 (warning: pre-Premier League) and their second league and cup double after 1971 (warning: pre-Ceefax), but in the first half of the season a series of Premiership stadiums suffered floodlight failures and games were subsequently abandoned. First, at Derby's new Pride Park in August, then Upton Park in November and Selhurst Park in December. Bang, pop, darkness. On each occasion the match was called off, a record for a Premier League season, with, it eventually emerged, a shady Malaysian betting syndicate behind the latter two.

You should feel sorry for Neil Shipperley, whose two goals for Palace against West Ham counted for nothing once the game was abandoned, although he did score one in the rearranged game (albeit in a 4–1 defeat). The scorers for West Ham in the game that never was were John Hartson and competition legend Frank Lampard, whose final career tally of 177 Premier League goals would have been one higher had it not been for some pliers-based skulduggery.

Arsenal's title win in their first full season under French revolutionary Arsène Wenger seemed pretty unlikely given they were 13 points adrift of Manchester United at one point, and their total of 54 points with 10 games to go remains the lowest by any Premier League champions at this stage of a 20-team season. But 10 successive wins between March and May showed the power of consistency and Wenger's range of innovative pasta recipes, and a team who featured Isaiah Rankin, Paolo Vernazza and Gavin McGowan, lifted their first Premier League crown.

A fascinated horror has been a growing trend over the past two decades when confronted with the gap between English football's first and second tiers, but 1997–98 remains the only Premier League season in which all three promoted teams have gone straight back down. Barnsley's demotion was little surprise: the Yorkshire side had conceded seven, five and six goals in matches by the end of October and were in the bottom three from then until the end of the season. Crystal Palace, in contrast, were 13th at Christmas despite somehow failing to win a home game until late April. By that stage, the bald dome of Italian winger Attilio Lombardo was in charge of the team, but a team who were doomed to go down amid the sort of turmoil that would characterise the club for the next decade.

Bolton were the unluckiest of the three relegated teams, going down merely on goal difference while Everton survived. That was particularly significant as those two sides had drawn 0–0 in the first ever league game at the Reebok Stadium, back in September 1997 (a match in which TV showed Bolton had scored, although referee Stephen Lodge judged it hadn't crossed the line using nothing more than his eyes). In our modern world, shaped as it is by goal-line technology, human errors like this have been eliminated by moral robotics, although Everton live on.

Finally, as revealed in last year's book, but so good it must be repeated, Andy Roberts buckled the space-time continuum and played against Arsenal four times in a single league season, twice for Palace and twice for Wimbledon, those four matches accounting for 5 per cent of his entire Premier League career. Andy Roberts is our friend; he plays Arsenal.

Three Things We May Have Learnt About 1997–98

When Leicester were good (version one)

Leicester City, under Martin O'Neill, managed the rare feat of winning away at Anfield and Old Trafford in the same season, something achieved on only two other occasions by Premier League teams who didn't end the season as champions. Those were Wimbledon in 1992–93 and Martin O'Neill again, at Aston Villa in 2009–10.

The battle of Oakwell

Barnsley may not have survived but they certainly left their mark. The Tykes' match with Liverpool in late March was the first Premiership game to see a team reduced to eight men, after referee Gary Willard sent off home trio Darren Barnard, Chris Morgan and Darren Sheridan. Play was suspended after the second of those red cards after a berserk fan got on to the pitch and tried to attack Willard, and the hunted official ended the game needing a police escort. Only two teams since have been reduced to eight players, and none with as much raw fury as seen on that spring day at Oakwell.

End of a golden era?

Although not a particularly low-scoring campaign (2.68 per game), no individual player managed to score more than 18 and the top scoring duties were shared by a yeoman trio of Michael Owen, Dion Dublin and Chris Sutton. It continued the Premier League's record of having only English top scorers up to this point (indeed the only non-UK/Irish top scorer in English football's history at this point had been George Robledo for Newcastle in 1951–52), but in 1998–99 Dwight Yorke and Jimmy Floyd Hasselbaink would join Owen at the top of the charts. The era of the stylish overseas hitman was about to begin.

Verdict

If there is one season in the Premier League that marks the transition from an old First Division-style affair to the cosmopolitan global brand we now know, 1997–98 is probably it. The first foreign manager to win the English league was the start of the future, while the past, represented by Barnsley's snarling rage, was gently ushered back into the lower reaches.

3.

You are Liverpool
(You Haven't Won the Title for 27 years)

1990—91 (it is one year since you won the league title)

You are Liverpool, *the reigning champions*, and you start the season in exceptional form. Title-winning form. Imperious form. Liverpool form. You start the season with 12 wins and a draw from your first 13 games. 'This time it seems Liverpool are determined not to let potential rivals for their League title even dream a little,' the *Guardian* says. 'Liverpool yesterday illustrated that they have not only the strongest squad in the Football League but also the finest tacticians,' purred *The Times*. It remains, even after all this time, the joint best opening 13 games in English top-flight history. Your defence has let in only seven goals at this stage. In early December you lose 3–0 at Arsenal (who had recently been deducted two points for their part in a royal rumble at Old Trafford), with six recognised defenders in the team: Ablett, Burrows, Nicol, Venison, Gillespie, Hysen. Six defenders, three goals conceded. That's OK, no one can go through an entire season unbeaten in the modern game. The crowd at Highbury know that.

You end 1990 with a defeat against Crystal Palace, who had shocked you in April in the FA Cup semi-final. Still, you're Liverpool. The *reigning champions*. Make the most of it, it's not happening again any time soon. Think about this: at least two clubs whose name begins with L are going to win the league before you do again (while you started the season with eight straight wins, Leicester lose seven of their first eight in the second tier and will finish 22nd of 24 clubs. They are going to be champions of England before you are again. Leicester City. Champions. It will happen).

People in the future will focus on the resignation of Kenny Dalglish in late February as the beginning of the beginning of the end but you'd won only four of 11 league games before he quits. In the turmoil that follows you lose at Luton, you lose at home to Arsenal (their harvesting of six points against you is a fairly major factor in them winning the title by seven points), you lose at home to QPR (QPR! Their only ever top-flight win at Anfield, 20 per cent of their top-flight goals at Anfield come on this one day, in March 1991), you lose at Southampton, at Chelsea, at Forest. You lose the title. It's not coming back any time soon. 'Liverpool are the reigning champions.' Not any more. Not for a long time.

1991–92 (it is two years since you won the title)

Graeme Souness, Liverpool icon, Liverpool legend. Graeme Souness, Liverpool manager, Liverpool pariah. Graeme Souness, appointed earlier in 1991, sees his Dalglish-built team fail to win the title. Graeme Souness, decides to rebuild Liverpool FC, starts spending money. Dean Saunders comes in, Peter Beardsley goes out. Last season you scored 77 goals, this season you score only 47. Only once (1970–71) have you scored fewer in a 42-game season. Forty-seven goals, as many as Ian Rush scored in all competitions in 1983–84. European champions in 1984, diminished horizons in 1992. Forty-seven goals, and 11 of them come against Notts County and Oldham.

Forty-seven goals, and two of them are cherished. The two that come on 26 April that end Manchester United's hopes of winning the title. You can't win the league any more but you can stop others from doing so. Your season is, an FA Cup win against Second Division Sunderland aside, not one for the ages, but United have gone 25 years without winning the league. Twenty-five years: unimaginable. After a decade finishing in the top two, you end sixth. Liverpool FC in sixth place. People look at the league table just to marvel at such a curiosity.

1992–93 (it is three years since you won the title)

The FA Premier League, brand new start, brand new approach, same old decisions. Which team is shown live on the first Super Sunday? Liverpool, of course. The big guns. Centenary Year. New badge. The champions-in-waiting. The actual champions, Leeds (they beat you last week in the Charity Shield, you conceded four goals, three to Éric Cantona, he looks up for it), get a three o'clock Saturday kick-off. Against Wimbledon. There's no glamour in Leeds in August 1992, no glory in the side streets. Super Sunday is on the banks of the Trent. Clough and Liverpool, all over the 70s, all over the 80s, all over in the 90s.

That defeat to Forest on the opening weekend (Sheringham scores but will soon be away, just like Cantona the previous week) sets the tone. Two wins from the first 10 games. A 5–1 defeat to Coventry (Coventry) just before Christmas. The FA Premier League doesn't respect Liverpool FC. The First Division was where you belonged. Aston Villa and Norwich (Norwich) are setting the pace, Manchester United are facing up to their 26th year without a league title by trying to win a league title. Liverpool FC are not. Liverpool FC are 17th in the FA Premier League in early March. Who put them there? Manchester United, by winning 2–1 at Anfield. Revenge tastes sweet. Still, that lot have won the league only seven times. Come back when you've won 18. A gulf. A chasm. Thirty-six points after 30 games is your worst record since the league changed to three points for a win. You stave off the threat of relegation (Liverpool, staving off relegation) with seven wins from the last 12. Come back when you've won 18. Spurs are destroyed 6–2 on the final day. Liverpool are back. Back in mid-table. Come back. Come back when you've won 18.

1993–94 *(it is four years since you won the title)*

The world is changing, but some things stay the same. It's 1993–94, roll the dice. Nigel Clough and Neil Ruddock come in. Can men called Nigel and Neil foster change? (Might Roy Keane have been the better purchase from the Nottingham Forest relegation fire sale? Not that he would have come. Or would he?) The signs look good, four wins from five at the start of the season (five goals against Swindon, how little you know). Then four defeats in a row. Here comes inevitability again. That title challenge you felt in your hands? Balsa wood and porcelain.

More steel in defence perhaps? Ruddock is joined by Julian Dicks. Dicks is a penalty expert, scoring 15 from 16 taken in his Premier League career. He's also a malevolent force when it comes to winning back possession, yet is sent off only once in his Premier League career. Dicks has the honour of being the last Liverpool player to score in front of the standing Kop but by this stage, April, the man who brought him to Anfield, Souness, has gone. Dicks is his last signing. Dicks does not have much of a future at Liverpool FC. Roy Evans thinks Dicks is bad. Roy Evans doesn't want a team full of Dicks.

John Barnes is little help, his two assists this season being the lowest total he records at Liverpool but Robbie Fowler, whispered about for so long, emerges into the light, even though the five goals he scores in his second appearance at Anfield take place in front of only 12,541 paying fans. For the last game in front of the standing Kop a host of legends, Albert Stubbins among them, parade on the Anfield turf. The current players cannot prevent Norwich City easing to a 1–0 win. Jeremy Goss scores the last goal in front of the standing Kop. He gets a standing ovation. Because you can't sit down. Not yet.

1994–95 (it is five years since you won the title)

Three wins in a row to start the league season (it will be 19 years before this happens again) and the signs are good. Are Liverpool back? Probably not, but you are willing to spend many millions of pounds on Phil Babb and John Scales. They form a defensive trio with Neil Ruddock that is expensive, if not watertight. Ruddock will end his career at Anfield having made 115 appearances, five more than Luis Suárez. Razor enjoys a bite as much as the next man.

Where once you had pretenders to your eternal dominance of the league, now you hope to be a challenger to the almighty Manchester United, but Alex Ferguson is much more concerned about Blackburn Rovers, managed by the last man to win a league title for Liverpool FC, and Newcastle United, managed by the man who played up front for you and then was successfully replaced by the last man to win a league title for Liverpool FC.

Slow improvement, then, to fourth (a League Cup, your first trophy in the Premier League era, helps ease the numbness, feel the weight of the silver), but the fact remains that almost 10 per cent of your goals came on the opening day, and your final-day victory against Blackburn almost hands the Premiership title to Manchester United for a third year in a row. Except it doesn't, and things feel slightly more bearable again. Blackburn Rovers, champions. Two weeks earlier, Robbie Williams joins the squad on the team bus for the trip to Aston Villa. Everything changes. It is half a decade since you won the title.

1995–96 (it is six years since you won the title)

You start the season in white-hot form, with five wins from the first eight games. You end the season in white suits, eternally cast as the flimflam team when compared to Manchester United, who beat you in the FA Cup final and record their second league and cup double in three seasons. They've gone from behind you to ahead of you in league and cup doubles in the space of two years. They'll not catch you in terms of league titles though, no chance. That's the one that matters. Real history takes time. Come back when you've won 18.

The country is swept up by Newcastle United, or told to be by television. Anfield icon Kevin Keegan drives the Magpies to the top of the table early in the season and keeps them there until spring. You, in contrast, start December in eighth place, before a run of 34 points from 14 games pushes you into third place and the nearest side to Newcastle and the relentless Manchester United, who are hunting Keegan, probing Keegan, destabilising Keegan.

3 April: Newcastle come to Anfield. 3 April: Newcastle leave Anfield empty-handed. 3 April: Liverpool beat Newcastle 4–3. 3 April: Satellite TV football has its founding moment, its legacy. 3 April: Liverpool all but guarantee Manchester United will win their third title in four seasons. 3 April: Collymore closing in. 3 April: Keegan slumped over the advertising hoarding. 3 April: you win the battle but you lose the war. Three days later you lose at Coventry. From the sublime to the ridiculous.

But memory remains unreliable. The Spice Boys lost the 1996 FA Cup final two months before the Spice Girls' debut single was released. So, really, you didn't. The Spice Boys were unreliable, and yet you used only 19 players all season in the Premier League. Things aren't perfect, but they are better than they were. It is six years since you won the title.

1996–97 (it is seven years since you won the title)

Fourth in a two-horse race. The seven-year itch. The big chance. You blew it. Top at Christmas, top at New Year. With five games to go, you travel to Everton knowing a win by two goals will take you top. Instead you draw 1–1 and have Robbie Fowler sent off. Three days later you host Manchester United, another chance to go top. You lose 3–1. Fowler-less for the last three games, you pick up just four more points. Four. Fourth place. Fourth in a two-horse race. United win their fourth title in five years (the last team to win four of the previous five titles was Liverpool in 1986). Nevertheless: come back when you've won 18.

Going forward, your team is often pleasingly reminiscent of those decades of dominance. Defensively, your team is invariably not up to it. Goalkeeper David James looks unable to catch crosses. The numbers bear this out: his total of 14 dropped catches in 1996–97 is at least three more than any other goalkeeper in the Premiership that season. The crucial defeat to Manchester United in April is sealed when James misjudges a wide ball, leaving Andy Cole with a simple chance to give the swaggering, trophy-gorged canal-building visitors a two-goal lead. This is the grand era of crossing; Beckham, Giggs, even your own Jason McAteer are regularly swinging quality balls into the box. Every club needs a goalkeeper who can deal with them. You don't have one. Fourth. In a two-horse race.

1997–98 (it is eight years since you won the title)

Those golden seasons in the 1980s, when each year Manchester United would be talked of as title contenders, only to flatter to deceive. Is that you in the 1990s? Are you that team now? At this rate Liverpool, Liverpool FC, will go 10 years without a league title. Ten years. Liverpool Football Club, 10 years without a league title. Bridesmaids.

Third place is technically an improvement on fourth a year earlier but, really, it's not. Last year you were contenders, perhaps even the rightful winners (you know this phrase means nothing but this is the sort of language you have to use now), but this season you're chasing, chasing, and end the season 13 points behind Arsenal and 12 behind Manchester United.

Michael Owen, though. Steve Heighway's system keeps unearthing diamonds for you. McManaman, Fowler, David Thompson, now Owen. And they say there are some more in there. Owen in 1997–98 is a whirlwind. Eighteen Premiership goals and 10 assists, it's his most productive Premier League season (he'll never score more than 19 goals in a Premier League season and never assist more than five, other than in 1997–98). Owen is 18 years old, he plays 36 league games followed by a World Cup. Those hamstrings will never be healthier, those smiles will never be wider.

You end the campaign at Anfield with a 4–0 thumping of new champions Arsenal. Demob happy, they don't care and neither should you. Arsène Wenger is being praised for transforming the London side's diet and training. Graeme Souness tried the same here and got chastised by the pie loyalists, by the fish and chip loyalists, by the continental lager on the team bus loyalists. It is eight years since you won the title.

1998–99 (it is nine years since you won the title)

Arsène Wenger has made an impression. The French are revolutionising the English league like they revolutionised the English language. There's no camouflage hiding them in 1998. Manchester United are still mourning Éric Cantona's retirement, Tottenham are increasingly reliant on David Ginola and Arsenal have *Le Professeur*, Wenger. It's time to go French. But slowly. In comes Gérard Houllier, a technocrat, to join Roy Evans, an Anfield man since the 1960s. Chalk and cheese. *Craie et fromage.*

Ten points from the first four games puts you top of the Premiership. The experiment is . . . working? One win from the next nine is the answer, and puts you firmly in 12th position. By this point Evans has resigned and Houllier is in sole charge of the club he watched as a lowly teacher in the city in the 1960s and 1970s. Liverpool FC have switched from back-bench evolution to French revolution.

You experience some highs (your 7–1 win against Southampton in January is the 17th time you've scored seven or more goals in a top-flight game. It has not happened since) but more lows (your final total of 54 points is the fewest you've recorded since the three points for a win rule was introduced. It will be 2012 before you go lower than this). Seventh place is the lowest finish since the Souness era. Manchester United are champions once more. Their 12th league title. Come back when you've won 18.

1999–2000 *(it is 10 years since you won the title)*

Your first full season with Gérard Houllier in sole charge and he tries to fix the defence. In comes Sami Hyypia (who will go on to play more than 300 Premier League games for Liverpool, more than any player other than Jamie Carragher and Steven Gerrard), out goes David James. Defensively it works; your total of 30 goals conceded is the best return since 1988–89. But it comes at the expense of the attack. The idea of Liverpool isn't defence. The idea of Liverpool is attack. The idea of Liverpool is league titles.

The opposition is nullified but so are you. You don't score in any of your final five games of the season and slip from second place to fourth, missing out on a Champions League place. Your final win (and goals) of the season come in a 2–1 win at Wimbledon in mid-April. The Dons are done for. Twelve years after humbling Liverpool in the FA Cup final, the Dons are down. Revenge is best served cold but this is meagre fare that's cold because it looks unappetising. In 1988

Liverpool were unrivalled; in 2000 Liverpool take what they can get. Manchester United collect another league title. Thirteen now.

2000–2001 *(it is 11 years since you won the title)*

The 21st century. Liverpool, a 20th-century team with a 20th-century trophy cabinet. This club demands honours and you deliver them in 2001. Gérard's game. Three proper pots (League Cup, FA Cup, UEFA Cup) and two baubles (Charity Shield and Super Cup) follow in late summer. The famous five, the quintet of hope. Still no league title though. Chalk another one up to the men who play at Old Trafford. Fourteen. Come back when you've . . . well, best not tempt fate.

Thirty-eight wins in a single season, though. Thirty-eight wins. Twice as many as there had been two seasons earlier. Eighteen of them come in the cups (that tends to happen when you win three competitions). The plastic treble, they call it, but that's three more trophies than a lot of clubs win in their entire history. Memories though, like plastic, last for ever.

2001–02 *(it is 12 years since you won the title)*

Your manager has a heart problem, he needs to convalesce. No such worries about the team in the autumn, the wins come flooding in. Ten from the first 14. Top in December, the title talk is on. If you can win every other trophy in 2001, why not the big one in 2002? Liverpool FC, champions. It's been a while. Caretaker Phil Thompson is a link with the old days.

Caretaker Phil Thompson falls out with Robbie Fowler in the summer. In November caretaker Phil Thompson sees Robbie Fowler sold to Leeds. Robbie Fowler, the bright spot of the 1990s, gone to Leeds. Owen and Heskey are left. Owen will get 19 league goals this season; he'll never score 20 in a single campaign. Heskey will score nine times this season; he'll reach double figures only once more in his career. For Birmingham City. Robbie Fowler will reach double figures only twice more in his Premier League career. The three of them together was a strike force. Take one away and the triangle evaporates. There are three sides to every story.

Caretaker Thompson oversees an unkempt Christmas. One win in nine plunges you from top of the table to fifth. Is this a title challenge or just a decent autumn? Thirteen wins from the last 15 is the answer: sensational form to end the season. But just when you are turning teams over like it's 1984, Arsenal and their alternative French manager are doing the same. Thirteen wins to end the season takes the title to Highbury for the third time since you were last champions. Plus ça change. Thirteen wins from 15 and you still don't win the title. Not even finishing above Manchester United for the first time since 1991 makes it much better. It does make it better, but only a bit. There are children playing football in the park in Liverpool shirts who have never seen Liverpool win the title.

2002–03 (it is 13 years since you won the title)

Manchester United: fading force. Arsenal: haven't retained the title since the 1930s. Leeds: no. Newcastle: bridesmaids. Chelsea: they've run out of money. So 2002–03 is the one. This is your year. Is it?

Nine wins and three draws (all the draws are 2–2 and they are in consecutive games, this is not usual) is a fine start. Bonfire night, Liverpool are top of the league. Title talk. Houllier's cracked it. Then 11 games without a win. Seven goals in 11 games. Five points from 11 games. Liverpool are seventh. No more title talk. Houllier's cracking up.

Years before Arsenal perfected having the same season every season, you're having the same season as you did last season. A spring recovery, Michael Owen scoring 19 goals. Champions League qualification. A 6–0 win at West Brom in the 36th match is a sign you're going to overhaul Chelsea. Except no. Going into the final game at Stamford Bridge, you know a win will hand you fourth place. You take the lead. You lose the lead. You lose the game. You lose Steven Gerrard to a red card. You lose the chance of fourth place. Chelsea make the Champions League. Chelsea get bought by Roman Abramovich. Chelsea begin thinking about league titles. Chelsea, who've only ever won the league once, thinking about league title. Oh, and Manchester United are up to 15 now. Come back when you've won 18.

2003–04 (it is 14 years since you won the title)

The vagaries of football. The league table never lies. Last season 64 points gave you fifth place; this year you'll end up with 60 points and take fourth. You'll be in the Champions League in 2004–05. That will be something. Sixty points from 38 games, 1.58 points per game for a chance to become champions of Europe. Modern football. You'll take it all day long. Sixty points from 38 games. Fourth place. The average for fourth in the Premier League era is 69 points. Sixty points is the lowest points total to earn fourth place since they started handing out three points for a win in 1981–82.

The 2003–04 season will be a touchstone of English football history for eternity. The season Arsenal went unbeaten. You thought you were going to do it in 1987–88 until that 30th game. Until that game against Everton. The 30th game. Arsenal, though, they do it. Thirty-eight games. No defeats. You've lost six times before the Christmas trees go up. French managers have never been so revered. Your one, though, he's gone. Souness, Evans, Houllier. Three men who were going to bring the title back to Anfield. Three men who didn't bring the title back to Anfield. Now it's going to be Rafael Benítez's turn. From Scotland to England to France to Spain. Your appointments are going south. Your title hopes are already there.

2004–05 (it is 15 years since you won the title)

Everyone makes choices. Benítez decides to come. Owen decides to leave. Liverpool's first Champions League game of the season is a qualifier in Austria with Owen on the bench. Don't cup-tie the prodigy. Liverpool's final Champions League game of the season is the final in Istanbul with Owen on Real Madrid's bench. Everyone makes choices.

A fifth European crown makes everything OK, of course it does, it's the Champions League. But those fans who normally insist that the Champions League is not the same, not as pure, as the European Cup are strangely quiet about your presence that year being down to a fourth-place finish on 60 points.

The league season brings the unthinkable for Liverpool

fans: finishing below Everton for the first time since 1987. The league season brings the unthinkable for Everton fans: a hard-won Champions League spot potentially consumed by a Liverpool team, this Liverpool team, winning the European Cup.

Your top scorer in the league is Milan Baroš, with nine goals. He's the first Liverpool top scorer to score fewer than 10 since Jack Cox in 1904 (also nine, and Steven Gerrard will do the same in his final season with the club).

The season will go down as one of your greatest. A hungry man savours thin gravy. You've won it five times.

2005–06 (it is 16 years since you won the title)

You are the champions. Champions of Europe. But they make you start your defence in the first round of qualifiers, punishment for becoming the champions of Europe while being only the fifth best team in England. It means you'll end the season having played 62 games, two more than you did last season. In the 1990s you were averaging only 53 games a season. It's harder to win the league with all these extra distractions (in 2013–14, when you come close to finally landing a Premier League title, you'll play only 43 games; you last played fewer than that in 1914-15).

These are changing times in the Premier League. The door to the league title is never even ajar this season, as Mourinho's Chelsea win 20 of their first 22 games. Twenty wins by mid-January (Chelsea won 20 games in a 42-game season in 1954–55 and still won the title). Twenty wins. It's not like you slacken off, your total of 25 wins by the end of the season gets you third place; no team has got more wins and finished third in a

38-game season. Based on three for a win, 82 points was more than you got in 1901, was more than you got in 1906, was more than you got in 1922, was more than you got in 1947, was more than you got in 1977, was more than you got in 1983, was more than you got 1984, was more than you got in 1990. What you did get in those years was the league championship. What you get this year is the FA Cup.

These are changing times in the Premier League. The door to the top four is never even ajar. This is the time of the Big Four. The Grand Slam Sundays. *All Four Majors*, the man on the television says. If all anyone worries about is getting into the Champions League, does it even matter who comes top? Of course it matters who comes top. It's never Liverpool who come top.

2006–07 (it is 17 years since you won the title)

Goals. No one in the mid-2000s wants much to do with goals. This is the era of Mourinho and Benítez, the dark princes of neo-pragmatism, the high priests of nullification. For a fourth league season in a row you will score fewer than 60 goals, something that hasn't happened since 1897–1902. After 15 Premier League games you have 15 goals, the worst return since 1991–92. That season was saved by a cup final and so will this one be. For the second time in three years Benítez, somehow, takes you to the European Cup final, to the Champions League final. But although he is a miracle worker, he can't win you the Champions League for a second time; this time Milan get their revenge. Liverpool and Milan in the biggest club game in the world. It doesn't sound fanciful but in 10 years it will. In 10 years' time Leicester City will get closer to the Champions League final than either of you can even dream of.

The Big Four shuffle their chairs and finish in this order: United, Chelsea, Liverpool, Arsenal. Ferguson's first title for four years; 16 of them in the trophy cabinet at Old Trafford now. Squint and 16 looks very similar to 18. Too similar.

2007–08 (it is 18 years since you won the title)

What does two Champions League finals in three years get you? Money. What does finishing in the top five for eight years in a row get you? Money. What does money get you in summer 2007? Fernando Torres. The thirst, the ache, the need for a 20-goal-a-season striker is sated. For the first time since Robbie Fowler in 1995–96, one of your players scores more than 20 goals in a league campaign. Torres is so money.

Is there a more effective Iberian in the league? Unfortunately, yes. Cristiano Ronaldo at Manchester United scores 31 times. Manchester United retain the league title. Manchester United win the Champions League. The four semifinalists were Manchester United, Chelsea, Liverpool and a team not from the Big Four (you had knocked Arsenal out in the quarter-finals). The Big Four are untouchable, the Big Four are unbeatable. You have not won the league for 18 years.

2008–09 (it is 19 years since you won the title)

Since you were last champions, humans have been born, gone through school and reached adulthood. There is a generation who know what Liverpool are but also what Liverpool are not. There is a generation who want to see Liverpool challenge for the title. Not start well and fade. Not pick up some form in the spring. A proper tilt.

They get one at last. As if the thought of Mr Ferguson's United drawing level on 18 was the final ignominy, Liverpool are back. Fact.

Top at Christmas, top at New Year, top on 9 May. Second on 24 May. Your manager criticises Manchester United's manager in January, shortly before you drop six points in the next three games. Are these connected? Probably not but the impression lingers. Ten wins from the last 11 games includes a 4–1 annihilation of the champions-in-waiting at Old Trafford, but it's not quite enough.

Eighty-six points is not quite enough. Rafa's cracking up. Except he isn't.

Six Gerrard assists for six Torres goals is not quite enough (none of them comes away from Anfield).

Two defeats all season (United lose four). It is the only time a team has lost this rarely and not won the title. It's not quite enough.

Manchester United have won the league title 18 times. Your historic lead, so vast, so huge, was not quite enough. Come back when you've won 18. They've come back. With 18.

2009–10 (it is 20 years since you won the title)

Short-term memory trumps long-term memory. People remember the titanic battle of the spring and tip Liverpool to challenge again. With United losing Ronaldo to Real Madrid, surely you're the favourites to land the title. You must be. Liverpool FC, title contenders. It's in their DNA.

Long-term memory is shut outside, shouting, hollering, banging on the door. It's roaring 'in 1991 we came second then finished sixth a year later. In 2002 we came second then came fifth a year later. In 2009 we came second . . .' Long-term memory slumps to its knees. It knows what's coming. You can't sustain two title bids in a row. Five red cards after only one in the previous three seasons belies the frustration that consumes the club on and off the pitch. Even long-term memory doesn't know what's actually coming, though.

What's coming is seventh place. No more Champions League (you exit in the group stage anyway, with five goals in six games). No more Rafa Benítez. No more Big Four. Since you last won the title your average finishing position is four and a quarterth. There's no Big Four and a Quarter. It's over. It's 20 years since you won the title. It's a fifth of a century since you won the title.

2010–11 (it is 21 years since you won the title)

Roy Hodgson. The fifth post-Dalglish manager to try to win you a title.

Roy Hodgson with his functional football, his pass completion of 78 per cent.

Roy Hodgson with his win percentage of 35 per cent at Blackburn, of 34 per cent at Fulham, of 35 per cent at Liverpool. What's sauce for the goose is not good enough for the gander. (Hodgson will later record a win percentage of 36 per cent at West Brom to much acclaim.)

Roy Hodgson with his League Cup exit to Northampton, with his signing of Paul Konchesky (the millennial Dicks), with the arrival of Joe Cole. They say Joe Cole can do things with a tennis ball. He needs to do them with a football.

'I think it would be a sad day for football and for Liverpool if someone who had been brought in with the pomp and circumstance, and the money it took them to release me from my previous contract, and being feted as one of England's best managers – if after eight games people are deciding this guy has got to go,' said Roy Hodgson.

Roy Hodgson. They decided you had to go.

It is 21 years since you won the title. You are no longer the club with the highest number of league titles. Manchester United have won 19 titles. Manchester United. Nineteen.

2011–12 (it is 22 years since you won the title)

Kenny Dalglish. The King. Return of the King. King Kenny. The sixth manager to try to win the title since . . . himself. A steady hand after Hodgson's bleak interim, this season will be a glorious dance with nostalgia. Or that, at least, is the plan.

In the domestic cups you can bathe in the glow of a Dalglish retrospective, with a run to both finals (League Cup: win. FA Cup: defeat to Chelsea) but the league form is meek. In his original spell at the club, Kenny's Liverpool finished 1–2–1–2–1, like a strutting soldier, but now you resemble a hobbled veteran, unable to move past former glories, weighed down by medals from a bygone age.

Six wins at Anfield all season is the worst return since the 1948–49 season, the shot conversion rate of 9 per cent is the worst in the Premier League by a distance; you hit the woodwork 33 times, nine times more than any other side and 11 per cent of the total in the division. If you had finished like Manchester United this season you'd have scored 98 goals. There are goals in this squad, this is a squad that includes Luis Suárez, but they can't be winkled out. Not yet.

Manchester City win the title with the last kick of the season, the sixth club to win the league since you last managed it. Back at home, King Kenny is dethroned after the cup final. Regicide at the Reds. We go again. You go again. It's 22 years since you won the title.

2012–13 (it is 23 years since you won the title)

Brendan Rodgers, the seventh manager to try to take Liverpool back to the top of the league. Loquacious Brendan with his buzzwords and his plans. Garrulous Brendan with his hopes and dreams. It's a long way from the bootroom to the envelope shop but everything's worth trying.

Despite three defeats and two draws in the first five games, something happens. A raft of teenagers (Ibe, Sterling, Suso, Wisdom, Coady) and the 20-year-old Philippe Coutinho are the vanguard of a new generation (you name three teenage players in six starting XIs in 2012–13; no other Premier League team does this even once).

It is a long slog (defeat to Stoke on Boxing Day leaves you 10th) but three defeats in the last 17 pushes you to seventh. Small signs of progress but who can be bothered to nurse tender green shoots when the vast agri-business at Old Trafford harvests another title. Ferguson's last. United's 20th. This is the end of an era but just as your fans were unable to see what was coming (or not coming) in 1990, the same is true as the most successful league club in English football history (check it, they are. They are now) prepare to welcome David Moyes.

2013–14 *(it is 24 years since you won the title)*

Roy Evans had his chance. Gérard Houllier likewise. Rafa Benítez came closest of all in 2009. Now Brendan Rodgers gets his shot at the Premier League crown in 2013–14, the unlikeliest and unluckiest of the lot.

Goals, endless, relentless goals; 101 by the end of the Premier League campaign. It is the first time you have reached three figures in a top-flight campaign. One hundred and one goals, with Luis Suárez unplayable, unstoppable, uncontrollable. He scores 31 and assists 12 more. He scores 10 times in December alone, a Premier League record. The days of your top scorer finishing with nine goals are over, for this season at least.

The league is a battle between yourselves, Arsenal and Manchester City. Manchester United are nowhere to be seen, battling their own demons as the vacuum left by Alex Ferguson's retirement engulfs them. Come back when you've won 20, someone probably says.

Fourteen wins and two draws from New Year's Day until 20 April means the title is in your hands with three games to go. The broadcasters start filming your team bus arriving at Anfield just for the sheer spectacle of it. The raw heritage of Liverpool pounding, gloriously lurching their way to the league title. The television producers adore the scenes; they remind them of their youth. Just keep winning (we go again, we do not let this slip). You've won the last 11 games in a row (we go again, we do not let this slip). You're at home to Chelsea (we go again, we do not let this slip), José Mourinho's Chelsea (we go again, we do not let this slip). One error, one slip, one mistake and it's over. Steven Gerrard is so desperate to make amends that in the Chelsea match he has eight shots from an average distance of 27 yards.

You don't go again. You did let it slip. The dejection is total. One hundred and one goals. Second place. It is 24 years since you won the title.

2014–15 (it is 25 years since you won the title)

Just as it was after those other seasons when you came second, the media tip you to go one better the next season, but seasoned Liverpool FC watchers know that the hangover will be brutal, endless, astonishing.

Rodgers' team still can't defend but with Luis Suárez departed to Barcelona, the goals virtually halve. From 101 to 52. Last season Suárez and Sturridge scored 52 times by themselves. A muddled Champions League campaign only compounds a league season in which you have one point fewer after 16 games than Roy Hodgson did four years earlier. From strutting general to beleaguered wonk. Your manager is under pressure.

The 2013–14 'success' wasn't solely down to Luis Suárez, but you certainly make a big effort to make it look like it was. By the spring the main concern is Steven Gerrard's impending departure from the club. His final match will be the game at Stoke on the final day of the season. You hope for a goal from the captain at least (he delivers, and joins Jack Cox and Milan Baroš as nine-goal leading scorers in a Liverpool league season). At the other end of the pitch Stoke humiliate you by scoring six times (13 per cent of their goals for the entire season), the first time you've let in six or more goals in a top-flight game since losing 7–2 to Tottenham in 1963. As farewells go, Gerrard's is a rotter.

A year is a long time in football. So is a quarter of a century. It is 25 years since you won the title.

2015–16 (it is 26 years since you won the title)

Memories of United's run of 26 years without the title. Memories of banners and songs. What goes around comes around. And it's virtually all United have to hold on to, as they slide into sterile irrelevancy under the technocratic sludge of Louis van Gaal.

It is 26 years since you won the title yet your stature and reputation, built in those two decades when you were the continent's finest club, last longer than even the polished glass in the trophy cabinet. The list of potential replacements for Brendan Rodgers when he is sacked, and his dismissal was inevitable after the final game of last season, is better than it should be for a club who have finished in the top four only once in the past six seasons.

The appointment of Jürgen Klopp, the eighth manager to try to bring the title back to Anfield, injects the club with an enthusiasm it needs. Two (unsuccessful) cup finals in his first (partial) season is, apparently, evidence that, finally, here is a man who can do what is necessary to put English football in its ordained order. Liverpool FC, champions-in-waiting. Frozen dreams, waiting to be defrosted. Let it go.

Klopp's immediate and vivacious mastery of the other major clubs in the league is accepted with delight. His habit of losing to teams from the lower reaches less so. Leicester City become the seventh team to win the title since you last did. Leicester City, champions of England. Liverpool FC, still champions-in-waiting. Still out in the cold.

2016–17 (it is 27 years since you won the title)

Klopp is the man. Klopp is your man. A man for the big occasion. Liverpool FC have a lot of big occasions. Even now. It is 27 years since you won the title but a Liverpool game is still a big event. Bigger than ever with the new main stand at Anfield open for business. Business time. Title business?

Autumn is a time for renewal. In the fall you rise. A total of 24 goals in your first eight competitive games of the season is your most rampant opening since 1895. The goals, they're coming like someone's turned on a tap. Klopp's turned on a goal tap and you're bathing in goals. Between 10 September and 6 November you score 25 in eight league games, ending the run with a 6–1 win against Watford. The thwacked Hornets were lucky to escape this lightly. You muster 17 shots on target against them. Seventeen in one game. Burnley have had only 26 all season at this point, yet are the only team to beat you so far. You end the day top of the table for the first time in nearly a thousand days. Liverpool on top of the league. Doesn't look fanciful.

People on the street. People on the television. People in the papers. They're saying it's Liverpool's year. The title's coming back. Jürgen Klopp. Liverpool FC. The title's coming back.

Except it isn't. One point from two games on the south coast at Southampton and Bournemouth, the cold sea spray kick-starting all the old rustiness. Klopp in the *clásicos* is peerless, unbeaten against the Big Six all season. Klopp in the bread and butter games is rudderless, losing to Burnley, to Bournemouth, to Swansea, to Leicester, to Palace. You take four points off the eventual champions, you fail to score in four games against Southampton, which includes a wasted League Cup semi, missing the cash prize of United at Wembley in the final, while the FA Cup is ransacked by Wolves. The run-in becomes a slow-motion attempt to finish in the top four, which, to Klopp's credit, he achieves ahead of big-spenders Manchester United (it is four years since they won the league title). Top four, top four. That modern mantra, top four.

Chelsea win their fifth Premier League crown. Their sixth league title, level with Sunderland. Six titles, a third of the way to 18. Come back when you've won 18.

You are Liverpool Football Club. You haven't won the title for 27 years.

Premier League season No. 7: 1998–99

Is it still called the Premiership? UNDOUBTEDLY

Champions: Manchester United

Relegated: Nottingham Forest, Blackburn Rovers, Charlton Athletic

Top scorer: Jimmy Floyd Hasselbaink/Dwight Yorke/Michael Owen (18)

Most assists: Jimmy Floyd Hasselbaink/Dennis Bergkamp (13)

Biggest win: Nottingham Forest 1–8 Manchester United

Overview

If the period between August 1997 and May 2004, when Manchester United and Arsenal shared seven league titles (four and three respectively) and battled and wound each other up incessantly, is the Premier League's heroic era, then 1998–99 was when the empire struck back. United's winning total of 79 points was the third season in a row that the champions had recorded fewer than 80 points (that hasn't been done since, and was the first time it had been done three years in a row, based on three points for a win, since before the First

World War), and by now we all know that low winning-points-totals mean close battles at the top and bottom. Both Manchester United and Arsenal drew often, the former's total of 13 the most they had recorded in the Premier League era until 2016–17, and ties were a theme of the season. The 49 goalless draws remains the most seen in a 20-team season, with Arsenal responsible for seven of them (only Everton, with eight, had more).

Here's the thing, though. No one remembers the conveyer belt of goalless draws; what they recall instead is a compelling conclusion (again, the empire strikes back) and this is what the top two provided. From Boxing Day until the end of the season, Manchester United won 14 and drew the remainder of their 20 games, while Arsenal won 15 of their last 20 matches, crucially losing just once, to Leeds in the penultimate game, which meant that United, after a draw with Blackburn a day later, would head into the final game in first place and with the title in their hands.

At Christmas neither side were in the top two, with the pace being set by John Gregory's band of English warriors (see below) and that version of Chelsea you remember thinking were entertaining but couldn't ever imagine winning the title (their top-scoring players were Gianfranco Zola, Gustavo Poyet, Tore André Flo and . . . Bjarne Goldbæk). At the other end of the table, the season marked Nottingham Forest's last taste so far of top-flight football, their 18 subsequent seasons in the lower reaches now as many as Brian Clough spent with the club between 1975 and 1993. Charlton's only real contribution to the season was convincing everyone that Clive Mendonca scored a hat-trick against Southampton on the opening day, even though it actually came in week two. The third team to go down were Blackburn, just four years after

Jack Walker's iron-ore-soaked cash had propelled them to the title.

Three Things We May Have Just Learnt About 1998–99

Old Yeller

For a man who spent the 1980s playing for Manchester United, Barcelona and Bayern Munich, Mark Hughes could have been forgiven for winding down after he was eased out of Old Trafford in 1995 at the age of 31, yet he went on and played for another four Premier League clubs, continuing well into the 2001–02 season. His second club after leaving United were Southampton, and although the spectacular volleys and horizontal scissor-kicks were a rarer sight (Hughes by this point had been reinvented into a menacing midfield presence), he converted this musculatory prowess into robust tackling. Hughes's total of 14 yellow cards in 1998–99 (11 for fouls, three for dissent) has never been surpassed in the Premier League era, although three players have subsequently matched it. It was indicative of the season as a whole, with the total of 1,404 yellows being an all-time record, as the refereeing standards became stricter before the memo had necessarily reached the players' legs.

Villa's full English

Predating the birth of Brooklyn Beckham by five days and the death of Rod Hull by 18, 27 February 27 1999 marked the last time a Premier League team named 11 English starters and made three English substitutions. It came as John Gregory's Aston Villa took on Coventry City at Villa Park; Gregory naming a starting XI of Oakes, Watson, Southgate, Dublin, Scimeca, Grayson, Wright, Hendrie, Merson, Taylor and Joachim. The three players to come on were Draper, Collymore and Barry. In what could be seen as a pointer for the future of all-English teams, the visitors won 4–1 (the last time Coventry scored four or more goals away from home in the top flight), with all four goals coming from foreign players. Rampant globalisation of the English game made it seem that February 1999 would remain a marker for ever more but, with post-Brexit player registration still a thing of mystery, perhaps we will soon be able, once again, to tuck into a full English on a rainy Saturday.

Sullivan builds a wall

Everything has a start point, and performance data for the Premier League emerged in the late Bassett era (also known as the Brian Little Ice Age). From its dawn (1996) to the present day, Neil Sullivan's total of 203 saves in 1998–99 remains the most by any goalkeeper in a Premier League season. Across his 38 appearances, that works out as 5.2 a game and it's no wild exaggeration to say that Sullivan postponed the Dons' inevitable relegation from the division by 12 months.

Verdict

Like Ant or Dec, the 1998–99 Premier League season is rarely studied just on its own merits, instead it's usually the

hors-d'oeuvre in Manchester United's much studied and celebrated treble. But, despite the relative lack of goals, it stands
up on its own as one of the most compelling Premier League
seasons of the 25. Arsenal's title win under their revolutionary
foreign manager the previous season clearly provoked Alex
Ferguson into a furious and effective reaction but it was close.
Replay this season a hundred times and Arsenal would win
plenty of league and cup doubles, and beer and trophy-themed
lederhosen sales in Bavaria in late spring 1999 would be much
higher.

Premier League season No. 8: 1999–2000

Is it still called the Premiership? VERY MUCH SO

Champions: Manchester United

Relegated: Watford, Sheffield Wednesday, Wimbledon

Top scorer: Kevin Phillips (30)

Most assists: Nolberto Solano/David Beckham (15)

Biggest win: Newcastle 8–0 Sheffield Wednesday

Overview

There isn't a campaign to twin different Premier League seasons but should such a thing arise, I'll be canvassing for 1999–2000 and 2012–2013 to be the inaugural entry. The reasoning? In spring 2000 Manchester United exited the Champions League at the hands of Real Madrid but soothed their pain by securing the title on 22 April with four games remaining. Fast forward 13 years and Manchester United exited the Champions League at the hands of Real Madrid but soothed their pain by securing the title on 22 April with four games remaining.

But while the 2013 version of events ended Alex Ferguson's

last chance of landing another European Cup, in 2000 his team were caught in a strange limbo: furlongs better than any other Premier League team, but wedded to an approach that left them exposed against the better sides in Europe. The league title was secured by a monstrous margin of 18 points (based on our old pal three points for a win, only Aston Villa's advantage over Sheffield United in 1896–97, of 19 points, was bigger) but their defence of the other elements of their treble was clouded by failure in Europe and evaporation in the FA Cup (the club being persuaded to pull out of the competition so they could compete in the World Club Championship in Brazil, a move for which they have often been unfairly held solely accountable over the past two decades).

The deranged commitment to attack (they scored three or more goals in half of their league games) that was United's undoing in the Champions League was evident in the Premier League also. Their defence conceded 45 goals, more than any other Premier League champions, and, along with Derby in 1974–75, it was one of only two instances of a championship-winning team conceding 45 or more since the 1960s, with six wins hoovered up despite conceding two or more goals in the game. Four teams – Chelsea, Aston Villa, Liverpool and Leeds – kept more clean sheets than the champions.

At the foot of the table we waved a final goodbye to Wimbledon, whose unlikely run of 14 successive seasons in the top flight was ended after their experiment with a foreign manager, Norway's Reepian direct-pass enthusiast, Egil Olsen. The south Londoners also managed the impressive feat of conceding a penalty in each of their first five games of the season. Fittingly, given their reputation for rural play, the Dons' pass completion in their final Premier League campaign was a dire 59 per cent (lower than most third-tier teams that sea-son). The club staggered on for four more years in the second tier before morphing into a new entity elsewhere.

Three Things We May Have Just Learnt About 1999–2000

Sent to Coventry

Coventry's ability to survive top-flight relegation was as much a part of the late 1990s as B*Witched and they stretched it, just, into the new millennium by pulling off another what football law states must be called a 'great' escape in the first few months of 2000. Fourteenth place looks reasonably com-fortable for the Sky Blues but they achieved this without winning a single away game, the only team to have done such a thing and avoided the drop in the 20-team Premier League era. They actually lost only three of their opening 10 road trips (seven draws, obviously) but from February through until May they lost nine in a row, including one at rock-bottom Watford on the final day. Curiously, or not, Coventry then opened up the 2000–01 season by winning their first two away games. The good times were back. Or perhaps not because by May they were relegated, and have not looked like returning to the top table since. C'est la vie.

Baldock life

In the mid-1990s the only person to have heard of Baldock was Keith Baldock, the mayor of Baldock, but the emergence of Kevin Phillips as the Hertfordshire town's favourite (only) son soon put it on the map. Phillips's barrage of goals in 1998–99 had earned him an England cap from the depths of the second tier and he carried on in the same vein in the top flight. His final total of 30 remains the most recent occasion an Englishman has cracked the 30-goal barrier in the top division and, until Harry Kane did so in both 2015–16 and 2016–17, Phillips was the most recent English Golden Boot winner. Particularly impressive, other than the fact that Phillips was playing for Sunderland, was that he scored 16 times away from home, which remains a Premier League record, with Alexis Sánchez and Sergio Aguero (both with 15 in 2016–17) the most recent stars to come close to Phillips, but not close enough.

Rock of ages

Bradford's 4–0 defeat at Goodison Park in April 2000 looked like it had condemned the team to doing a Barnsley: a single sorry Yorkshire-based season in the Premier League. But 10 points from their final five games allowed City to squeak above Wimbledon. At the time, Bradford's goal difference of minus 30 was the worst by any team who had avoided relegation but, among contemporaries, more was made of the creaking demographics of their players, with their average age of 30 years and 126 days being the oldest yet seen in the Premier League. At the other end of the scale, but still within Yorkshire, Leeds' average age in 1999–2000 was just 24 years and 162 days, which remains the youngest in a Premier League season. The only other season to have such a wide spread of average ages was 2012–13, with Fulham representing the pensioners and Aston Villa the youth. As I said earlier, these seasons should be twinned.

Verdict

A romp for Manchester United, but an entertaining one. This was the era when only Arsenal, occasionally, were truly capable of challenging the Old Trafford hegemony, and in seasons in which the Gunners were not on their game, United galloped away into the distance. The relegation of Wimbledon can possibly be seen as ending the last links with the rustic First Division era, and gave the steady rise in average attendances a further shot in the arm.

Premier League season No. 9: 2000–01

Is it still called the Premiership? IT'S THE ONLY THING I STILL HAVE FAITH IN

Champions: Manchester United

Relegated: Bradford City, Coventry City, Manchester City

Top scorer: Jimmy Floyd Hasselbaink (23)

Most assists: David Beckham (12)

Biggest win: Manchester United 6–0 Bradford City

Overview

Was this Manchester United's least significant title win under Alex Ferguson? On paper this was the moment his team joined that exclusive band (made up of Huddersfield, Arsenal and Liverpool) of clubs who had won the English title for three years in succession, but after the drama of 1998–99 and the *golazo* blitzkrieg of 1999–2000, this season saw United clocking in and doing enough to win the league by 10 points, but not enough to live too long in the memory.

Their total of six defeats remains the joint worst of any 20-team Premier League champions and, significantly perhaps, three of them were inflicted by their nearest challengers Arsenal (once) and Liverpool (twice). To be fair to the champions, Arsenal were bludgeoned 6–1 at Old Trafford in February and half of United's defeats came in the final three dead rubbery games of the season, but even that low-key end just added to the sense that this was a good team, doing nothing more than they needed to do to dominate opponents who just weren't at their level. It was also another year in which they were bested in the Champions League, this time by the Bayern side they had so dramatically beaten two years previously.

Also of significance was the fact that, for the first time since the introduction of the award, the Premier League manager of the year was not handed to the man who had led the champions to the league title. People were looking elsewhere for inspiration, and they found it in the form of preening tactician George Burley at Ipswich Town. The Suffolk outfit were back in the top flight for the first time since 1995, were naturally tipped to struggle, and yet made an unlikely bid to secure one of the Premiership's three Champions League spots.

It wasn't as if Ipswich started the season in fine form and then held on. They took only four points from their first five matches, but seven wins from nine between October and mid-December propelled them into the inconsistent pack sullenly chasing Manchester United. They never really outclassed anyone (they didn't score more than three goals in any of their league games) but the 19 goals from Marcus Stewart, a kind of West Country proto-Jamie Vardy, kept them in the hunt.

Stewart, like Ipswich themselves, faded badly the next season, scoring six times as Ipswich succumbed to the relegation most had forecast for them a year earlier. But, for one season, Portman Road was an exciting alternative source of

Premiership joy, with journalists crowding trains at Liverpool Street every other Saturday. Burley's once-unique achievement of becoming Premier League manager of the year despite not winning the title has since been matched by Harry Redknapp (2010), Alan Pardew (2012) and Tony Pulis (2014) in what looks slightly like a latter-day attempt to offer some crumbs of success to UK-born managers.

Three Things We May Have Just Learnt About 2000–01

Sub-prime football

The 2000s ended with the City in turmoil, the global financial crisis its gift to the world. But the decade began with the Cities in turmoil, notably those of Manchester, Coventry and Bradford. Not only was the 2000–01 season the only instance in English top-flight history of three City-suffixed teams getting relegated but they did so without much hope of salvation, the eight-point gulf between Manchester City in 18th and Derby County (see below) in 17th being the biggest gap between the drop zone and the safety zone in Premier League history. For these three teams, this season was markedly sub-prime.

County Feedback

Another institution to crash and burn like the economy in 2008 was Derby County but the 2000–01 vintage were not much better, despite their relatively comfortable survival margin (see above). In fact, after 13 games of the season, Derby looked like they were doomed: seven draws, six defeats and a giant, glowing zero in the won column. Only two teams since the Second World War – Leicester in 1975–76 and Sheffield United in 1990–91 – had gone so long without a win from the start of the season and survived, yet Derby did and became the only team to do it, so far, in the Premier League era.

Vintage Becks

The 2000–01 campaign marked the culmination of four seasons of peerless David Beckham creativity. From August 1997 to May 2001, Beckham assisted 51 goals (13, 11, 15 and 12 per season respectively). It has become fashionable, indeed almost obligatory, to promote the other elements of Manchester United's turn-of-the-century midfield (the growling driving force of Keane, the effervescent wing-play of Giggs, Scholes hitting a tree in training) but Beckham's consistency in this period was unparalleled, with 15 more assists than any other player (Dennis Bergkamp is second, Giggs and Steve Guppy joint third). He also scored 30 times, only four fewer than fading prodigy Robbie Fowler in those four seasons. But after that, just as his global reach was expanding endlessly, his local impact was on the wane. Only 16 more assists (quite good, but this is David Beckham we're talking about) followed in his final two Premier League campaigns, before he was shipped off like a nascent virus to Real Madrid in 2003.

Verdict

Another season when a lack of real challengers to Manchester United resulted, unsurprisingly, in a lack of drama and vigour.

There were signs of progress at Arsenal, where Thierry Henry's 17 league goals would prove to be the last time he scored fewer than 20 in a season for six seasons, but the Gunners needed another 12 months before returning to the top table. More than the league, it was instead the cups that provided the memories in 2000–01, with Liverpool winning a knockout treble (FA Cup, League Cup, UEFA Cup), third-tier Wycombe reaching the FA Cup semi-finals and Leeds making it to the Champions League semis. Three years later both Wycombe and Leeds would suffer relegation. Leeds were probably the bigger shock.

4.

Comedown – Football's Worst Title Defences

'Never regret thy fall,
O Icarus of the fearless flight
For the greatest tragedy of them all
Is never to feel the burning light'

– Oscar Wilde

After the champagne comes the headache. There was little chance of Leicester City retaining their Premier League title in 2016–17 and it was clear by the autumn that the Foxes had applied their surprising-performance vouchers wholly to the Champions League and had returned to relative domestic league obscurity.

What Leicester's 2016–17 season did show, though, was that retaining a league title can be even harder than winning one. There are quite a lot of famous instances of small or unfancied sides swooping in from the fog and plundering a league championship but doing so in successive terms takes a much stronger team and mindset, and probably an epoch-defining manager or two. The teams who have done it in England bear this out.

Dynasty digest

Preston in the 1880s

The dominant team as league football was founded in England was Preston North End. Their fans must have been mad as hops (official Victorian celebration terminology) in spring 1890 as they celebrated their second title in two years. Runners-up in the following three seasons, North End fans would have laughed if you'd said their team would shoot into the brown (official Victorian etc.) for the next 100-odd years and fail to land another league title.

Sunderland and Aston Villa in the 1890s

As Preston's Invincibles faded into obscurity (the term mothballed until it was reanimated in 2004 for an Arsenal team that never managed to win two titles in a row), Aston Villa and Sunderland emerged as the first superclubs of the 19th century. Sunderland won titles in 1892 and 1893, were succeeded by Villa in 1894, won the title back in 1895 and then saw the Birmingham side win two in a row in 1896 and 1897. All in all, the Rokermen and the Villans, possibly the two most consistently depressing sides of the 2010s, won nine of the 11 league championships between 1892 and 1902. If only you could have Instagrammed with a box camera, think of the engaging social content they could have produced.

The Wednesday in the 1900s and late 1920s

Our old favourite definite article 'The' has been largely forgotten in modern football, occasional snarling references on fan YouTube channels to 'The Arsenal' being all that remains of its proud tradition. Go back to the start of the 20th century and things were different, with Yorkshire powerhouse The Wednesday winning the title in 1903 and 1904. Three of their four titles came as The Wednesday, with all four coming as two pairs (and 1929 and 1930). Crucially, perhaps, the club changed their official name to Sheffield Wednesday in 1929 and, after creeping to a fourth title a year later, have never again won English football's biggest prize. From The Wednesday to Everyday Wednesday.

Liverpool and Huddersfield in the 1920s and Arsenal in the 1930s

After The Wednesday's proud pair in the early 1900s there was anarchy (and a World War that decimated football among other things) in the First Division, with no titles retained until the 1920s, when there was a sudden flurry from Liverpool (1922 and 1923) and then the first team to win three in a row, Huddersfield (1924–26), guided by managerial great Herbert Chapman for the first two. Chapman then decamped to Arsenal, invented the W-M formation and won two in a row at the London club, before dying of pneumonia, which didn't prevent the Gunners matching Huddersfield's three in a row in the 18 months after his death, something only two teams, Liverpool and Manchester United (twice), have since emulated.

Post-war Pompey

Like fellow P-based outfit Preston, Portsmouth's only two league titles came in a pair, namely in 1949 and 1950, in a brief period when they shone brightly (apt for the team who would subsequently take part in England's first floodlit league match). Since then, a third place in 1955 is as close as the only island city (it's true) to win the English league title have come. If you're looking for a Leicester-like story, where the club actually managed to retain the title, this is probably as close as you can get.

Manchester United and Wolves in the 1950s

As floodlights were installed and European competition crept slowly into existence, the English title was retained twice in four years by Manchester United (1956 and 1957) and Wolves (1958 and 1959). These were great teams constructed by legendary managers (Matt Busby and Stan Cullis respectively), yet their periods of dominance were not maintained and they presaged the anarchic 1960s and 1970s, when only one club, Liverpool, was able to win back-to-back championships.

Liverpool

English football has seen two long-term dynasties and the first of these was Liverpool. Between 1973 and 1990 the club won 11 of their 18 league titles, with consecutive successes in 1976 and 1977, 1979 and 1980, and three in a row between 1982 and 1984. After that, the Red Machine was still able to land titles, but never consecutively, a sign of their waning powers. The same thing happened to Manchester United at the end of the Ferguson era.

Manchester United

The second long-term dynasty in English football came in the 1990s and 2000s under Sir Alex Ferguson at Manchester United (you possibly remember it). More than perhaps any manager in the history of English football, Ferguson was able to construct and reconstruct his teams, and chivvy them into not just winning but then retaining the title. A pair in 1993 and 1994 was interrupted by nouveau riche Blackburn in 1995 but was then followed by another brace in 1996 and 1997. Between 1999 and 2001 United became the fourth club to win three titles in a row, something they repeated under a supercharged Cristiano Ronaldo between 2007 and 2009. Then, even when his teams and his powers were in decline, Ferguson could coax a title win out of them (see 2003, 2011 and 2013), something that his managerial successors must look at with envious awe.

Mourinho's Chelsea

The only other team to retain the English league title were Chelsea in José Mourinho's first two seasons at the club, in 2005 and 2006. Modern-day Mourinho has lost some of his lustre but in the mid-2000s he was a superstar sergeant who sneered his way to two dominant league campaigns, before it all started to crumble. Even so, as one of only a handful of managers to land successive titles, he certainly justified his club's decision to replace his predecessor, Claudio Ranieri.

Which, of course, brings us back round to the essence of this chapter, the many teams who were not able to do what the clubs above did, and follow up their glory with more glory. And that's nothing to be ashamed of, it's the standard outcome. But there are failures and then there are *failures*, and as Leicester's dice with relegation in 2016–17 showed, there are levels to which league champions really shouldn't sink.

★

There aren't too many candidates for terrible title defences in the 19th century as, first, league football was a recent concept, and, second, there weren't many countries who were engaged in such a new-fangled football club ranking system. But, just before the 19th century gave way to the 20th, Sheffield United unhappily obliged.

Blunted

United had won the league title in some style in 1898, finishing five points clear of Sunderland, less than a decade after their formation. Life was good and the players celebrated in the traditional Victorian manner (posed photographs and a variety of pipes). However, like the many teams who would follow in their good year/bad year footsteps, fortunes were about to take a turn for the worse.

Ostensibly, the 1898–99 season began reasonably well for the defending champions, with United unbeaten until late October and top of the table (albeit largely owing to the disappointing lack of uniformity in 19th-century fixture scheduling;

the Blades had played three games more than second-placed Aston Villa at this point), but when your record after 11 games is W3 D8, then there are signs that your title challenge may not be sustainable. In the year the design of the paperclip was perfected, everything at Bramall Lane was about to fall apart. Or maybe that should be everything away from Sheffield United's home base as, starting with a defeat at Anfield on 29 October, the Blades proceeded to lose every single away game for the rest of the season, a run of 12 in a row. In the first season to have automatic relegation between the First and Second Divisions, this was not an ideal development for the reigning champions.

Fortunately for United, their home form kept them afloat and meant they were never quite in danger of joining rivals The Wednesday in dropping into the second tier and being replaced by little Glossop, the smallest town to have played in the English top flight. Wins in their final three home matches, by an aggregate of 12–2, cancelled out the depressing run of away defeats and ensured they would reach 1900 in the premier division. Indeed, United bounced back in 1899–1900 to finish second behind Aston Villa but they are still waiting for their second league title and, alongside Preston, are the only team to have been champions of England but whose success came wholly in the 19th century.

Goodison to Badison

The next major mishap by a defending champion came 30 years after Sheffield United's meltdown, and this time it came from Everton. The Toffees' 1927–28 season was an all-time classic, Dixie Dean's 60 goals (more than half of the team's total of 102) a record that stands to this day. Perhaps the sheer extravagance of that campaign took its toll on Everton but they then embarked on a mini-period of absolute rollercoaster mayhem. First, in 1929, they defended their title by finishing a lowly 18th, with away form, like Sheffield United before them, the main issue (seven defeats in 1927–28, 13 a year later). But where the Blades had bounced back after their bad defence, Everton plumbed new depths by getting relegated in 1930 (despite scoring 80 goals), securing promotion in 1931 and then reclaiming the title in 1932. Furthermore, Dixie Dean stayed with them for the entire period, the very concept of a relegation release clause being as fanciful as artificial turf.

Fear Wild's heaven

But if Everton began the 1930s like a footballing vaudeville act, the decade would throw up the ultimate in bad title defences. Manchester City's league title in 1936–37 was achieved with them scoring 107 goals, the 10th and final team of the decade to reach triple figures (no club would manage the feat again until Manchester United scored 103 in 1956–57, and it's happened only 16 times since then). Goalscoring remained on point for the Sky Blues in 1937–38, as they ended the season with 80, more than any other side. All well, you might think. Nothing to see here. Well . . . no. City, despite scoring more than any other team and ending the season with a positive goal difference (although goal average was the tie-breaker of choice at the time), were relegated. Demoted, flung out of the top flight, bodied into the second tier. They remain the only team to be relegated as reigning champions of England, an unimpressively impressive achievement.

For City, like so many of the other struggling champions (including Leicester last season), it was the decline in performances away from home that put them in trouble. Wilf Wild's City team actually won their last two home games of the season by an aggregate of 13–3 but defeat on the final day to Huddersfield meant they dropped from 17th to 21st. There were eight teams who could have gone down on the final day in 1938, just think of the alliterative name 7 May would have been given by modern television (suggestions: The Hateful Eight, Mayday, Dimanche of Doom).

You've never had it so bad

The 1950s and 1960s were generally a benign time for English sides defending their league titles but two instances stand out and, like modern-day Leicester, both were teams defending their first league championship.

First, Chelsea in 1955–56. They came 16th a year after landing their first title (it would, of course, be 50 years and take the invention of Joe Cole before they landed another). That triumph, although welcome, did come from a total of only 52 points, a low point that had previously been seen only in the pre-war era, and never since. A season later the Blues were eighth at the end of February, despite winning only one of their opening nine games, and not seemingly in much trouble, but a run of five successive defeats pushed them towards the drop zone, before five points from their final three games guided them clear. They picked up only 13 points fewer than they had the season before, but in the two-points-for-a-win era, such margins could be the difference between glory and gloom.

The 1960s produced possibly the closest analogy with Leicester City in the shape of Ipswich Town, champions from an unfancied location soon after promotion. Town were led up the divisions and to the title by Alf Ramsey, a manager whose tactical experimentations gave his team a short-lived but glorious advantage, demonstrated by their 3–1 win over the defending champions at White Hart Lane in March 1962, arguably the result that gave their title push the legitimacy it needed (strikingly similar to Leicester's win at Manchester City in February 2016). But after the success came the reality: an early European Cup exit to AC Milan and news that Ramsey had agreed to become England manager at the end of the season. Whether it was their lame duck manager or their opponents coming up with a way of countering Ipswich's regimented approach, or a mixture of both, the reality was that six defeats from seven games between Boxing Day and March (the small number of matches due to the harsh winter of 1963 that paralysed football in the UK for months) pushed Town to 21st place and the relegation zone by 19 March. And, owing to their geographical location, Ipswich had suffered less from the frozen conditions than their rivals and had played up to six matches more than teams around them in the table at this point.

But just when they looked doomed to join Manchester City as the second champions to get relegated, they reeled off six wins and just two defeats from their final 12 games to finish, relieved, in 17th place. It was only a temporary reprieve, however, and 12 months later they finished rock bottom of the First Division and, in the season Ramsey took England to their only World Cup win, Ipswich finished 15th in the second tier.

Altitude sickness

Statistically, the biggest fall of the 1970s by a reigning champion was Everton in the first full season of the decade. The Merseysiders had won the league shortly before England jetted off to Mexico for the 1970 World Cup, and had supplied the team with four players for the tournament: Alan Ball, Tommy Wright, Brian Labone and Keith Newton. Some Evertonians maintain that the efforts that those key Everton men made in the rarefied Central American air (they played more than 1,000 minutes combined) had a detrimental effect on them in the following league season. Without scientific data this is clearly impossible to verify but it's perhaps notable that Arsenal, who won the double in 1970–71, did not supply any England players for that World Cup.

Whatever the reasons, Everton started their title defence abysmally, failing to win any of their opening six games before a spell of four victories in a row pushed them into a mid-table berth, where they largely remained all season. Between the start of October and the end of the campaign Everton were always somewhere between ninth and the 14th place they eventually ended up in. Dreary.

Villa not so rosy

If Everton were the only defending champions to finish outside the top 10 in the 1970s, Aston Villa were the only team to do so in the 1980s, although they did counter this with the ultimate in consolation prizes, the European Cup. Their league title in 1980–81 was a triumph of teamwork and man-management, famously using only 14 players in their entire league campaign, with seven of them playing all 42 league games. Manager Ron Saunders, who used to get the apprentices on the bench to count his players' tackles in a rudimentary nod to data collection, left the club halfway through the following season after a contractual dispute, and although Tony Barton led the Villans to that unlikely European Cup win against Bayern, the brief glorious spell was over and five years later Villa were relegated to the second tier.

Looking for Éric

Straddling the end of the old Football League structure and the start of the Premier League, Leeds United's title win in 1991–92 owed almost as much to Manchester United's insecurities as to their own ability. Alex Ferguson's team were one point behind Leeds with two games in hand in mid-April but were undone by fixture congestion, having to play five league games in 11 days, a spell from which they picked up just four points, the final ignominy being a defeat to Liverpool at Anfield that handed Leeds their first league title since 1974, and the secretive society of English football managers their most recent championship success in the shape of Howard Wilkinson.

A season later everything had changed, and not just the name of the competition that Leeds and Manchester United were playing in. The first Premier League campaign in 1992–93 was the start of the Old Trafford side's domination of the game and they began by stealing Éric Cantona from Leeds. The Frenchman had played only a minor role in the Whites' title win, scoring three league goals in the second half of the season, all at home against bottom-half sides, although he had started 1992–93 with a hat-trick against Liverpool in the Charity Shield. But while Cantona was undoubtedly the spark for Manchester United's improvement that season (once he moved across the Pennines in November), Leeds' problem was a rank inability to win away from home. A 4–1 defeat at promoted Middlesbrough in August didn't augur well, a defeat at Old Trafford in September likewise. Leeds then went on to concede four at Portman Road in October and four at Maine Road in November in a spell of nine successive away defeats. The first away clean sheet of the campaign came at Highbury in late February, Arsenal being managed by George Graham, who would bring his unique brand of defensive football to Elland Road later in the decade.

A 3–3 draw at Coventry on the last day of the season (albeit a match in which they were 3–1 down in the 88th minute) ensured that Leeds ended the season (and remain) as the only reigning champions in England to fail to win an away game. Had home games alone counted, Leeds would have finished third. Had only matches away from Elland Road mattered, Wilkinson's team would have finished six points adrift at the bottom. Their drop from first to 17th is the joint third worst fall of any reigning champions and equal first with Ipswich in the post-war era. Losing Cantona seems fairly minor in that context.

Reigning champions – away wins

Season	Team	Games	Away wins
1992–93	Leeds United*	21	0
2016–17	Leicester City	19	2
1897–98	Aston Villa	15	2
1898–99	Sheffield United	17	2
1900–01	Aston Villa	17	2
1901–02	Liverpool	17	2
1936–37	Sunderland	21	2
1937–38	Manchester City	21	2
1968–69	Manchester City	21	2
1970–71	Everton	21	2

In a curious continuation of their away woes in 1992–93, Leeds' only win in Europe away from Elland Road came at a neutral venue (the Nou Camp) in a deciding game against Stuttgart after the Germans had played an ineligible player in the second leg of the original tie. Even when they won away, Leeds weren't technically away.

The madness of Mourinho

The pre-eminent bad title defence of the modern era, before Leicester, came just 12 months earlier, when Chelsea under José Mourinho buckled in a way that no one envisaged. While their title win in 2014–15 lacked the excitement of the Manchester City v Liverpool race of the previous campaign, it was a solid, professional operation that reeked of Mourinho's well-honed methods. The following season it was the complete reverse, with Chelsea losing nine times in the league under the Portuguese between August and December, only one fewer than he had suffered in his entire first spell at the club between 2004 and 2007. The Blues ended the campaign in 10th place, not quite as bad as their slump to 16th in 1956 but with a considerably more expensive squad. Their total of 50 points was, until Leicester, the lowest by a defending champion in the Premier League era. Mourinho's complaints about lack of quality were undermined by the fact that Chelsea did at least end 2015–16 with the longest unbeaten run of the season (under caretaker Guus Hiddink) and then by their sensational revival, with largely the same set of players, under Antonio Conte the following season.

Global meltdown

It's not just the English league, though. Across the planet there have been teams who have flown too close to the sun and then plummeted a year later. Every calm nation can harbour a Wilf Wild.

In Germany the best example comes from the late 1960s, when Nürnberg won the Bundesliga in 1967–68 before being relegated the following season. Austrian Max Merkel, who seems to have been a central European version of Aston Villa's Ron Saunders (both men with deep respect for the art of tackling and suspicious of players who couldn't graft), guided the team to the title in 1968 but the following campaign was a disaster, with many of the ageing, title-winning team jettisoned and replaced with seemingly inferior players. The result was the club's longest period outside of the German top flight.

Finland deserves a mention owing to events of the mid-1990s. In 1994 Tampereen Pallo-Veikot won the Veikkausliiga, the Finnish top flight, only to be relegated in 1995. Meanwhile, in

1995, they were replaced as champions by Haka Valkeakoski, who were then relegated themselves in 1996. Of course, with only 14 teams (in 1994 and 1995, it went down to 12 in 1996) the chances of this happening are increased but reigning champions being relegated for two consecutive seasons is still deeply impressive, in a disastrous way. Haka's fortunes at the turn of the century were as follows: 1995, champions; 1996, relegated; 1997, promoted; 1998, champions; 1999, champions; 2000, champions.

Staying in Scandinavia, Leicester's success in 2016 must have brought back memories of Danish side Herfølge Boldklub's equally unlikely title win in 2000, under player-manager John Jensen (yeah, that one). A tiny club compared to the usual suspects in Denmark, they are one of only four teams to win the Danish title just once. Needless to say, given the subject matter of this chapter, they were relegated in 2001 as well as being knocked out of the Champions League qualifying stage by Rangers.

Moving away from Europe, Algeria's ES Sétif won the country's top flight in 1987 only to be relegated the following season. And yet while a second-tier side, they won the 1988 African Cup of Champions Clubs (having qualified as Algerian champions) and remain the only club in Africa to have won the continental tournament while not being a top-flight side.

For Fox sake

Nobody really expected Leicester City to establish a glittering Premier League dynasty but as the 2016–17 season approached there was no strong consensus on how football's ultimate surprise package would do. New rules allowed kick-offs to go backwards but would the Foxes do the same? Claudio Ranieri's team kicked off the new campaign in the early game (one of those modern tweaks designed to feel like it's a historical tradition) away at Hull and lost 2–1, a result that not only meant Leicester had, after 90 minutes of the season, racked up one-third of the total defeats they suffered when winning the title the previous season, but also partly nudged Hull into making the decidedly rash decision of appointing Mike Phelan as their full-time manager.

Between the start of January and 10 April 2016 Leicester conceded only six goals in 14 games, but leaked 31 in the opening 18 games of 2016–17, a run that left them bobbing dangerously in 16th. As we've seen with so many of the other examples in this chapter, it was a deep and sudden collapse in their ability to compete away from home that was the main force dragging them down. One point from their first eight away games was the worst such start by English defending champions.

And yet while the Foxes were being hunted down and exterminated domestically, in Europe it was a completely different story. In October they became the first English team, and one of only five in total, to win their opening three games in the Champions League; at times in that month they had more points in their group than they did in the league. Meanwhile, four clean sheets in their opening four games was something that no one had ever done before in the Champions League. Europe had to deal with power-Leicester while domestic fans were treated to a team posting (by late November) the worst start by champions since Ipswich in the 1960s.

If Leicester fans were hoping for even a slight improvement as 2017 dawned they were sorely disappointed. Between Boxing Day and 12 February, City scored one goal in eight games (becoming the first top-flight side to fail to score in their first five games of a new year since Tottenham in 1986) and the last match in that sequence, a 2–0 defeat at Swansea, now their relegation rivals, ultimately ended Ranieri's tenure as manager, to much wailing and pantomime brow-beating among fans and journalists alike. There was no way to logically explain Leicester's march to the title and the same rules applied when they dismissed the Italian. If he had had little actual influence on the Foxes' success then sacking him shouldn't have made any difference. And yet if he truly was the mastermind behind the Midlands side's glory then surely he must also have been responsible for their subsequent rapid decline as 2016–17 progressed. Keep him, sack him, bin him, back him: there was no right or wrong thing to do (this is also known as the Nigel Adkins conundrum).

What transpired under caretaker manager Craig Shakespeare was one of the oddest reactions to a team improving their form seen in the annals of English football. As Leicester followed five league defeats in a row (under Ranieri) with five wins in a row (under Shakespeare, making the best start by a British manager in Premier League history) he and the players were variously labelled as rats, bums and snakes for deigning to improve under a (mainly) new regime. Twelve months earlier Chelsea had undergone a similar recovery under Guus Hiddink but had escaped censure. Leicester, as always, are radical pioneers in their field.

By the end of the season Shakespeare had eased Leicester into a mid-table position they seem suited to yet seem determined to avoid each year. The additional wealth and kudos that their title has brought them could and should set the Foxes up for a spell of relative stability but, as they have demonstrated all too well in the past 36 months, anything can happen.

For two successive years the Premier League champions dispensed with their managers in the following campaign. Whether this is an example of modern football's impatience or instead an indictment of the tolerance of mediocrity that existed in older generations is a debatable point, but ultimately debate is at the heart of the game. Very few things in football are unarguable but a club's honours are set in stone, so whether you win the title for one, two or nine years in a row, you've made it. Leicester's title wasn't tarnished by sacking Ranieri; it served only to make their season of wonder sparkle that little bit more. And they got to avoid relegation as well. Win/win.

Premier League season No. 10: 2001–02

Is it still called the Premiership? PERHAPS FOR EVER

Champions: Arsenal

Relegated: Leicester City, Derby County, Ipswich Town

Top scorer: Thierry Henry (24)

Most assists: Robert Pirès (15)

Biggest win: Blackburn 7–1 West Ham United/Liverpool 6–0 Ipswich Town

Overview

The Invincibles luxuriate in their copyrighted glory but there's a reasonable argument that Arsenal in 2001–02 were the best of Arsène Wenger's three Premier League title-winning teams. In summer 2001 the Gunners, humbled by Manchester United for two league campaigns in a row, tempted Sol Campbell from Haringey to Islington, despite the higher council tax. Wenger justified possibly the most sensational transfer in Premier League history (certainly one of the last deals where not even the most well-connected members of the press had an idea of who was about to be unveiled) by saying: 'I was told many times that I had to improve my defence.' How times change.

But although Campbell did improve Arsenal's defence (slightly: they conceded 36 goals, two fewer than in 2000–01 but claimed an additional 17 points), it was their continued development as an attacking force that turned the Gunners back into title contenders. Unfairly forgotten by many people, Arsenal scored in all 38 games, the only time this has been done in the top flight in the modern era (Bolton and Everton both did it in 22-game seasons in the 19th century). Is scoring in every game harder and/or more impressive than not losing? It's hard to be definitive but Arsenal fans got the chance to find out in the space of three seasons. By 2017, sections of the club's support were accusing Wenger of 'killing the club', which seems a little ungrateful given the Frenchman's extraordinary legacy.

Manchester United began the season looking to become the first team to win the English league title for four seasons in a row but ended up finishing outside the top two for the first time since 1991, as Alex Ferguson's project to turn his team into one who could consistently challenge in the Champions League, signified by the signing of Juan Sebastián Verón for a British transfer record, went sour. Verón, who was vociferously defended by his manager, ended the season with one assist in 26 league appearances, putting him level with Charlton goalkeeper Dean Kiely.

Instead it was Liverpool who pushed Arsenal closest, with their final haul of 80 points the first time they had accrued that many since the glorious 1987–88 campaign, and one more than they had earned in 1989–90, the last time they had been champions.

At the foot of the table, Ipswich's demise a year after they had been the nation's plucky darlings was a surprise (probably less so after Town won only one of their first 17 league games), but it looked like they had recovered when a win at Goodison Park in February took them up to 12th. Over the final 13 games they collected just one more win, however, and they slipped into the second tier, where they have been ever since. Joining them were Derby and Leicester, all of which meant that 2002–03 would be the first top-flight season with no representatives from East Anglia or the East Midlands since 1956–57. The 2001–02 season was also the first in the Premier League era to see all three promoted teams stay up the following season, with the tenacious trio of Fulham, Blackburn and Bolton all remaining in the top flight until the next decade.

Three Things We May Have Just Learnt About 2001–02

Relentless

Teams who end the season well tend to be remembered more fondly than those who play their best football in the first half of the season (Manchester United in 2012–13 being a good example of the latter). Arsenal in 2001–02 ended the campaign with 13 wins in a row and, between 23 December and their final match in May, dropped just six points (via three drawn games) in their final 21 games. A win in the opening game of 2002–03 set the English top-flight record of 14 successive victories while at a few points in September and October Wenger's team had collected 59 points from their last 21 games (a rolling total), which remains the greatest run of form in top-flight history. Runners-up Liverpool almost matched Arsenal with 13 wins from 15 under stand-in manager Phil Thompson to end the season. It would be the Reds' last genuine title tilt for seven years.

Toonacious

Think of Newcastle's Premier League glory years and the mid-1990s is the correct response from your brain. But Bobby Robson's 2001–02 team is often overlooked as a genuine force. Not only did the Magpies reach the Champions League by ending the season in fourth but they topped the table at Christmas and showed admirable resilience throughout the entire season. In fact, their total of 34 points won from losing positions remains the most a team has recovered in a Premier League season. Almost half (48 per cent) of their points that season, therefore, came in games in which the opposition had led. Bobby Keegan. Sir Kevin Robson.

Topsy-turvy

While in 2001–02 a goalkeeper scored in the Premier League for the first time (Peter Schmeichel netting for Aston Villa away at Everton, the first keeper to score in the top flight since Coventry's Steve Ogrizovic in 1986), the outfielders responsible for tucking away penalties had a torrid time. Only 48 of the 73 spot-kicks awarded in 2001–02 nestled in the net shortly afterwards, a conversion rate of only 65.8 per cent, the lowest yet seen in the Premier League. (2001–02 is, unsurprisingly, the only season to see fewer than 50 penalty goals.) Chief culprits were Charlton, who failed with all three of theirs, while Derby could score only two of the five they were given.

Verdict

After two seasons of generic Manchester United formality romps, 2001–02 was a genuine thriller, with the title race alive until the penultimate round of fixtures. Arsenal's title win should, really, have been the first of their own three-in-a-row, but in 2002–03 Alex Ferguson employed all of his dark (and light) arts to regain the upper hand in his increasingly embittered battle with Arsène Wenger, stoked to fever pitch when the Gunners had the temerity to win the title at Old Trafford.

Premier League season No. 11: 2002–03

Is it still called the Premiership? I'VE CHECKED AND YES

Champions: Manchester United

Relegated: Sunderland, West Bromwich Albion, West Ham United

Top scorer: Ruud van Nistelrooy (25)

Most assists: Thierry Henry (20)

Biggest win: West Bromwich Albion 0–6 Liverpool

Overview

Master and commander. Has any manager other than Alex Ferguson ever won the Premier League when they really shouldn't have? (NB, I'm saying that Leicester in 2016 is just too odd to be included in this.) Keegan in 1996, Benítez in 2009, Rodgers in 2014; there are numerous examples of title-worthy teams who just couldn't quite get across the finishing line in first place, but at least three, possibly four, of Manchester United's 13 Premier League titles were prised from rivals with a determination and doggedness that came, undoubtedly, from their fierce manager. His 2002–03 triumph is possibly the finest example, as United hunted down Arsenal in their breezy Wengerian pomp and sowed the first tiny seeds of the mental disintegration that would hamper the Gunners for more than a decade.

With nine games to go Arsenal were eight points clear of United, having cruised past Charlton at home, with Highbury seemingly an impregnable fortress and Manchester United still to visit. In that eagerly awaited fixture, Arsenal led their great rivals 2–1 but a late Ryan Giggs goal gave Ferguson's team parity. Soon after, Arsenal faced a trip to Sam Allardyce's Bolton Wanderers, a phrase that could send southern-based progressive midfielders into a mental breakdown in the early 2000s. The Gunners squandered a 2–0 lead to draw another match 2–2. United's relentless progression, accompanied by the chant 'we want our trophy back', saw them eviscerate Charlton 4–1 on 3 May, leaving Arsenal eight points behind, albeit with two games in hand.

But the next day, relegation-haunted Leeds shocked Highbury with a 3–2 win that sent the Premier League trophy back to Old Trafford. Arsenal followed up in midweek with a rueful 6–1 romp against Southampton, notable for two hat-tricks (from Pirès and Pennant, two of four Arsenal players to score hat-tricks in the Premiership in 2002–03) and the fact that it was the first game in their 49-game unbeaten run. As recoveries go, that's a good one.

At the time, Manchester United's total of 31 days atop the Premier League was the shortest amount of time spent there by a title winner, and their form after losing to Middlesbrough on Boxing Day (15 wins and three draws) was breathtaking, if hard to take for Arsenal. Paul Scholes, in the era before he had transformed into a deep midfielder who could impress Cristiano Ronaldo by kicking balls against trees, scored 14 goals, his best return in a top-flight campaign, while David Beckham, in his final appearance for the club, scored with a direct free-kick, the 18th of his Premier League career, a total that has never been beaten.

Three Things We May Have Just Learnt About 2002–03

Blunderland

While Manchester United spent the first half of 2003 hoovering up victories, Sunderland's concurrent decline was even more astounding. Having sacked Peter Reid after a defeat to league leaders Arsenal in October, the club, who had finished seventh in 2000 and 2001, appointed Howard Wilkinson, the last Englishman to manage a side to a league title. One defeat from his opening five matches suggested he could be the man to keep the reeling Wearsiders up, but alas not. Nine defeats from his last 10 games (including a 3–1 defeat against Charlton to which Sunderland contributed not one, not two but three own goals, a Premier League record that has been matched only by . . . Sunderland in 2014), led to the club appointing their third manager of the season, genial Hiberno-Englishman Mick McCarthy, who promptly led the club to defeat in their remaining nine games, meaning they ended the season with 15 defeats in a row. When the club eventually returned to the Premier League in 2005–06 they lost their opening five matches, extending their record to 20 top-flight defeats in a row, which may never be beaten.

Earn your stripes

The 2002–03 season was the second in which the Premier League had four qualifying spots for the Champions League (or, more accurately, two for the Champions League and two for the qualifiers), and it was, naturally, around this time that the fetishisation of finishing in the top four emerged. Three of the top four sides (Manchester United, Arsenal and Chelsea) in May 2003 would go on to form that most 2000s of entities 'the Big Four', with Newcastle making up the quartet. The Magpies' third place in 2003 remains the last time that a team wearing stripes has finished in the top four. A hundred years earlier, stripes were a sign of respectability, with the design claiming 10 of the 18 league titles between 1892 and 1909, but in the 21st century, their impact has been as narrow as their own essence.

Beachcombers

One virtual guarantee in the modern Premier League is the quality of the pitches. Even when clubs with smaller grounds such as Bournemouth make it to the top flight, the playing surface is invariably immaculate. But 2002–03 featured almost certainly the worst ever Premier League pitch and possibly a top-flight low (though no doubt a Victorian side played at least once on gorse). The stadium was Stamford Bridge and the match was Claudio Ranieri's Chelsea against Charlton; long before the Italian was tearing up the rulebook in 2015–16, he seemingly oversaw the removal of all turf at the Bridge, with Charlton claiming that a home official had told them that what they had played on was the base for a new pitch, rather than an actual . . . pitch. The Addicks demanded that the game, which they lost 4–1, should be replayed, but their request wasn't granted and they were left instead to rue their lack of penetration on Chelsea beach. (NB, a tabloid newspaper's response to this event was to stage a rematch involving donkeys on Blackpool beach, complete with 'Clopta Stats' on the game. A different time.)

Verdict

Fourteen years may have passed but the memories of Manchester United hunting down reigning champions Arsenal and pulling off an unlikely win are still powerful, with the heat of the tussle in 2002–03 fanning the flames for further battles in 2003–04 and a wounded United's ending of Arsenal's invincibility in 2004–05. As the nation, and increasingly the world, focused on the Gunners and the Red Devils, early in July 2003 a Russian businessman called Roman Abramovich purchased Chelsea. The Wenger/Ferguson era of twin dominance was nearing its end.

Premier League season No. 12: 2003–04

Is it still called the Premiership? THE NAMING CONVENTION SEEMS INVINCIBLE

Champions: Arsenal

Relegated: Wolverhampton Wanderers, Leeds United, Leicester City

Top scorer: Thierry Henry (30)

Most assists: Muzzy Izzet (14)

Biggest win: Portsmouth 6–1 Leeds/4 games ended 5–0

Overview

It shouldn't be underrated. It can't be underrated. Whether it deserved a special golden trophy is not a debate for these pages, but you can see why the metallurgy experts were engaged. The 2003–04 season is nothing without those Invincibles. A glance at the table shows Arsenal winning the league (played 38, won 26, drew 12, lost . . . you know) by 11 points but it wasn't a runaway victory, not until the last few weeks at least. Arsenal's campaign contained Thierry Henry's greatest goal haul, with 30 (22 of them coming at Highbury) and it remains a stunning achievement. Even so, if you had suggested in the long summer of 2004 that Arsenal would go at least 14 years without another league title, you'd have been thought insane.

As befitted the great Arsenal–Manchester United war of the early century, Sir Alex Ferguson's churlishness about the London side's achievement was as remarkable as it was unfounded. 'It wasn't championship form from Arsenal; they had too many draws,' he said. 'Normally you're going to lose about four games a year when you win a title but, with all the draws they were getting, four defeats would have cost them first place. You can use religion but they adopted remaining undefeated as their great cause. It was a one-off, I don't expect it to be repeated.'

While he was right (so far) about it not being repeated, Ferguson's insistence that 12 draws was unusual wasn't true. Arsenal were, in fact, the 22nd English champions to record 12 or more draws (although Leicester in 2015–16 are the only club to have done it since), including three of Ferguson's own champions (1993, 1997 and 1999, with United recording a whopping 13 draws in the latter season; would he accept anyone saying that the treble winners hadn't demonstrated 'championship form'?). What's not recorded is whether anyone told Ferguson about 1978–79 in Serie A, where Perugia went unbeaten (with 11 wins and 19 draws) yet came only second to Milan. Now *that* is too many draws.

Ferguson's mind games, so beloved by the media and so revered since his retirement, were designed to detract from his own team's failings. Two wins and three defeats in their final six games ensured United finished outside the top two and marked the true start of their manager's toughest rebuilding job (adding Cristiano Ronaldo in summer 2003 was a

reasonable start), with even an FA Cup win slightly under-
played given that it came against second-tier Millwall.
Meanwhile, seventh-placed Charlton recorded the highest
top-flight finish with a goal difference of zero since Stoke in
1936 (when goal difference didn't even count). It remains the
last time the Addicks finished as one of the top 10 clubs in the
country, their mid-2000s complaints about a lack of UEFA
Cup qualification now just a cruel footnote to their decline.

At the bottom of the table fans were treated to a super-rare
three-way relegation draw, with Wolves, Leeds and Leicester
all ending the season on 33 points (Leicester drew 15 games;
#toomanydraws). This is the only time in English top-flight
history when three teams have gone down on the same
points. At the time, you would have expected Leeds to return
soonest, given that only three years earlier they had contested
a Champions League semi-final, but they have been out of the
top tier ever since, while Wolves and Leicester (the latter in
outstanding fashion) have bounced back.

Three Things We May Have Just Learnt About 2003–04

We need to talk about Kevin

As reinventions go, the Kevin Davies remake of 2003–04 (director: Sam Allardyce) was a good one. The striker's spells at
Southampton and Blackburn had been frustrating, and most
had given up on the former Chesterfield starlet coming good
in the Premiership, but at Allardyce's Bolton he flourished. In
2003–04 he both scored and assisted nine goals (nine assists
was more than either Robert Pirès or Dennis Bergkamp managed for champions Arsenal that season), but he also gave his

team a physical edge that his manager relished. Davies ended the season having conceded 98 fouls, and then reached the magical three-figure mark in 2004–05, 2005–06, 2008–09, 2009–10 and 2010–11. Why choose between beauty and the beast when you can have both in one package?

How I learned to love the Bootboys

It passed unnoticed at the time but 2003–04 was the last time the great Alan Shearer scored 20 league goals in a season, clocking up 22 as Newcastle came fifth (missing out on the top four thanks mainly to their total of 17 draws; *#toomanydraws*). But while the total was impressive, and second only to Thierry Henry, seven of Shearer's 22 came via the penalty spot, the former England man scoring more spot-kicks than 17 of the 20 Premiership teams. In fact, with only 110 shots all season, almost 10 per cent of Shearer's shots in 2003–04 came from the penalty spot (he took 10, missing three). It was a telling change in his game as injuries started to take their toll on the battering ram who had bludgeoned the defences of the 1990s. For Newcastle, it would be a long wait for another player to score 20 or more league goals, with no one managing it until Dwight Gayle in 2016–17.

Jonesing for action

Were 2003 and 2004 the most eventful years of Paul Jones's goalkeeping life? You'd have to say yes (you don't have to, but I'm saying it's a fair shout). In May 2003 he became the first substitute goalkeeper to appear in an FA Cup final. Then, in

2003–04, Jones became the second, and possibly final, player to play for three Premier League clubs in a single season (arcane registration regulations from barmy bureaucrats have since made this almost impossible to replicate). Jones started the season as Southampton's No. 1 before an emergency move to Liverpool in January, where he made two appearances, keeping one clean sheet. Then, just a couple of weeks later, he moved to Wolves, where he appeared 16 times as the Midlands side dropped out of the big league.

Verdict

Let it be said: Arsenal's 12 draws do not undermine their achievement in going an entire league season unbeaten. They had three successive games in the closing weeks of the season where they edged nervously to draws, unusual to see in champions-elect. But this was *precisely because they were chasing the seemingly impossible*. The tension around those final few games that season (even for non-Arsenal fans) was palpable. People knew they might be about to see something epochal. And they did.

5.

The Blueprint for a Perfect Match

'It's one of them days when you just say "it's one of them days"'

– Ian Wright

Your name is _____. You are a football manager. You are 59 years old. You spent most of your playing career in the second tier. You have had a successful career as a manager for the past 22 years. Your ambition is to manage the England team one day. Your team is playing an FA Cup match on Saturday. Your team played a European game in midweek. You are under pressure to get results after a difficult period. You know that defeat in the forthcoming cup game will almost certainly get you sacked. You do not want to be sacked. What can you do to ensure you come through the cup tie and keep your job, for another week at least?

Thursday morning (two days before the game)

You meet your assistant manager before light training (you played in northern Portugal on Tuesday night and landed at Luton airport at 01:25 on Wednesday morning). He has noticed that you've lost three times after playing in Europe this season and wants to discuss this. You've asked your club's data scout to compile a report. Here are his findings.

2000–2017	Pts difference post-Europe
Arsenal	-0.02
Chelsea	-0.20
Liverpool	-0.16
Man City	-0.29
Man Utd	-0.08
Tottenham	+0.09
Overall	**-0.10**

It seems that generally there is a slight penalty after playing in Europe, with major teams averaging about 0.1 points per game less in games after European matches than they do overall. He notes that the worst performance in his study was Chelsea in 2002–03, who averaged only 0.5 points per game after European matches, down 1.26 on their seasonal average. This was the final season before Roman Abramovich's takeover of the club and the management were restricted in terms of squad depth.

You note that you are in a similar position and, although the forthcoming game is a cup match, injuries and the need to progress as far as possible mean you are restricted in changing the team much from the midweek game. Your data scout agrees with this approach but you sense some resistance from your assistant, who you suspect is keen to supplant you.

Friday morning (one day before the game)

Friday's edition of the *Daily Mail* carries an article by a columnist, a former professional who played under you, claiming that you are tactically outmoded and haven't adapted to changes in the modern game.

He notes that supporters have complained about your insistence on playing a defensive 4–5–1 system, and this is accompanied by a table that shows that it has the lowest win percentage of the six main formations used in the Premier League, just 20 per cent. The ex-player suggests a series of foreign managers who are out of work who could replace you either immediately or in the summer. You notice he thinks Shakhtar Donetsk are a Russian team.

You see that 4–4–2, a formation you used heavily in the late 1990s when you were regularly lauded as one of the brightest young managers in the English game, is not used very much any more in the Premier League, but it does have a reasonable win percentage of 36 per cent. You consider bringing in an additional striker for the cup game tomorrow, although you are not confident your second- and third-choice forwards are up to the task.

Formation	Games	Wins	Win %
3-4-2-1	73	43	58.9%
3-4-3	80	37	46.3%
4-1-2-1-2	73	33	45.2%
4-2-3-1	1,618	698	43.1%
4-4-2	509	185	36.4%
4-3-1-2	25	9	36.0%
4-3-3	444	159	35.8%
4-4-1-1	376	116	30.9%
3-4-1-2	35	10	28.6%
4-3-2-1	14	4	28.6%
4-1-4-1	254	72	28.4%
3-5-2	70	17	24.3%
5-3-2	32	7	21.9%
4-5-1	125	25	20.0%
5-4-1	21	3	14.3%
3-5-1-1	29	3	10.3%

Friday evening (one day before the game)

Your team is at home in the cup game tomorrow, so you are able to relax at your executive-style home on the outskirts of a town that lies 17 miles from the town the team you manage play in. Your weary wife is walking away from the telephone, which is ringing. It is your chairman, who is reminding you of the importance of tomorrow's game. You agree with the chairman. He notes that the game is not being shown live on television in the UK, as they expect that your opponents, who are in the second tier, will not be able to knock out the Premier League side on their home ground. He hopes they are right. You agree with the chairman. He mentions the piece in the *Daily Mail* and says that negative coverage of the club isn't helpful. You agree with the chairman. He wishes you luck for tomorrow. You say goodnight to the chairman.

Friday night (one day before the game)

You get an email on your iPad (you are unwilling to link your email account to your phone as you are not entirely sure how it works and you do not want to send anything by mistake; a former team-mate once sent his resignation letter to the *Mail on Sunday* by accident) 10 minutes before midnight. The email is from the data scout at the football club. He has compiled a report looking at the history of top-flight teams playing Second Division sides in the FA Cup. You are slightly annoyed that it has come late, but you remember that he watches a lot of these American sports so is often most active at this time of night.

The results show that since the Second World War (your usual cut-off point for most studies), top-flight teams playing at home (in the first game at least) have progressed three-quarters of the time, rising to almost 80 per cent in the Premier League era.

You drift off to sleep and sleep uneasily, the number 79 and your assistant's leering face infiltrating your dreams in a series of unexpected and uninteresting ways.

FA Cup 1946–2017 unless stated	
Ties between top-flight and second-tier teams	1241
Progression rate of top-flight side	72%
Top-flight team at home to second-tier team	576
Progression rate of top-flight side at home	75%
Home ties in PL era (Jan 1993 onwards)	214
Progression rate of top-flight sides at home	79%

Saturday morning (day of the game)

In a parallel universe, today's game is already under way. A television company has used the long history of this particular cup competition to leverage a significant broadcasting contract in Asia, and has requested that one game in each round of fixtures should kick off at 11 a.m. GMT, so it can be shown on Saturday evening in the new market, but so far the organisers have refused to acquiesce.

As you journey to the ground you think back to the start of your managerial career, when the Premier League experimented with kick-offs before 12 p.m., occasionally because of police advice but mainly for broadcasting reasons. Between 1993 and 2005, 29 games kicked off at 11 a.m., 11.15 or 11.30, with the matches producing a healthy 3.1 goals per game, 0.5 more than the average.

In November 2000, those global viewers were able to enjoy Mark Viduka scoring all four goals as Leeds defeated Liverpool 4–3 in a match that began at 11.30 a.m. In something that became semi-typical of these morning kick-offs, Liverpool keeper Sander Westerveld was forced to wear a cap because of the low winter sun that hung over Elland Road. You reflect that in trying to please viewers in the land of the rising sun, star players were made to deal with one that had already climbed too high.

This won't be an issue today, though. The kick-off is at three o'clock and it is already raining.

Saturday lunchtime (day of the game)

You have decided to play two forwards in this game. You know some people will think that this is a reaction to the *Daily Mail* article but you have actually been thinking of doing it for some time, even if you haven't articulated it. Some two-bit smart alec on Twitter has said that no team playing with two out-and-out strikers have lifted the FA Cup since 2006,

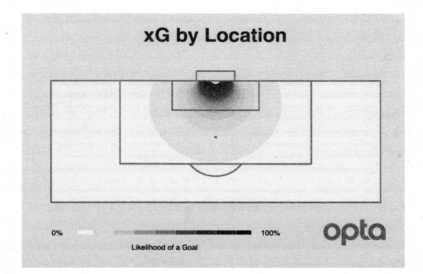

and even then Liverpool won on penalties, but you reassure yourself that this isn't an FA Cup final. Not yet anyway.

You deliver your pre-match briefing after lunch at 12:51 as you have for the entirety of your career. You reiterate your long-held mantra that shooting from outside the box is not productive and you'll fine any player who does it twice in a game.

You engage your assistant in a conversation the players have heard many times, but repetition helps people remember things. It helps you remember things.

'What are the odds of scoring from a shot inside the box?'

'Fourteen per cent, boss,' he replies, a little monotonously.

'Sounds good to me. What about outside the box?'

'Just 3 per cent.'

'Three per cent sounds lower than 14 per cent.'

'Quite a lot lower, boss.'

'Yes, just as being fined £0 sounds lower than being fined £1,000. Do you think that sounds lower?'

'Yes, boss, definitely sounds lower to me,' he adds sullenly, turning away from the team before the sentence is even finished.

'Heroes shoot from inside the box, never forget that. Heroes shoot from inside the box.' You end the speech by thumping your right fist into your left hand but most of the players are fiddling with their socks or their laces and don't see the gesture.

Saturday 2 p.m.

Your pre-match obligations include a five-minute chat with sponsors and corporate fans. It is your least favourite part of the working week. Recently, you have suffered criticism in this slot for your defensive approach to games. You have the lowest number of shots on target in the Premier League and you've either won or lost 1–0, or drawn 0–0 in 74 per cent of your league games so far. One of the sponsors has been vociferous about how his company's brand is associated with entertainment and yet he rarely sees any when he comes to games. You have asked for some data to back you up in case the point is raised again. It is.

'Manager, can you assure us that you and your team are committed to attacking play?'

'I can assure you we're committed to getting the best result for this football club.'

'Through attacking play?'

'Through *winning* play. Winning games is our aim. Attacking play helps us win games, but attacking too much can cause us to lose games. The chairman doesn't like us losing games.' You smile, ruefully, remembering the incident at the Christmas party in 2009. How were you to know, how were you to know?

Snapping out of the unpleasant reflection, you quote the data you have been given:

2012–2017	Comeback win %	Comeback win or draw %
Big Six team	24%	47%
Other team	7%	24%

'The fact is, for teams outside the Big 6 going behind makes victory extremely unlikely. Stopping our opponents scoring is paramount to our success as a football club. Teams who have had five or more shots on target win 57 per cent of their games;

teams who allow the opposition two shots on target or fewer win 62 per cent of their games. Gentlemen, my defence is the defence. Continue to attack me and I will prevail.'

You walk out of the room without looking back. The game is imminent.

Saturday 2.50 p.m.

The last few minutes before the match. You rarely offer any advice at this point; it's too late to make tactical changes, and you've found that impassioned speeches are best saved for key moments in a season that may come along only once or twice, if at all. For a group of people who enjoy publishing inspirational quotes on social media, footballers are largely immune to oratory.

Saturday 3 p.m.

You sit in your dugout and ponder the fact that football is one of the few sports where the person who controls the team has a hindered view of the action. In 2008 you campaigned against proposals to ban TV monitors in Premier League dugouts, but lost the vote. As you see it, the tyranny of the referees' association won out, officials fearful of live feedback during games. The technical zone was, ultimately, stripped of replay technology invented in the mid-1950s. You have seen coaching staff at other clubs surreptitiously hunched over smartphones looking at pixelated goal clips and data feeds.

You also notice that the pre-match rituals have caused a slight delay to the kick-off, as usual. You are unaware that in the Premier League in 2016–17 6 per cent of 3 p.m. games kicked off at least a minute late, but it's certainly something you'd enjoy.

Saturday 3.12 p.m.

The early stages of the game have not gone well. Your beloved firewall of allowing the opposition just two shots on target has already been breached and the new formation isn't working, the two strikers having touched the ball only four times between them, two of them from the (traditionally taken) kick-off.

You know this is bad because Premier League teams, despite their addiction to player rotation in the FA Cup, allow about 0.4 shots on target fewer in the FA Cup than they do in league competition. This is not the start you were looking for. You look up at the directors' box. The chairman is staring straight back at you. Your assistant is smiling to himself, breaking off only to aggressively harass the fourth official about encroachment.

Saturday 3.25 p.m.

Here it is, the opening goal. Your defence will blame the goalkeeper, your goalkeeper will blame the defence. You will blame . . . yourself. A set-piece goal is always a stab to the ego. Open-play goals, well they come from brilliant chaos, but set-piece goals are eminently preventable. Around 14 per cent of the goals in Premier League history have come from corners or indirect free-kicks and you can guarantee that each one of them has been pored over, discussed, diagnosed, rewound and regretted.

This goal came from a corner. You mark zonally as you have for more than a decade. You are English so you are at least rarely criticised for it by the national media, who nonetheless still seem to view zonal marking as an aberration from the culprit-based man-to-man marking system. In the 2000s Andy Gray said of zonal marking: 'I'm not saying it's a shocking system, but it is flawed and that makes it very difficult to blame people who are marking space,' making it clear that in the English game, identifying and punishing players after a set-piece goal is conceded is both expected and necessary. And, implicitly, that the true issue with zonal marking is that it means that punishment must be attributed to the abstract system and the collective team and not to an individual.

As Michel Foucault said: 'It is the certainty of being punished and not the horrifying spectacle of public punishment that must discourage crime,' but this is a concept that is yet to reach analysis of defending set-pieces.

Saturday 3.42 p.m.

Disaster. Your goalkeeper goes down with a head injury in a melee following a corner (your team's defending of set-piece situations in this game continues to be a serious concern), and the physio has indicated that he cannot continue in the game. Last year you trended for 15 minutes on social media in the United States after stating that 'in my experience, a bash on the head is no worse than a kick on the shin'. You remember that someone in Connecticut called you a 'medically illiterate whackjob'.

Your reserve goalkeeper looks aghast as he realises he'll have to come on. He conceded five goals in his last appearance, a League Cup tie in the autumn. You look aghast as you remember this game.

From the recesses of your mind you recall a study of substitution impacts you requested from your data team. The information showed that first-half substitutions and goalkeeper substitutions were relatively positive in win-percentage terms. Unsurprisingly, there were relatively few (<50) occasions when a goalkeeper was substituted, but more than 400 first-half substitutions, and it seemed to be a better move than a half-time switch, where the win-percentage was noticeably lower. This was almost certainly because the majority of substitutions before half-time would be due to injury rather than a dire game situation, whereas at half-time the opposite would almost certainly be true.

The two most obscure substitution scenarios were making three changes at once or no changes at all. Both, in different ways, are gambles and thus rarely seen. As you discovered, the only team to win without making any substitutions in the last five years were Hull City against reigning champions Leicester in August 2016, and that was because they had barely any players to call on.

Premier League since 2012–13	Win%
Double subs	26.3%
Treble subs	18.2%
No subs	11.1%
First-half sub	35.9%
Half-time sub	25.1%
Keeper subs	37.8%

The other issue with substitutions is that you're largely limited to players who are either out of form or not good enough to make the team in the first place. The list of Premier League players with the highest proportion of goals from the bench is a case in point. Yes, they were impact players but the main impact they made was that they were not good enough to start games in the Premier League. The highest-scoring player in Premier League history never to score after coming on as a sub? Éric Cantona with 70. He started games because he was Éric Cantona and Éric Cantona was good. You didn't bench Éric Cantona so you could wait and see what happened.

Premier League	Goals	Sub goals	%
Matt Derbyshire	10	9	90.0%
Adam Le Fondre	12	8	66.7%
Stern John	10	6	60.0%
Robert Earnshaw	13	7	53.8%
Victor Anichebe	26	13	50.0%
Ryan Babel	12	6	50.0%
Geoff Horsfield	12	6	50.0%
Dan Gosling	10	5	50.0%
Hat Robson-Kanu	10	5	50.0%
Sylvan Ebanks-Blake	10	5	50.0%

That said, as your first-choice goalkeeper is carried off the pitch to lukewarm applause, you have no choice. Your reserve goalkeeper is putting on his gloves, and when this is complete he pulls his knees towards his stomach as he jumps up and down, in time-honoured substitute-preparing-to-enter-the-field-of-play fashion. A cursory studs check from the assistant referee and your new custodian is plunged into the game.

Saturday 3.47 p.m.

Half-time. You are still trailing by one goal. Your (first-choice) goalkeeper has already left for hospital. The plucky lower league side almost scored from another set-piece just before half-time, but your (second-choice) goalkeeper made a (first-class) save to keep you in it. As you walk into the dressing room you overhear someone saying that conceding just before half-time is the worst time to concede, something that has enraged you ever since you were told it is not really true. Conceding in the 80th minute, for example, is slightly worse.

Defeat % when conceding a goal in [xx] minute			
45+	10	80	90+
68.2%	58.5%	69.9%	67.1%

A screen in the dressing room shows data from the first half, although half of the screen is covered with what the club shop calls an anthem jacket. Even so, you can see your team have already allowed the opposition four shots on target. You prepare to show your displeasure to the team, although you see your assistant speaking to one of the strikers while covering his mouth with his hand. What is happening to the game?

Saturday 4.12 p.m.

Your three-minute, eight-second rant at the players at half-time has had no discernible effect yet. You still trail 1–0. The opposition have already had two more shots on target. Your (second-choice) goalkeeper has doubled the number of saves he's made all season in around 13 minutes of action.

Your assistant is staring blankly at the pitch, although he has made a threatening comment to the fourth official, something to do with a car park and a . . . yoga mat? You shake your head in what you think is an imperceptible way, but within 83 seconds there's a gif of this head shake being shared on various social media channels. You try to remember the information you were given about game states.

After a worrying pause, you remember the detailed information you were given about game states in Major European Leagues.

Game state	% of plays ending in a shot	Passes per possession	Time per possession
Winning	7.28%	3.07	12.62
Drawing	6.93%	3.12	13.19
Losing	7.71%	3.36	14.04

Specifically you remember being asked (by a slightly supercilious man) whether you thought teams had more shots when they were winning or losing. You, to the man's apparent delight, said winning, and you were incorrect. Teams generally shoot more when they are trailing, which did make sense when you thought about it. Possession time is also higher for trailing teams, which again seems logical, as teams who have the lead are likely to value their shape and solidity more than trying to open up their opponents.

Applying this to your current situation, you call over the left midfielder and tell him to remind the rest of the team to ensure they shoot only in good positions. The age-old advice of 'stay calm, don't panic' is what you are saying, albeit backed up with actual evidence.

Saturday 4.43 p.m.

Drama at the death. Your (first-choice) centre-forward is shoved in the back and falls gracefully to the ground. It's traditional to say that the referee didn't hesitate but this time he did, for what seems like minutes but is actually less than four seconds. Eventually, with an exaggerated sense of self-importance, he points to the spot and your staff and unused substitutes erupt. You sit still, hoping your clear instructions will be followed. Your assistant shouts 'that's what's been coming, you mugs' to no one in particular.

The fouled centre-forward picks himself up and looks around to see where the ball is. He is your designated penalty taker but only in situations when he has not won the penalty. The reasoning is that the conversion rate of players who take penalties they have won themselves, in the Premier League at any rate, is lower than when another player takes it. Not by a huge margin, but enough to hang a club policy on.

You can see your other main penalty taker, the Irish full-back, making this point to the centre-forward. The striker is shaking his head but seems to be handing the ball to his teammate. The Irish full-back is left-footed and you once harboured negative views towards left-footed penalty takers, but once you were shown there is minimal variation in conversion rates between left- and right-footed players, you were happy to change your stance. On a related note, you once tried to sign Obafemi Martins and considered asking him to nominate a chosen foot for penalties in his contract as he scored with both feet in his career and you felt it was unnecessary showboating.

Premier League 2012–2017	Success rate
Taken by player who won penalty	73%
Not taken by player who won penalty	81%
Taken right-footed	80%
Taken left-footed	77%

Saturday 4.45 p.m.

The penalty area is empty of players other than your full-back and the opposition goalkeeper. You know that your player has scored with seven of his last nine penalties and prefers to go low and to the left. If the goalkeeper moves in that direction during his run-up he'll switch, otherwise it will be low left. This goalkeeper plays for a club who rarely have need to scout Premier League goalkeepers so you are reasonably confident he'll go low left. According to a report you received from your data scout, high penalties are rarely reached by the goalkeeper but, understandably, do carry a greater risk of missing the target. Low left will do. Frankly, anything will do.

Premier League 2012–2017	Success rate
High left	97%
High right	97%
High centre	100%
Low left	79%
Low right	81%
Low centre	80%

Only includes penalties hit on target and not those wide and/or high

The Irish full-back goes low left, the goalkeeper stands still and watches the ball hit the back and side of the net simultaneously. 1–1. You look up to the directors' box. The chairman is not in his seat.

Saturday 5.01 p.m.

Extra-time (a new experiment at this stage of the competition, as part of the great fight with fixture congestion), which brings the unedifying scenes of dispensing managerial advice and guidance on the actual playing surface. Your main aims are to assess who is struggling (you have by now used two of your three substitutions) and to crystallise the team's set-up in the additional 30 minutes. As you see it, there are two ways to approach extra-time. Option one is to carry on as normal, and treat the additional time as a further opportunity to win the match. Option two is to close down the game and make reaching penalties the primary aim.

Since penalty shoot-outs were introduced to the FA Cup in 1991, around 57 per cent of the games in the first round or later that have reached extra-time have been settled in the additional period, with the remainder going to penalties. Between 1991 and 1998 second-tier teams won on penalties against top-flight sides in the FA Cup on three of six occasions but since then the Premier League sides have won seven in a row.

You decide to hedge your bets and tell your team to keep probing but to keep it tight as well. The conditions have tired both sides and you are confident your side's fitness levels are superior. You reiterate your rule about not shooting from long range. People remember Steven Gerrard's goal in the 2006 FA Cup final, but his total of eight, unsuccessful, shots from outside the box as Liverpool blew their title chances against Chelsea in 2014 is a more telling tale.

Saturday 5.32 p.m.

Extra-time is over, extra-time was abysmal. Your opponents, tantalised by the prospect of the penalty shoot-out, parked a bus of such solidity and immovability that you managed only three shots, all of them from outside the penalty area; 3 per cent of sheer ineptitude. The other team's manager looks delighted as the referee ends the second period of extra-time, punching the air and hugging his staff. His team reminds you of England in Euro 2012, who, in their knockout game against Italy, managed only 15 passes in the second period of extra-time. Fifteen passes in 15 minutes, there can't have been many more today. The crowd is grumbling, the players look dejected, the chairman, back in his seat, looks inscrutable. The penalty shoot-out is upon you.

You at least have a body of research behind the decisions you are about to take. From what you can see, your opposite number looks as if he's going with the default method of preparing for a penalty shoot-out by repeatedly asking 'who fancies one?'.

After exiting the League Cup to a lower league side three seasons ago, you commissioned some research into penalty shoot-outs, which you have since enthusiastically applied to training, although this is only the second chance you have had to test it. The key points you have hopefully drilled into your staff and players is that penalty success drops about 10 percentage points in a shoot-out, compared to a penalty during the game. Being the team to take the first penalty is statistically an advantage, and success rates decline as the shoot-out progresses (with the eighth penalty having been missed most often at World Cups), although if a player is taking a penalty to win a shoot-out the chances of scoring it rise significantly (to around 90 per cent), whereas with a penalty to avoid elimination the success rate falls below 50 per cent.

As such you have instructed your captain, if he wins the toss, to choose to go first, and you have named your best taker (your centre-forward who won the penalty during the game) fourth in your submitted list. The rest is down to other people.

Saturday 7.53 p.m.

You finish your post-match duties and responsibilities. You have, as is customary, shared wine (red but light, possibly a Gamay) with the opposition manager. Your team have progressed to the next round, his team have been knocked out, but his (heroic) cup exit is already being praised more than your (fortunate) progression. This is the way it goes. There are five unread text messages from your assistant manager on your phone. There are four days until you play again and you have to be back at 9 a.m. tomorrow to prepare Monday's schedule and speak with your medical team. The average tenure at a Premier League club is around 60 games. You've done 184 at this club. It's been a good run. You can feel a level of fatigue that no amount of sleep will cure. We go again. We have to.

Premier League season No. 13: 2004–05

Is it still called the Premiership? PATIENCE, CHILD

Champions: Chelsea

Relegated: Southampton, Norwich City, Crystal Palace

Top scorer: Thierry Henry (25)

Most assists: Frank Lampard (18)

Biggest win: Arsenal 7–0 Everton

Overview

The one with the Special One. At the culmination of 2003–04, Arsenal's hegemony looked established. The first team to go unbeaten in an entire top-flight league campaign since 1889 (you may have heard about this), Arsène Wenger's side started 2004–05 in the same positive fashion, equalling Nottingham Forest's 42-game unbeaten run with a 5–3 rollercoaster of a game against Middlesbrough, a match in which the Gunners were 3–1 down at one point but looked as concerned as a grown man faced with an ant. But just as it looked as if they would make it to 50 games without a loss, Wayne Rooney and Manchester United took huge delight in ending their run at

49, with ensuing pizza-based mayhem (incidentally, Wenger's thematic move from pasta to pizza was, in a way, illustrative of Arsenal's fading grip on the Premiership crown).

One defeat doesn't shape a season, but after that Manchester United loss Arsenal showed early onset modern Arsenal by winning only one of their next five games (albeit a 5–4 humdinger against Tottenham in which a Premier League record nine players scored), and letting Chelsea ominously replace them at the top of the table. José Mourinho's side lacked the panache of Wenger's Arsenal but their league title in the Portuguese's first season was arguably the most impressive ever seen in the English top flight. Not only did the Blues end the campaign with 95 points (the only 38-game season in English history to see a team get 'more' was Bristol City in Division Two in 1905–06, with 96, although they actually got 66 points as it was two points for a win, of which they recorded 30, please keep up), they also conceded only 15 goals all season (see discussion below), and two of those 15 came after they had wrapped up the title. In the end, Chelsea finished 12 points clear of Arsenal, who lost four more Premier League games after their cloak of invincibility had been torn to shreds at Old Trafford. Incredibly, it was the last time Arsenal would finish in the top two until 2015–16.

While Chelsea dominated at the top, the battle at the bottom was an unpredictable classic. West Brom became the first team since Sheffield United in 1990–91 to be bottom at Christmas and not go down (and the first team since Crystal Palace in 1969–70 to win only six games and not suffer demotion) and, going into the final day of the season, no team had yet been relegated. Norwich were in the relative luxury of 17th place, but proceeded to lose 6–0 at Fulham, one of only 12 instances of a team conceding six or more in the Premier

League in May. They were joined in demotion by Southampton and Crystal Palace to complete the most southerly drop zone combination in the competition's history.

Three Things We May Have Just Learnt About 2004–05

When 15 is more than zero

Arsenal were given a special golden Premier League trophy for remaining unbeaten in 2003–04 but Chelsea were unrewarded for conceding only 15 goals in the subsequent campaign. The Gunners were happy to adopt Preston's Invincibles tag from the 1880s but Chelsea matched their number of goals conceded and, like Arsenal, played 16 more games. Chelsea's only defeat was to Kevin Keegan's Manchester City in October and a team derided for being functional and dour ended the season with only one goal fewer than Arsenal had scored 12 months earlier. And, unlike the Gunners, who have never added to that title, Chelsea defended their title successfully and then went on to win the Premier League on three further occasions.

Agent Penalty

Just like *Die Hard* had two Agent Johnsons, the Premier League has had two Andy Johnsons, and nothing says Andy Johnson more than the 2004–05 season when one of them (the small striker one) ripped up the rules on how many penalties a player can possibly win, persuading referees to give him eight, while taking a Premier League record 13 and scoring 11.

Even relegation cannot take the gloss from Johnson's extraordinary total of 11 penalty goals in one season. Since he did it, Frank Lampard and Steven Gerrard have come close (10 apiece in 2009–10 and 2013–14 respectively) to Johnson's bumper haul, but it looks set to remain a shining beacon in the penalty community for some time to come. The final irony was that penalty-laden Palace were relegated on the final day away at Charlton, who didn't get awarded a spot-kick all season.

King power

Among England's glut of excellent central defenders in the late 1990s and 2000s, Ledley King was possibly the most talented. He was certainly the most unlucky, with a chronic knee problem that severely limited how much he was able to train and play. The 2004–05 season, then, was King's finest effort, especially off the back of some strong performances for England at Euro 2004. The Tottenham man proceeded to play all 38 of his club's Premier League games the next season, the only time he ever achieved a 100 per cent appearance rate. Oh, and his goal after 10 seconds against Bradford in December 2000 remains the fastest ever seen in the Premier League.

Verdict

Arsène Wenger was the undisputed king of English football in 2004, but a year later the Mourinho era had begun. Along with Rafa Benítez (who led Liverpool to an unlikely Champions League win in this campaign), Mourinho fundamentally changed the approach of top teams in England, with low scoring but tactically adept teams dominating both the Premier League and, in particular, European football. Chelsea became only the fourth club to win the Premier League and their financial strength, combined with their star manager, suggested that they would dominate a division in which both Arsenal and Manchester United looked to be fading forces. The 2005–06 season would only underline that feeling.

Premier League season No. 14: 2005–06

Is it still called the Premiership? CHANGE IS COMING (NOT YET)

Champions: Chelsea

Relegated: Sunderland, West Bromwich Albion, Birmingham City

Top scorer: Thierry Henry (27)

Most assists: Didier Drogba (11)

Biggest win: Arsenal 7–0 Middlesbrough

Overview

A romp for the ages. Chelsea became only the fifth club to retain the title since the war (after Portsmouth, Wolves, Liverpool and Manchester United; the latter two, naturally, on more than one occasion) in a league campaign that was not just dominant, but virtually over by early autumn. The Blues won 20 of their first 22 games, the only time this has happened in English top-flight history. After that 22nd game, José Mourinho's team were 16 points clear at the top of the table, with the prospect of being caught as distant as the Ken Bates era of financial struggle. So routine did Chelsea's title gallop seem that Mourinho didn't even win manager of the month at any point during the campaign, something that wouldn't happen again to a Premier League-winning manager until 2014–15.

Chelsea were rarely challenged by their domestic opponents, and this, combined with their manager's safety-first philosophy, saw them score 72 goals, exactly the number they had registered in Mourinho's first season (his third title with the club in 2015 would see them expand hugely to 73 goals). The 2005–06 campaign represented the mid-point of the great defensive era of the Premier League era, with all champions from Arsenal in 2003–04 to Manchester United in 2008–09 conceding fewer than 30 goals. It hadn't happened in any of the 12 seasons prior to 2003–04 and has happened only once since. Eagle-eyed readers might notice that these seasons of defensive prowess coincided with the last period of English dominance in the Champions League, almost, somehow, as if the two things were connected.

But while the Big Four, led by the militant 4–3–3 of Chelsea, exerted a tighter grip on the league, the rest of the teams increasingly looked like they were there only to make up the numbers. The 76-point gap between Chelsea in first place and Sunderland in 20th was an all-time top-flight record, equalled two years later by Manchester United, who went on to become European champions in the same season, and a Derby County team who . . . well, we'll come to that.

Elsewhere, newly promoted Wigan were the early season sensation, maintaining second place in the table until mid-November, when they had 25 points from 11 games, before an understandable second-half-of-the-season slowdown meant they ended the season (after an appearance in the final league game ever at Highbury) in 10th place. Sunderland were relegated in mid-April (see below) and joining them were West Midlands pair West Brom and Birmingham, the first time two clubs from the region had gone down together since the same pair 20 years earlier. You could almost call it second city syndrome, but for the five miles between West Bromwich and Birmingham.

Three Things We May Have Just Learnt About 2005–06

Black Catastrophe

Sunderland established new frontiers in 2005–06 by losing 29 of their 38 league games, the first time a top-flight team had been defeated so often in a 20-team division. Three years earlier the Black Cats had sunk out of the Premiership with 19 points and 15 straight defeats but the 2005–06 outfit were even worse, ending the campaign with just 15 points and just three wins. It's sometimes hard to work out which of Sunderland's many terrible seasons was which, as their ineptitude can blend into one catastrophic rollercoaster of memory, but 2005–06 is a fair shout, especially given that no player scored more than three (three!) goals for them all season (what meagre credit there is should go to Dean Whitehead, Liam Lawrence, Anthony Le Tallec and Tommy 'Tommy Miller' Miller).

The doyens of the d'ockyard

At the other end of the country from Sunderland, Portsmouth were enjoying themselves by playing a series of players with apostrophes in their name. In 2005–06 Andy O'Brien, Gary

O'Neil, Franck Songo'o and Andrés D'Alessandro all featured at some point, with the following season bringing the arrival of Rodolphe M'Bela Douala (often known just as Douala but stay with me). The maximum number of apostrophe players in a single Portsmouth game in this era was three, a number that has been matched by only one other club, Sunderland themselves in 2015–16.

Everton 1–0 Opposition

Everton began the season in the Champions League qualifiers thanks to a fourth-place finish in 2004–05 that was wildly overshadowed by neighbours Liverpool's Champions League win in Istanbul. The 2005–06 campaign was not as memorable for David Moyes's dogged side, who failed to make it even to the group stage in Europe's premier competition and could finish only 11th in the Premiership. Just how functional the Toffees were in 2005–06 is best illustrated by the fact that, of their 14 wins, 10 of them were 1–0 (European champions Liverpool also recorded 10 1–0 wins in 2005–06). Only a year earlier Chelsea had recorded a Premier League record 11 1–0 wins on their way to the title. And people reckon the mid-2000s were boring.

Verdict

In football, drama is often valued higher than excellence, and long-term memories of 2005–06 seem to bear this out, with Chelsea's sleek, professional, effortless march to a second title in two years virtually consigned to the footnotes of the history books, such was the lack of challenge from any other team. In summer 2006, with Mourinho seemingly invincible in league football and his restrictive credo being hastily adopted by other clubs throughout the division, the future looked like one in which the number of goals would decline as fast as transfer fees and wages were going up.

Premier League season No. 15: 2006–07

Is it still called the Premiership? THIS IS THE FINAL COUNTDOWN

Champions: Manchester United

Relegated: Watford, Charlton Athletic, Sheffield United

Top scorer: Didier Drogba (20)

Most assists: Wayne Rooney/Cesc Fàbregas (11)

Biggest win: Reading 6–0 West Ham United

Overview

They call him CR06–07. After a three-year title drought, Manchester United reclaimed the crown, led by Cristiano Ronaldo and Wayne Rooney in tandem, and after a summer when the media had predicted the pair would never speak or function together again after what was known to contemporaries as the 'World Cup winking storm'. After just 19 minutes of United's opening game of the season, against Fulham, Sir Alex Ferguson's team were four goals up, with the fourth scored by Ronaldo and created by Rooney in a neat encapsulation of how the season was about to go.

Ronaldo (17 goals and eight assists) and Rooney (14 goals and 11 assists) were the bedrock of a newly energised United side, who shrugged off their manager's typically blunt removal of Ruud van Nistelrooy (95 goals in 150 Premier League games but only two in his final 10 appearances) in the summer. While United had binned their top scorer, double title holders Chelsea added Andriy Shevchenko to their success-gorged squad. The signs were clear: José Mourinho's Chelsea were going to win a third Premiership in a row, United would continue to stagnate under a manager from an older generation who was being outwitted by the chiselled thinker from Portugal. Instead, the Red Devils scored 83 goals, their third highest total under Ferguson at that point, while Shevchenko managed just four league goals in his first season with Chelsea, leaving him level with Phil Jagielka and one behind Matt Derbyshire for the campaign.

Few teams could match the attacking verve United showed in 2006–07 (four of their five defeats came against Arsenal and West Ham, the six points conceded to the Hammers enough to keep the east Londoners, Carlos Tevez et al, in the top flight). Nine successive wins from Mourinho's Chelsea in the new year (two more than any other club managed in 06–07) closed the gap to three points with five games to go but then they drew their final five games, including a dreary 0–0 with the newly crowned champions at the Bridge, with both sides playing a weakened team (United included Dong Fangzhuo for his only top-flight appearance: three shots, none on target). Liverpool and Arsenal completed the top four as the Big Four era (2006–07 was to be the first of three successive seasons when English sides made up three of the four semi-finalists in the Champions League) moved into its holy period.

Newly promoted Reading took the biscuit by not only

finishing eighth in their first top-flight season but also record-ing the biggest win (6–0 v West Ham) and the longest game (107min 44sec v Chelsea, courtesy of the serious head injury to Petr Čech that led to Mourinho laying into the South Cen-tral Ambulance Service).

At the bottom, even after all this time, Sheffield United's relegation still rankles in South Yorkshire, with their demo-tion confirmed after Tevez, signed via an illegal third-party agreement, scored the goal at Old Trafford that kept West Ham up. Two years later the dispute was settled out of court for a reported £20 million but, even though the Hammers have been down and back up since, and now occupy the plainly monikered London Stadium, the Blades have never returned to the top table and 2016–17 was their sixth consecu-tive season down in the third tier. The irony about Tevez's hot streak at the end of the season was that he took so long to actually get going. His signing, along with that of Javier Mascherano (kept out of the team for considerable periods by Hayden Mullins, a player yet to be converted into a centre-half by Barcelona), was a late summer sensation in 2006, but Tevez failed to score in any of his first 16 Premier League appearances, a period in which he had 36 shots (with only six of them on target). He finally netted for the Hammers in early March against Spurs, the first in a run of seven goals in 10 games that swung the relegation battle in the London side's favour.

Three Things We May Have Just Learnt About 2006–07

How low can you go?

Harry Kewell's penalty for Liverpool against Charlton after 89 minutes and 47 seconds was typical of 2006–07 in two senses. Firstly, it was one of only four goals in the last 20 minutes of any of the 10 games played on the final day, a period when, in usual times, most goals are scored. In fact, the total of 931 goals in 2006–07 remains the lowest total ever scored in the Premier League and the smallest figure in the top flight since the 904 in 1904–05. Secondly, Kewell's goal was also the 112th penalty of the season, which remains a Premier League record. Overall, 9.3 per cent of the goals in 2006–07 came from the penalty spot; it may have been the season in which Cristiano Ronaldo discovered his shooting boots but he was typically atypical on that score.

Barbarism begins at home

While the overwhelming majority of Manchester City fans must revel in their team having the likes of David Silva and Sergio Agüero in it, a few must hark back to the altogether more Cityish olden days, when the club seemed to lurch from crisis to disaster via the A-road of farce. The 2006–07 season featured a ground-breakingly dire run of home form from the club, with their 2–1 home win against Everton on New Year's Day somehow being the last goals City would score at home in that campaign. After that, season-ticket holders got to enjoy the following scorelines: 0–3, 0–2, 0–1, 0–1, 0–0, 0–0,

0–2, 0–1. Somehow, Stuart Pearce's team ended the campaign in 14th despite scoring only 29 goals (top scorer: Joey Barton with six). And for that, we salute them.

Quadrantphilia

British crowds remain lusty supporters of the concept of the corner kick, if not the invariably disappointing outcome from the classic 1872 restart rule. Short corners are still seen as a tacit lack of ambition rather than a neat way of retaining possession, fans unwilling to see the traditional arched delivery for the hit-and-hope heavy artillery that it is. It's apt therefore, that the record number of corners taken in a Premier League game (2006–07 onwards) came on November 11 2006 when Portsmouth won 20 of them in their home game with Fulham. 20 corners and their only goal of the game came from open play. Fulham, meanwhile, scored from a corner. Even a broken clock tells the right time twice a day.

Verdict

After two clinical, metronomic wins from Chelsea, Manchester United's return from seemingly terminal decline was a refreshing change, with the new champions playing with a fluid verve that belied their campaigns of struggle in the mid-2000s. Overall the league seemed in fine fettle, with Liverpool, never even contenders in the domestic league, still making their second Champions League final in three seasons.

6.

Where Next for the World Cup?

*'I can see a time, not that far into the future, when all the
biggest games will be between clubs, not countries'*

– Franz Beckenbaeur, 1998

'What's the first World Cup you can remember?' is one of
those questions that is asked when people want to either rem-
inisce about football or subtly indicate their age relative to
other people in the conversation. Or both. Your first experience of the World Cup might have been grainy images from
Brazil in 1950, or crowding round the TV to watch the 1990
semi-final on ITV or BBC (OK, BBC), or perhaps it was the
release of *Rio's World Cup Wind-Ups* in 2006. Whichever it was,
the first World Cup leaves an impression that rarely departs.
In an industry where broadcasting of live football has moved
from occasional to seven days a week, the fact that World
Cups still occur with the same four-year gap that was introduced in the 1930s means it can be a rare delight that excites
every time it comes around.

But could that rarity in fact be lessening the World Cup's
cultural resonance? Once upon a time, the World Cup was
the one period when football became centre stage, two or
three games per day for a couple of weeks and then a week or

so of heavyweight clashes largely featuring players that you had only read about or stuck in an album. It seemed like a feast after a relative famine, rather than what can, in the modern era, feel a bit like the leftovers from a season of fine dining on club football that culminates in the rich fare that is the Champions League final.

This is, understandably, very much a European viewpoint, possibly even one limited to England, and it should not be forgotten that what, in codified football's original continent, might be seen as unnecessary tinkering with the World Cup (the continued expansion in the number of teams, for example), is regarded as wildly overdue on the rest of the planet. Even so, UEFA continues to supply the highest number of teams and has provided the winners in four of the past five tournaments, the most dominant spell yet seen by a single confederation.

Euro 2016 showed, via the examples of Wales, Northern Ireland and Iceland, the joy and unity that can arise from an unexpected and successful tournament display, and yet none of them advanced the game particularly, merely themselves. Where international football once broke new ground (Hungary in the 1950s, the Netherlands in the 1970s), it has now become a more functional version of the great club sides, who can amass players without the limitations of national boundaries. Even the greatest international side of the 21st century, the Spanish team who won three successive international competitions between 2008 and 2012, were in essence a slightly watered down version of Barcelona. Barcelona without Messi, essentially, while the man himself was also weakened by being forced to play with inferior team-mates for Argentina. No one ever looked at the Brazil 1970 team and wondered whether Pelé was being held back by Wilson Piazza or whether he'd be tired out when the domestic season returned.

Whether you subscribe to the view that modern World Cups are less fundamental than they once were or not, there are few ways to examine the different eras in any depth. There is at least one, though, and that is deep inside the Opta vaults, namely analysis of every game in every World Cup from 1966 onwards (there is no Anglo-partisan reason for the starting point of 1966, just that this was the first World Cup where every game was televised, and the analysis is impossible without actually seeing what happened. If anybody gets cross and states that 'football didn't start in 1966', the correct answer is 'no, it ended').

Six hundred and sixty-eight games, from England's goal-less draw with Uruguay on 11 July 1966 through to the 30 minutes of extra-time in Germany's win against Argentina on 13 July 2014; 1,712 goals, 6,633 shots on target and more than half a million passes (530,637 if you want precision, and I can't help but feel that you do). But raw numbers are all very well. What do they actually tell us?

Rocket, take your turn

Apart from the research conducted by Charles Reep (see Chapter One), the Opta analysis of the 1966 World Cup is one of the few sources of football data from the 1960s. An era when woollen shirts and the ball itself competed to weigh more than a battleship understandably had a lot less running than the game does in the 2010s, with a corollary of that being less closing down of the opposition. The Dutch pressing of the 1970s was a revolution precisely because pressurising the other team wasn't the done thing.

And what transpires when people don't get closed down

very much? Shots, lots of shots. Perhaps, buried (like a Bobby Charlton rasper) deep in the collective consciousness, this is what people are looking for from their World Cups? Here are the raw numbers, anyway, showing that the four earliest tournaments for which we have full data have the highest number of shots, with 1970 just edging it ahead of 1966 (presumably because it's harder to run around in the Altiplanicie Mexicana than it is at Ayresome Park). The 1970 and 1966 tournaments are also the leaders when it comes to long-range shots, the only ones to see, incredibly, more than 20 per game. In a 90-minute game at Mexico 1970, you could expect to see a long-range effort every three and a half minutes. Even allowing for the thin air, that seems an unproductive way to play the game (quick task: think of a famous long-range shot from World Cup 1970. OK, it went just wide, didn't it? Unlike Xabi Alonso at Kenilworth Road).

World Cup	Shots/game	Long shots/game
1970	42	26
1966	39	23
1974	34	19
1978	34	19
1982	33	18
1994	30	17
1998	30	15
1986	30	17
2006	29	15
2010	29	15
2002	28	14
1990	27	14
2014	27	13

For pure, unadulterated shot action we need to head to the 1966 World Cup final, a seminal moment in England, a minor annoyance in (West) Germany. The Germans have subsequently reached 12 more finals; England zero.

Almost as if the players knew this was the only real shot at glory the nation would ever have, the boys of '66 peppered the goal throughout the final at the Empire Stadium, hitting 40 of them in the 79 minutes and 28 seconds of the game that the ball was in play. The West Germans responded with 37 of their own, bringing up a frightening total of 77, almost one for every minute of play. It remains 25 more than in any other subsequent World Cup final, with the 2014 edition, also featuring extra-time and the Germans, seeing a mere 20, 57 fewer than in 1966. 'Bobby belting the ball' was not just a line in 'Three Lions', it was a way of life. (NB, Bobby Charlton hit 24 long-range shots in 1966, second to Eusébio's total of 38, which was five more than Brazil managed in total.)

So, we've established that lovers of (possibly indiscriminate) shooting should be harking back to the 1960s and 1970s and, before we move on, contemplate the fact that the winners always set the narrative. Alf Ramsey's dismissal of Argentina as 'animals' after England edged past the South Americans in the quarter-final set the tone for more than 50 years of rivalry between the two teams, with the 1966 game remembered as much of an outrage in Argentina as the 1986 one is in England.

Were Argentina, snarling Argentina (described at the time by the *Sunday Telegraph*'s David Miller as 'a side with cultured feet and kindergarten minds') right to feel aggrieved about their treatment in a game that ended with the opposing manager refusing to allow his players to exchange shirts? The foul count at the end of the game suggests they may have a case, with England having committed 35 fouls to Argentina's 19. The English, however, did not receive a single caution (not yellow cards, these didn't exist yet, although this game was a clear indication that they might be a useful device). In fact, England's total of 35 fouls against Argentina (Alan Ball being the chief offender with eight) is the highest figure recorded by a team in a World Cup game (1966–2014) without ever triggering any further punishment from the referee. There were animals on the pitch, sure, but perhaps not where you thought they were.

Your Cruyffs, your Pelés

Football's great figure at the start of the 1970s was Pelé, but the man who dominated the decade was Johan Cruyff, the originator of the double Dutch World Cup tilts in 1974 and 1978. Cruyff didn't play in the latter tournament but he did as much in 1974 as many other players do in their entire career.

In seven exalted games in West Germany in 1974, Cruyff created 36 goalscoring chances, the third highest total of any player in World Cups in the 1970s, despite playing in only one of the tournaments. Similarly, Pelé, who featured only in 1970, is sixth in the list from only six games, a period in which he assisted six times and scored four (and, confusingly, ended the 1970 World Cup as the player who had committed the most fouls, with 23). This was the era of the totemic hero, when players rose to the occasion at World Cups, rather than tried to get through it after an arduous club campaign.

Goalscoring chances created – World Cups 1970–78

Player	Team	Chances created	Games played
Kazimierz Deyna*	Poland	47	13
Wolfgang Overath	Germany	42	13
Johan Cruyff	Netherlands	36	7
Gerd Müller	Germany	32	13
Jairzinho	Brazil	32	13
Pelé	Brazil	28	6

*Among the established legends in this table, it's interesting to see Kazimierz Deyna at the top, a player very much in the mould of the 1970s playmaker. Looking like a combination of Eddy Merckx and John Noakes, Deyna remains a cult figure at Manchester City, where he played in the late 1970s, and is one of two players in this extremely short list to have featured in *Escape To Victory*, along with Pelé. The 1970 World Cup remains, on the (very) rudimentary basis of shots per game, the most attacking tournament from 1966 onwards, with an average of 42 per game, almost one every two minutes.

This era of plundering mavericks was not limited to the World Cup. After their creditable defence of the trophy in the gasping confines of Mexico in 1970, England then failed to qualify for either of the subsequent tournaments in the decade but, even away from the world's glare, the domestic game produced its own wayward heroes, such as Frank Worthington, Stan Bowles, Tony Currie and Charlie George, exponents of raw flair who collected a mere 31 England caps between them, four fewer than Stewart Downing won on his own.

It is ironic that Cruyff towers over the decade, given that he was part of one of football's greatest collectives. The Dutch system of *totaalvoetbal* (you do the translation) was never better illustrated than at the start of the 1974 final, when the

Netherlands strung together 16 passes from the kick-off, before winning a penalty that another Johan, Neeskens, blasted into the net, giving the Dutch the lead before the West Germans had even touched the ball. Yet while posterity has been kind to the men in orange, it's not like the rest of the teams were engaged in proto-neanderthal football; West Germany themselves had the two longest passing moves preceding a goal in the 1974 World Cup and, while Holland did indeed have more possession than any other side (58 per cent), three teams completed a higher proportion of their passes.

Four years later, without Cruyff, the Dutch once again reached the final and once again lost to the host nation. Only once since, in 2010, have they got to the last hurdle, and this time it was Spain who ended their hopes, although it should be noted that they did at least placate the gods of tradition in South Africa by becoming the first team since 1954 to wear numbers 1 to 11 in a World Cup final. An atypically orthodox move from a nation who have punched above their weight, largely through tactical innovation and a systematic refusal to follow the herd.

The political situation in Argentina, i.e., the military junta, during the 1978 World Cup seemed to engender an environment in which controversy thrived, with drug offences (Scotland's Willie Johnston), overeager referees (Wales's Clive Thomas) and Argentina's suspicious-but-not-proven-dubious 6–0 win against Peru in the second group stage that sent the hosts to the final. Peru goalkeeper Ramón Quiroga let in plenty that day but overall in 1978 he made 50 saves, which is 14 more than any other goalkeeper in any other World Cup since 1966. Not only ferociously busy between the goalposts,

Quiroga also found the time to be booked for a foul in the opposition half, setting a template taken up with rash aplomb by fellow South Americans such as Colombia's René Higuita in the 1980s and 1990s.

For fans growing into the game in the 1970s they had three stellar tournaments to absorb: Mexico 1970 with the shock of colour (television) and the images of Brazil's greatest generation; technocratic Netherlands putting on a techno show in the technocratic superhub of West Germany; and then the sinister, ticker-tape junta carnival of Argentina '78. In a world reeling from financial uncertainty and violence, these four-yearly jamborees were a mystical and memorable experience.

Diego

The decade may have advanced by one but the themes of the 1970s World Cups just carried on. You liked iconic but flawed teams like Cruyff's Netherlands? Well, sir, I think you'll enjoy this Brazil '82 we keep only for our most valued customers. Ah, you prefer the iconic players like Edson Arantes do Nascimento? Well, here's a promising Argentinian called Diego Maradona, he should have ripened to perfection by 1986, but please make sure you note the use-by date of December 1989.

At Spain '82 (possibly the most verbally pleasing World Cup to say out loud, with the exception of Italia '90) FIFA continued to taunt fans with not one but two group stages, yet there was no shortage of classic encounters. And although it was a Europe-based tournament with a European winner, both Brazil and Argentina were key protagonists in that hot Iberian summer.

Argentina were able to field Maradona in a World Cup for the first time and the junior maestro showed all aspects of his game. In the match against Hungary he scored his first World Cup goals (a game in which referee Belaïd Lacarne allowed the Hungarians to kick-off both the first and second halves for some reason), while in the second-round match with Italy, Maradona experienced the sort of roughhouse shackling he became accustomed to throughout his career. Claudio Gentile barely let his opponent have an inch during the game, fouling him six times (the only player he fouled during the game; he also successfully targeted Zico in the game against Brazil, fouling him five times). Then, in a winner-takes-all match with Brazil, and his side trailing 3–0, Maradona was sent off for a roundhouse groin lunge on João Batista, revenge for a high Brazilian foot moments earlier. Brilliance, bullying and badness. The three elements of Diego all on show.

Elsewhere it was a tournament made for highlight reels (not that Maradona being sent off wouldn't make it on to a highlights reel), with Brazil in particular offering a languid, romantic version of the game that still enchants almost 40 years later. This was the tournament with the best long-range shooting of any World Cup since 1966, with almost a quarter (22 per cent) of the goals coming from outside the box. Unsurprisingly, it was the Brazilians who bent and powered the adidas Tango into the net the best, scoring five of the 32 long-range goals. In the grey, air-conditioned world of the modern game, we know that shooting from long range is a fool's game but an alternative argument is Spain '82. In 1982 the fans expected goals and they expected them from distance.

World Cup	Goals outside box	% outside box
1982	32	22%
1994	30	21%
1970	19	20%
1978	19	19%
2010	27	19%
2006	26	18%
1974	16	16%
2002	24	15%
1990	15	13%
1966	11	12%
1998	20	12%
2014	19	11%
1986	14	11%

Another key element of what we all deem the perfect World Cup is a healthy dose of scheming skulduggery, and the 1980s were perhaps the ultimate period for this. The 21st-century German team have been rebuilt as a happy-go-lucky, smiling pool of eager nu-talent, but in 1982 the West Germans not only owned the concept of *schadenfreude*, but were happy to delight in it in real time. The first case was their group game with Austria. Both sides knew that a German win by one or two goals would see both sides progress ahead of Algeria. An early German goal led, predictably, to a farcical episode of to-me, to-you, with a distinct lack of chuckling from any neutrals (or Algerians) observing. How tame were the efforts of the two teams to convince the world that this was an actual contest? Well, the fact that the final shot of the game came in the

62nd minute tells its own story. *Nichtangriffspakt von Gijón*, you shall not be forgotten.

Of course, the West Germans then doubled down on the cynicism front when Harald Schumacher launched himself like a meat-seeking missile at France's Patrick Battiston in the semi-final. They were finally stopped in the final against Italy, Paolo Rossi's Italy. Rossi had scored a hat-trick in the final group match against Brazil, added two more in the semi-final against Poland and ended the tournament with six goals from seven shots on target. The romantic conclusion to Spain '82 would have been France against Brazil, but football rarely works like this. Still, you'd be hard pressed to find a more vintage tournament than this.

Four years later the jamboree was back in the Americas (Mexico) and Maradona was, this time, primed. It's become an established truth that Maradona carried his team to the World Cup in 1986, but he did, he really did. Of the 14 goals Argentina scored in Mexico, Maradona scored or assisted 10 of them (five apiece). He, and this is where it starts to look crazy, went on 90 dribbles (almost 13 per game); the next highest number by a player at that tournament was West Germany's Hans-Peter Briegel on 29. Maradona, to put it another way, dribbled as much in 1986 as Michael Laudrup, Enzo Francescoli, Jesper Olsen and Chris Waddle combined. Be it Maradona in 1986, or Paul Gascoigne four years later, what we want, what we *need*, from a World Cup is players dribbling, surging, gliding past the opposition.

It wasn't like Maradona's opponents didn't know what he was up to. He was targeted ruthlessly by almost everyone he played (he later claimed England had treated him fairly in the quarter-final, possibly as they were unable to get near him, although seven of their 16 fouls that day were indeed on Maradona), winning 53 fouls across the tournament, 26 more than any other player and two more than England won in total. By the time he left USA '94 in a drug-assisted outrage, Maradona had been fouled 152 times in 21 World Cup games. There's treatment and then there's treatment. Maradona got *treatment*.

Like Pelé, or Cruyff, Maradona represented not only himself or his nation but an entire way of playing the game. Sure, England fans waiting to watch the quarter-final in 1986 knew who Maradona was, and knew what he could do but he retained a mystical air, even though he had played in Europe for nearly half a decade. Perhaps if UK television viewers had seen Maradona go through the motions against Avellino in a league game then he would have seemed more normal, but you suspect not.

Love in the nineties

The 1990s gave us three World Cups and all three can stake their claim as super-iconic, for differing reasons. Italia '90 is the curate's egg tournament; loved and cherished in England and Ireland but largely dismissed in the rest of the world, in territories where Gazza's tears meant little and a severe lack of goals was a much more (de)pressing matter.

Let's get the lack of goals out of the way, because it cannot be ignored; there was a severe lack of goals at Italia '90. Ironically, it was the group containing England and Ireland that set the tone for this, with only seven goals in six games, England's 1–0 win against Egypt in their final group game being the only win in the entire section. The first three quarter-finals produced just two goals, before England and Cameroon served up five, while the two semis and the final added only five more. The negativity at least had a positive outcome, with the bleakness of 1990 serving as the inspiration for the back-pass rule that was introduced to the general footballing world in 1992.

World Cup	Goals/game
1990	2.21
2010	2.27
2006	2.30
2002	2.52
1986	2.54
1974	2.55
2014	2.67
1998	2.67
1978	2.68
1994	2.71
1962	2.78
1966	2.78
1982	2.81
1970	2.97
1958	3.60
1930	3.89
1950	4.00
1934	4.12
1938	4.67
1954	5.38

For England fans, though, 1990 remains a beacon tournament, a spirited display (the country's best away from the safe confines of their heritage HQ, Wembley) from a team who had faced derision after a dismal Euro '88 but who slowly come good in the hot Italian summer. Gary Lineker continued his tournament goalscoring streak that had begun at Mexico '86 but really it was all about Paul Gascoigne, the guiding force in what was, sadly and still unbelievably, his only appearance at a World Cup. He made 56 dribbles in Italy, 20 more than the next man (also a Geordie, Chris Waddle) and only Diego Maradona, who else, was fouled more often than Gazza.

But no image has encapsulated England in tournament football more than Lineker's concerned frown at the bench after Gascoigne's semi-final booking. Even though the midfielder passed to the forward only twice in 120 minutes, the two are linked indelibly. England came close, but instead West Germany made their third final in a row, and this time ended as victors. Perhaps England should have followed the blueprint laid down in 'World in Motion' a bit more closely. In May, John Barnes was adamant that 'there's only one way to beat them/get round the back' but, come the tournament, the Liverpool man delivered only one successful cross in five games. What you're looking at . . . wasn't the master plan.

England's absence four years later made barely a ripple at FIFA. The dream of a tournament held in the USA was realised and, while the football was becoming increasingly functional (38 per cent of goals were from set-pieces, a record high), the goals, however they were being scored, were at least flowing again after the blockage in the drains that was 1990. Yet for the first time since . . . (when?) no player dominated the tournament like a Maradona or a Matthaus. Even the cherished Golden Boot was part-won by a player, Oleg Salenko, who featured only in the group stage. Salenko's six goals (five of which came against a Cameroon team who were unable to repeat their heroics from 1990) were the only goals he ever scored for Russia and he never featured for them again after the conclusion of the 1994 World Cup. Ultimately, the moment of the tournament was a missed penalty. For some it's Diana Ross, for others it's Roberto Baggio. Either is a valid choice.

Four years later in France, the World Cup had been beefed up to 32 teams and the host country were finally ready to claim their first title, led by the skill of Zinedine Zidane and the positional play of Stéphane Guivarc'h. The increased scope of the tournament seemed to bring back a level of excitement that had been missing for a couple of editions, and the total of 13 last-minute goals in 1998 was a record until 2014 saw one more. Adding to the general frivolity, there was also a record six own goals, as the margins between defensive heroism and nation-shaming howler got ever closer. France '98 also remains the last time that England produced performances that united a nation watching at home. The turgid percentage-ball of the 'golden generation' in some of 2002, most of 2006 and all of 2010 is almost certainly a key reason why World Cups in England are increasingly seen as a chore more than a challenge but the second-round game with Argentina in 1998 remains a bona fide World Cup classic.

2001 AD: a lack of space odyssey

Like Martin Luther nailing his 95 theses to a church door, or Sian Massey's appointment as assistant referee at Molineux, the impact of some events becomes apparent only in retrospect. Similarly, the first game of the 2002 World Cup was, in some respects, the end of the heroic era of World Cups and the start of the modern, pragmatic one. The event in question? Reigning champions France losing to tournament debutants Senegal in the opening game of Japan/South Korea.

The game was obviously a gargantuan embarrassment for the French but it wasn't as if there hadn't been World Cup shocks before (a virtually identical scenario played out in 1990 when Argentina lost to Cameroon in the long shadows of a San Siro afternoon) but whereas Maradona rallied his reeling, splintered group to somehow reach the final, France in 2002 stunk out the entire tournament by following up the Senegal defeat with a 0–0 draw with Uruguay and then a 2–0 defeat to Denmark.

Thus the holders departed not only at the earliest possible moment but also without scoring a single goal. This was a squad containing Zidane, Henry, Trezeguet and Desailly, and marked the start of an era of national teams full of superstar club players failing to perform as a collective, with England possibly the finest, but certainly not the only, example. Consider that in the period from 1966 onwards, only three reigning world champions have failed to progress past the first group stage, France in 2002, Italy eight years later and Spain in 2014. Italy's display was arguably worse than the French one, given that they contrived to finish behind Rory Fallon's New Zealand. England, meanwhile, have won one of their seven World Cup finals matches since the departure of Sven-Göran Eriksson.

Other themes that have descended on the World Cup in the digital age are a functional safety-first approach, as international sides struggle to replicate the high-fidelity choreography of modern club sides, and a steady erosion of the mystical heart of World Cups, a direct result of the globalisation of the sport.

On the former, consider that in 2006 Italy conceded just

twice all tournament (once in the group stage, and Zidane's penalty in the final), while Spain in 2010 scored just four times in the group stage and then won all four of their knockout games by one goal to nil. Unquestionably the best side in the tournament, the Spanish nonetheless won the World Cup despite losing their first group game (the first time this had happened) and scoring only eight times (the lowest total by a World Cup-winning side). Germany, the 2014 winners, scored seven times alone in the semi-final, humiliating the host nation Brazil with their first home defeat for 12 years, with the biggest margin of victory ever seen at this stage of a tournament.

And Brazil's eventual evisceration at the hands of the Germans was symptomatic of the other element of modern World Cups, the sheer lack of mystery. As the table below shows, as the Premier League's influence and wealth increased, so did the number of Brazilians playing in it. Between 1994 and 2002 the English top flight didn't supply a single squad member for the most iconic of international teams, but by 2014 this had jumped to six. Whether Brazil's nervous, unconvincing run to the semi-finals on home turf was in any way connected with their influx of people who now knew what it was like to play away at Stoke on a cold Tuesday night is unknown, but the otherworldliness of Brazil 1970 or Argentina 1978 or Cameroon 1990 is probably gone for ever. No one ever drafted François Omam-Biyik into their FUT. The modern game is more accessible than ever, but it's not a zero sum improvement.

Premier League players in Brazil World Cup squads	
1994	0
1998	0
2002	0
2006	1
2010	1
2014	6

The end of history

If we go back to the Franz Beckenbauer quote that started this chapter, it's fair to say that at some point in the 19 years since he said it, we did indeed reach that point. The Champions League final, particularly since it was cannily moved to a Saturday night slot in 2010, now has the gravitas that once only the World Cup final did, and with the added bonus (not least for sponsors) that it happens every year. International football, meanwhile, continues to promise much more than it delivers, with tournaments struggling for goals (Euro 2016 had a mere 2.12 per game, and Cameroon won the 2017 Africa Cup of Nations despite scoring only seven times, in an edition that averaged only 2.06 per match). Club football is not suffering in the same way, with certain teams and players smashing goalscoring records on a record basis.

For reasons it's fairly easy to understand, certain key elements that went into forming a 'classic' World Cup have steadily declined over the past 30 years and a modern World Cup is a very different prospect to one in the 1960s, 1970s or 1980s. In the same way that cycling races such as the Tour de

France and Giro d'Italia were born partly as a way of educating and uniting people around the concept of their particular nation state, international football seems to thrive when it is allied to some sort of nationalism (see Italy in the 1930s, post-war Germany's reputational recovery or Argentina in 1978), so perhaps the political upheaval of the late 2010s will usher in a new era of World Cup competitiveness. Could Brexit be the final element England need to win a second world title? Logic would suggest not and that, instead, clubs will become more demanding in the 21st century, and that most tedious of decisions, the international retirement, will become increasingly common.

Premier League season No. 16: 2007–08

Is it still called the Premiership? SIT DOWN PLEASE. IT IS NO LONGER CALLED THE PREMIERSHIP

Champions: Manchester United

Relegated: Derby County, Birmingham City, Reading

Top scorer: Cristiano Ronaldo (31)

Most assists: Cesc Fàbregas (17)

Biggest win: Middlesbrough 8–1 Manchester City

Overview

More Big Four but good Big Four. After a sullen spell spent reeling at Chelsea's cocky entry into the hallowed title-contender space, Arsenal finally put up a proper challenge, for the first two-thirds of the season at least. After their 2–0 home win against Blackburn in early February the Gunners were five points clear of the chasing pack with 12 games to go and had lost just once all season. Leading the charge for Arsène Wenger were Cesc Fàbregas, who ended the season with a competition-leading 17 assists, and Emmanuel Adebayor, who scored 24 goals (the only time he scored 20 or more in a

Premier League season), with 14 of them coming away from home; only five players in Premier League history, most recently Alexis Sánchez and Sergio Agüero in 16-17, have scored more on the road than Adebayor did in 07–08.

Their position at the top had been helped by a slow start from the champions Manchester United, who became the first title holders to fail to win either of their opening two games since Arsenal in August 1991. In the second of the two draws United began their season with, away at Portsmouth, Cristiano Ronaldo was sent off for head-based antics with Richard Hughes ('It wasn't a Glasgow kiss,' said Hughes. 'I have received harder head-butts than that'), causing him to miss three games. When he returned with two more goalless appearances, questions were asked about whether he, and United, were spent after their efforts the previous campaign. He answered with 31 goals and six assists in the remaining 30 games he featured in, unleashing 77 shots on target overall, only 39 fewer than Derby managed all season. Ronaldo goals in six successive games in March and April allowed United to usurp their old rivals from north London.

Even so, as spring neared, the title was Arsenal's to lose and, given this was only four years since they had gone the entire season unbeaten, it did not seem as outlandish as it might in 2017. Their Waterloo came on a brisk afternoon at St Andrew's in late February, a game in which they not only conceded a last-minute penalty to draw 2–2 (along with William Gallas's associated overreaction) but lost striker Eduardo to *that* tackle from Martin Taylor early in the match. There was no happy outcome for either player involved; Taylor played only one more game in the Premier League, and Eduardo, who had played 90 minutes in four of Arsenal's previous five games, never completed a league match for them again after his long recovery from the sickening injury. Whether connected with the scenes that day or not, Arsenal won only one of their next seven games (including a season-ending 2–1 defeat at Old Trafford, a match the Gunners led and dominated) to not only finish below Manchester United and Avram Grant's Chelsea, but also find themselves having to watch those two sides contest the Champions League final in Moscow.

Three Things We May Have Just Learnt About 2007–08

Stretch out and wait

Derby. Derby County. Derby County 2007–08. Just the mere sound of those words brings to mind the enormity of their inadequacy: one win, 89 goals conceded, 11 points all season, 25 points adrift of safety. All teams promoted to the Premier League must fear that they'll be as unready as Derby but only Derby were as unready as Derby. In their only win, a 1–0 victory against Newcastle in September that lifted the Rams up to the extraordinary heights of 19th, the Setanta cameras missed Kenny Miller's goal as they were showing a replay of a Newcastle chance. It was that sort of season. They ended the campaign having conceded 8.9 per cent of the goals in the Premier League, a record for a single season, while 11 points was the lowest that any team had recorded in the top flight since Darwen in 1891–92 (who played only 26 games, with two points for a win, and, to be fair, in a season in which goal nets were making their debut. In contrast, Derby's TV revenue of £29 million in 2007–08 would have funded the cost of all shipping and other transportation during the Boer War).

Even the decision in the autumn to replace manager Billy Davies with Paul Jewell backfired, with Jewell earning the club just five points in 24 games, and ensuring that Derby ended the season having won none of their last 32 games. They remain the only Premier League side to have had their relegation confirmed before the end of March.

Portsmouth at sixes and sevens

For supporters, a regular reliable penalty taker is a thing of wonder. To see your main man step up in a high-pressure scenario and tuck home a spot-kick brings with it a deep sense of relief. But some clubs do not have such a figure. Portsmouth, in 2007–08, remain the club with the most varied approach to penalty kicks, with six players taking them, a record for a single season in the Premier League (here's the list for your Rotary Club Christmas sports quiz: Defoe, Kranjčar, Muntari, Benjani, Taylor and Kanu). Pompey also featured in possibly the most memorable game of the season, when they defeated Reading 7–4 at Fratton Park in September. The 11 goals made it the highest-scoring Premier League game of all-time and the most goal-laden top-flight game since Luton beat Oxford by the same scoreline in 1988. Bravo.

Santa's not real

Roque Santa Cruz ended the 2007–08 season with 19 goals, behind only Ronaldo, Adebayor and Fernando Torres in the charts. It was a healthy total for the Paraguayan, and one that earned him a move to Manchester City a year later for a chunky £17.5 million. But this season was an aberration, a goalscoring whirlwind that the player couldn't and didn't repeat. See if you can spot Santa Cruz's first season at Blackburn in this chronological list of seasonal goal tallies during his time in Europe: 5, 5, 5, 5, 5, 0, 4, 2, **19**, 4, 3, 0, 7, 8, 6, 3, 2. In 2007–08 Santa Cruz also became the fourth and most recent player to score a hat-trick in a defeat, when he netted a treble in Rovers' 5–3 defeat to Wigan (the others are Dion Dublin, Dwight Yorke and Matthew Le Tissier, twice).

Verdict

A blockbuster of a season with a proper title race, a series of quirky and/or entertaining side stories and a team so bad they have gone down in the collective memory of the entire human race. This was all capped off by the first and so for only all-English European Cup final. We'd never had it so good.

Premier League season No. 17: 2008–09

Is it still called the Premiership? IT IS NOT, NO

Champions: Manchester United

Relegated: West Bromwich Albion, Middlesbrough, Newcastle United

Top scorer: Nicolas Anelka (19)

Most assists: Robin van Persie/Frank Lampard (10)

Biggest win: Manchester City 6–0 Portsmouth

Overview: Three in a row No. 2. For the second time in eight years (and the second time in their history), Manchester United won three straight titles, although this one was grasped with the looming knowledge that they were about to lose the division's best player, Cristiano Ronaldo, to the increasingly swaggering environs of La Liga. Compared to his efforts in 2007–08, the Portuguese was subdued, with 16 of his 18 goals coming at Old Trafford. The only other venue where he registered goals in his final league season in England was the Hawthorns (he would score 13 goals at nine different away grounds in his first season in La Liga).

Instead of brilliance from Ronaldo and Rooney, United relied on a formidable defence that did not concede a single goal between mid-November and mid-February (Edwin van der Sar recording a Premier League record 14 clean sheets in a row). Early leaders Liverpool continued to snap at United's heels as winter dripped into spring, and a 4–1 win for Rafa Benítez's team at Old Trafford in March, the first time they had scored more than three in a top-flight game there since 1936, followed by a first defeat for United in 45 years at Fulham a week later, opened the door for the Merseysiders. However, a week later, the unheralded Federico Macheda rose from the bench to score a 90th-minute winner against Aston Villa in a game in which United had trailed 2–1 with 11 minutes remaining.

It was typical of a season in which Sir Alex Ferguson had to rely on his entire squad; in fact United's use of 33 players in 2008–09 is a record for a title-winning team in the Premier League (the average for champions is 25), with 13 players, including Macheda, playing four times or fewer. Ronaldo had the second highest number of appearances, but his 33rd and final match of the season was the last he would play for United in the league, ending his career there with 84 goals and 34 assists in 196 games. Good figures, for sure, but modest given what was about to unfold in the Spanish capital.

Elsewhere, Hull City escaped relegation in their first top-flight season despite collecting only 35 points. And of those 35, 20 came in the first nine games, a heady, whirling period in which they won away at Arsenal and Tottenham. In the words of Hull manager Phil Brown: 'this is the best trip I've ever been on' (disclaimer: in early autumn). From third in October to 17th in May, it doesn't matter how you stay up, you just need to. Fulham, meanwhile, scored as many goals as Hull (39) but finished 18 points and 10 places higher. So, on reflection, it seems that not conceding goals does matter.

Three Things We May Have Just Learnt About 2008–09

Everything changes, but you

Talking of Fulham, they were the epitome of a settled team in 2008–09. Under the tutelage of Roy Hodgson, who seemingly found peace by the Thames, the Whites made only 24 changes to their starting XI all season (the most is by Manchester United with 144 in 2013–14, their first season after the retirement of Sir Alex Ferguson). Three Fulham players – Danny Murphy, Mark Schwarzer and Aaron Hughes – played in all 38 games, while 11 players featured in at least 30. That Hughes didn't miss any games through suspension is no real surprise, given the defender conceded only 54 fouls in 196 Premier League appearances for the south-west London side.

Throwing in: the towel

A new trend arrived in the Premier League in 2008–09: the long throw. They had existed beforehand, of course, but after Stoke's promotion they were elevated into a new, yet somehow medieval, weapon that struck fear into the hearts of all visitors to Castle Britannia. In 2007–08 no team had unleashed more than 92 long throws, but a year later Stoke hurled 337 of them into cowering defences. Chief aimer of the Potters was, of course, Rory Delap, who seemed to spend much of his Stoke career trundling from one side of the pitch to the other, before drying his hands on an official club towel. He took 267 long throws in 2008–09, 189 more than any other player and 21 per cent of the entire amount in the Premier League, while his team scored nine goals from long throws, 32 per cent of the league's total. Delap would go on to hurl 665 more into play during the next two campaigns but nothing would match the sheer mechanical impact of the tactic in 2008–09.

The 100 club

It was 1 November 2008, the only date in Premier League history when two players reached 100 goals in the competition on the same day. Those men, for the record, were Frank Lampard and Emile Heskey, whose goals invariably came in different ways, but who are linked by the fact that both remain somewhat underrated given their career achievements. Forty-three days later a third player, Nicolas Anelka, reached 100 Premier League goals and it remains one of only three seasons when three players reached the landmark figure, along with Sheringham, Yorke and Le Tissier in 2000–01 and a Manchester United triple pack of Giggs, Scholes and Rooney in 2009–10. Currently we're in a relative drought, with only Sergio Agüero (April 2016) and Peter Crouch (February 2017) moving into treble figures in the past three seasons.

Verdict

While Manchester United would go on to win two more Premier League titles under Sir Alex Ferguson before he retired, 2008–09 feels like the last time that he had a dynastic squad at his disposal. With both Ronaldo and Carlos Tevez departing in summer 2009, much of the swashbuckle that had characterised the team in their late 2000s three-in-a-row evaporated. While this season had not seen as much attacking intent as the previous two, there was still a sense that United, as they headed to their second Champions League final in succession, were the best that the Premier League had to offer. But, as always, a new era was about to commence.

Premier League season No. 18: 2009–10

Is it still called the Premiership? STOP USING PREMIERSHIP IN YOUR EVERYDAY SPEECH

Champions: Chelsea

Relegated: Portsmouth, Hull City, Burnley

Top scorer: Didier Drogba (29)

Most assists: Frank Lampard (14)

Biggest win: Tottenham 9–1 Wigan/Chelsea 8–0 Wigan

Overview

King's Road Fantasia. Jonathan Wilson, writing about Claudio Ranieri's time at Leicester after the Italian was sacked in 2017, pointed out numerous times in football when a team that had been constructed by a disciplinarian then flourished, briefly, under a more liberal manager (Pearson to Ranieri, in Leicester's case). A similar claim could be made about Chelsea in 2009–10. With largely the team constructed by José Mourinho but now managed by the genial Carlo Ancelotti, they became the first top-flight team since Tottenham in 1963 to score 100 goals in a single season. That imperious spine of

Čech, Terry, Lampard and Drogba combined in a way that, in the closing weeks of the season at least, blew their rivals away.

So often, once sufficient time passes, people's only recollection of how league seasons went is based solely on the snippets they can easily recall from the anterooms of their memory. *Chelsea . . . 103 goals . . . must have romped home.* Instead, despite the deluge of goals, the London side sealed the title only on the final day, finishing one point above Manchester United, who came closer to what would have been a record fourth title in a row than Liverpool had in 1985 (Joe Fagan's team ending a massive 13 points adrift of Everton). A 1–1 draw at Blackburn in late March had left Chelsea third and seemingly out of the title race, but then came one of the most extraordinary runs of goalscoring in English league history, with 33 in their final eight games, an average of 4.1 per game (the run included a 5–0 win at Portsmouth, a 7–1 home win against Aston Villa and then 7–0 and 8–0 wins in their final two games at Stamford Bridge, against Stoke and Wigan respectively).

Chelsea became the first team to score seven or more goals in four top-flight games in a single season since Arsenal in 1934–35, with only Blackburn in 1889–90 doing it more often (five times). Didier Drogba, who had scored just five goals in the Premier League the season before, led the competition with 29, 28 of which didn't come from the penalty spot. Frank Lampard, meanwhile, led the league in assists and also became the first central midfielder in Premier League history to score 20 or more goals in a single campaign, something only Yaya Touré has since matched. Perhaps the most telling piece of information is that, at an average of 29 years and 75 days, the 2009–10 Chelsea are the oldest Premier League champions yet seen. This was a final flowering from one of the great squads in English footballing history, and what a display it was.

Elsewhere, Burnley, playing in their first top-flight season since 1975–76, looked set fair after taking 15 points from their first 11 games, but collected just 15 more in the remaining 27 matches to take the final relegation spot, ahead of Hull and Portsmouth, the south coast side beginning their subterranean odyssey to the fourth tier. Forget reaching 40 points for safety, in 2009–10 31 was enough to survive. Finally, fans of illegal ball interventions should toast Jermain Defoe, who in this campaign conceded 19 hand-balls, more by himself than three teams did and 4 per cent of the total for the whole league.

Three Things We May Have Just Learnt About 2009–10

Humdrum Brum

While Chelsea were setting new goalscoring boundaries at the top of the table, there were still more than a few teams committed to the 2000s ethos of low-scoring matches, even as the new decade began. Chief among them in 2009–10 were Alex McLeish's Birmingham City, who, with 38 goals in 38 games, remain the lowest-scoring team ever to finish in the top half in a Premier League campaign. City scored more than twice in only one of their games (3–2 v Wigan), and their attitude was exemplified by defender Roger Johnson, who made a monstrous 441 clearances but completed only 600 passes all season. Never has the phrase 'get rid' been more applicable.

Life's a breach

And while Birmingham secured a top-half finish despite rarely scoring, Wigan managed to avoid the drop somehow, despite ending the season with a goal difference of minus 42, the worst figure ever recorded by a team who didn't get relegated. Much of that gruesome margin came in the capital, with the 8–0 defeat at Chelsea on the final day that sealed the title for the hosts, and a 9–1 hammering at White Hart Lane in November, a match in which the Latics had trailed only 1–0 at half-time. Wigan Mathletics.

Steed off

The north-east loves a substitution. Not only is Newcastle icon Shola Ameobi the player to have been brought on most often (142 times), but in 2009–10 Sunderland's Steed Malbranque was replaced a record 26 times, four times more than he had been the season before. The Frenchman made 30 starts for the Black Cats in 2009–10 and, in 26 of those games, he looked up and saw his number (that number was eight, squad number fans) being held up. The breakdown of his 26 removals is one first half, five at half-time and 20 after the break. Will the record ever be beaten? Well, in 2015–16, champions Leicester substituted Okazaki 25 times and Mahrez on 24 occasions, and if 2015–16 Leicester can't best you then surely nobody can.

Verdict

If in the second half of the 2000s the leading Premier League teams had dominated Europe with a controlled, defensively rigid but invariably unromantic approach, 2009–10 was the first hint of the chaos and slapstick that was to come in the 2010s (even the referees got in on the act with a record eight red cards on a single day, on October 31). Of Chelsea's first four Premier League titles, this was the one not won under the stern tutelage of José Mourinho and is possibly the league win Blues fans remain most fond of; that crazy April and May when the goals fell like spring rain.

7.

12 Steps to Heaven – the Lionel Messi Debate

'Once they said they can only stop me with a pistol.
Today you need a machine-gun to stop Messi'

– Hristo Stoichkov

SCENE: The annual (they hate this) meeting of the 12 months is taking place at a calendar factory in southern Denmark. Each year (they prefer the term '12 months') the months meet to discuss any issues they've had over the previous year and plans for the next 365-day period. They end each gathering by having a keynote discussion that is broadcast online to other periods of time (the days of the week, obscure religious holidays, specific dates on which Dave Bassett has appeared on Sky Sports News to talk about a player from a league he has little awareness of). In 2017, the months have chosen Lionel Messi, the year he turns 30, as their topic of discussion. Here is what they discussed.

June: Lionel Messi, the greatest footballer in the history of the game. No doubt at all. And, it should be noted by all of you, he was born in June. My man, Lionel Messi.

August: Aha, June is it? Another summer boy to make mockery of the autumn supremacists. 'They're too small, they fall behind at school, the autumn boys are too powerful.' Well it didn't stop Alan Shearer did it. A delicate plate of artisan chicken and beans on a hot August day as the blackberries slowly ripen. Elysian fields, my friends.

October: You utter fool, August. In Argentina, June is the middle of winter. Leo was born in, I imagine, a howling gale, with hailstones as large as adidas Tangos. This lack of knowledge modern months show about the southern hemisphere really is embarrassing. In many thriving countries I'm celebrated as a period of renewal. Me. October.

June: Winter, summer, whatever. Lionel Messi was born, we can at least all agree on that. 24 June 1987, a different time. The main import into Spanish football that week was Howard Kendall resigning from English champions Everton to take over at Athletic Bilbao. Other footballers born on the same day as Messi include Rochdale goalkeeper Josh Lillis and . . .

March: Are you looking at Wikipedia, June?

June: Well . . . yeesss.

March: Come on. While a fine resource for dates of birth, no $10 donation will be enough to cover the career of the great man. Let's go deeper.

April: Can someone provide us with a quick overview of his early years in Argentina? We all know he moved to Barcelona when he was still a kid, but before that? He must have been good?

May: Small and very good. Or very small and good. His youth team in Rosario lost only a handful of games in four years and were known as 'The Machine of '87', which not only denoted the year they were born but sounds like it could be the most important post-rock album released in 2008. One issue, though. Messi stopped growing when he was nine and when he was four foot two. This wasn't something that could be solved merely by eating all your vegetables up. This needed medical treatment, specifically medical treatment with human growth hormone.

April: Human growth hormone? That's got a, er, reputation nowadays.

May: So would orange juice if you used it immorally. Messi had a medical condition and this treatment allowed him to move past that. He was just fortunate that he comes from a generation where there was a reliable medical solution. Before the mid-1980s growth hormone deficiencies had to be dealt with by removing the actual real stuff from actual real cadavers and injecting it into the actual real patient.

September: The treatment wasn't cheap, though, and when Newell's Old Boys said they couldn't, or didn't want to, fund it, Messi's father used his Catalonian roots to line up a move to Barcelona. Messi's European life had begun.

June: Yeah, yeah, rise through the ranks, the greatest of hopes in Barcelona's golden generation. We've all heard about this. I want to see hard facts. When did he start playing? Not for the D team, the C team, the B team but Barcelona. The A team. Not *The A-Team*, Barcelona's first team. You know, more than a club. All that.

October: Well let me come in here because Messi's first start came in October 2004 in a defeat against UDA Gramenet, who may sound like a late 90s internet service provider but were in fact embarking on a sensational cup run of the lower-league variety. Think Wycombe but with an Iberic museum instead of one displaying chairs. This was 11 days after his first appearance, as a late substitute in the Catalan derby against Espanyol, for whom fellow Argentine Mauricio Pochettino was playing.

May: Good one, October, but I can claim the first goal, scored in the closing stages of the 2004–05 campaign against Albacete, and in the closing stages of the game. It was assisted by Ronaldinho and scored with Messi's left foot from inside the penalty area. It was to be the first of many such finishes.

March: You're right about the distance, May. Of Messi's first 28 goals, only one came from outside the penalty area, and that was his first goal for Argentina on 1 March 2006. Less a foot like a traction engine and more one like a . . . what came after the traction engine and was more refined?

December: A tractor? Messi has a foot like a . . . tractor?

March: A small tractor . . . a child's tractor or perhaps a sit-on mower? I feel we're losing the point here. Messi scores mainly from visually pleasing angles inside the box, that's my take on this. A fantastic take, a huge take.

February: And despite those previously discussed height issues, he's scored more than 20 headed goals in his career, with the first coming in February 2006 against Real Zaragoza. I mean, when you score more than 500 goals a few are going to come with your head or your knee or your chest but even so . . .

January: I'd keep quiet about headers, Feb old pal. Remember that open goal, 45-degree headed miss from a penalty rebound against Manchester City in 2015? Straight out of *Sensible World of Soccer* that one.

August: Headed goals? Chested goals? Come on, this is Leo Messi we're talking about here, not Ian Ormondroyd. What about hat-tricks? Lots, yes?

March: Thirty-seven for Barcelona as it stands, and guess what. I've seen more of them than any of you lot, with nine, including the first, which came against Real Madrid, not a bad start, in 2007. And unlike, say, Matthew Le Tissier, Messi doesn't do pyrrhic trebles, scoring them when his team loses in other words. That first hat-trick against Real remains the only time he's scored three or more goals and not won (the game ended 3–3). Since then, 36 of them and 36 wins.

January: By the way, June, don't feel bad or anything but you're the only month Messi's played in for Barcelona and not scored a hat-trick. July, you can rest easy here, we all know how it goes.

June: Three games, man, get real. I'm not a club football sort of guy. And . . . wait, October, hear me out . . . Messi's scored braces in two of those three games. Not bad, pal.

October: Ah, don't let that northern hemisphere bias creep out again, June. You're making me cross.

April: I'd like to announce something. And that something is that the first time Lionel Messi scored more than three goals in a game came in April.

November: That's true but it was against Arsenal at the Camp Nou or Nou Camp, you decide. If you score four goals against Arsenal does it even make a sound?

April: That would have worked much better with Nottingham Forest. Anyway, painful as it is for me to admit, my old rival March can lay claim to the first and so far only time Messi has scored five in a match, against Bayer Leverkusen in the Champions League in 2012.

March: Yeah, and to put that into context, at the point he did it, only 11 teams had ever scored five goals in a Champions League knockout match. He's good you know.

October: He was the first player to score five goals in a European Cup game since, wait for it, Søren Lerby for Ajax v Omonia Nicosia in October 1979, and the only player to do it since Messi is Luiz Adriano for Shakhtar v BATE Borisov, also in October. Go me. Seriously, that is classic October.

SCENE: June serves a tray of Ubuntu Cola to the other months, although March has brought lemon squash as he is allergic to sparkling drinks.

November: Shall we talk about 2011–12, Messi's magnus opus? Seventy-three goals and 29 assists in 60 games; 102 direct goal involvements in a single season.

August: Well, he certainly started in the right way. Four games in August and he scored and assisted in all of them . . .

April: And yet, as usual, it was the business end of the season where he did best. Fifteen goals and assists in each of March and April. Fifteen in a season would be enough for most players . . . not our Leo, though.

February: Let's not forget that month-long scoring run he started in late February 2012 with four goals at home to Valencia. Sixteen goals in six matches remains the best spree he has ever experienced in his career, and he had 22 of Barcelona's 57 shots on target in that period, despite missing one of the games. Extraordinary.

May: Well, at least I can claim his final goals of that mighty season, the four he rattled home against Espanyol on 5 May 2012. Messi is, inevitably, the top-scoring player in the Catalonian derby with 15 goals. Those four took him to 50 for the season in the league, the only time the half century has ever been reached in the Spanish division. This isn't some joke league like England, where players such as Dixie Dean can rattle in 60 at will. Messi even ended the season with a goalless display against Betis, like some sort of human.

December: If we're talking Messi and records and 2012, can I mention the world goalscoring record in a calendar yea—

Others: No!

October: Calendar year stats are confusing and make people sad.

December: Well, yes, but Messi scored 91 times in 2012 and gave some memorabilia to Gerd Müller to honour the man whose record he had taken.

November: This is highly disrespectful to Zambia's Godfrey Chitalu, the Jimmy Dunne of the southern hemisphere. One hundred and seven goals in 1972 and he was never ratified. A poor show, imo.

December: You shouldn't actually say 'imo' out loud. Anyway, I'm feeding off scraps here. Messi's spent his entire career playing in a country that takes a winter break so his December achievements are naturally going to be a bit restrained.

November: Anyway, you're all forgetting the key date in 2012, 11 November.

February: Armistice day?

November: Well, there was no ceasefire in front of goal from Messi, that's for sure. He scored two goals away at Mallorca. 'Big deal,' you're thinking. 'Messi scores a brace. We're not going to get an emotional biopic out of this one.'

May: I see where you're going, November . . .

November: That's right, the next league game in which Messi would not score was on 12 May, almost exactly six months later. Messi ended up scoring in 21 consecutive league games, which is, frankly, insane. The run involved 31 goals, while Barcelona scored 64 goals overall.

March: Twenty-one games in a row. That's . . . improbable.

November: And yet we saw it with our own eyes. A 175-day period of brilliance, that's 102 days longer than the Falklands W—

March: Whoa, November. Not now, mate.

November: Fair point.

SCENE: The months briefly depart the stage for comfort breaks, except for March as he didn't drink his lemon squash because it was 'too strong and thick'.

February: Welcome back, everyone. Let's run through some landmark dates, shall we? I'll start with 17 February 2016, when he became the first player in La Liga history to reach 300 goals when he scored twice against Sporting.

April: It was the year for it. Two months later Messi reached 500 goals in his career for club and country. Five hundred goals! Most players struggle to reach 500 appearances.

December: I really hope you're not counting goals in friendlies and five-a-sides like some of those Twitter accounts.

April: Please.

February: By the way, I'm not saying Messi was nonchalant about reaching the 300-goal mark in the league but a few days earlier he caused outrage among those who don't truly understand or believe in the rules that govern direct free-kicks by passing a penalty kick to Luis Suárez against Celta Vigo, allowing the Uruguayan to complete his hat-trick and leaving himself on 299 goals.

June: Ah yes, the eternal 'passed penalties are disrespectful debate'. The one that Robert Pirés experienced in real time in 2005. The most existential moment in football history.

February: Indeed, but not a philosophical conundrum for Messi. His pass to Suárez was inch perfect, although, for clarity, it was still recorded as a penalty not scored, meaning that at that point in time he had scored with only two of his five spot-kicks in La Liga that season. Perhaps he should pass to a team-mate more often.

October: What about the Champions League? Messi's two hat-tricks in the autumn of 2016 took him to seven in his career, as many as five-time European champions Liverpool have ever managed.

April: True, but my close friend Cristiano Ronaldo matched this in May [*muffled 'thanks' from May off camera*] but it will aggrieve the wee man that CR7 became, in April 2017, the first player to score 100 goals in the European Cup/Champions League. A landmark for the Portuguese machine.

November: But Messi was the first of the pair to successfully hunt down Raúl's long-standing record of 71, back in November 2014, hitting his 72nd in what was his 91st game. Raúl must have thought he was unassailable for a long time. And then everything changed. For Raúl anyway. And people who run Raúl memorabilia businesses.

April: True, as we've talked about before, the existence of Messi and Ronaldo in the same domestic and continental milieu has prevented either one being the utterly dominant figure of his time but has arguably driven both on to greater heights than they could have achieved alone. Their total of nigh-on 200 Champions League goals between them would put them 10th in the list of teams with most goals, ahead of teams such as Dortmund, Inter and Valencia.

January: Is there anything that Messi can't do? [*Makes popular double-handed worshipping gesture.*]

July: Guys, I can think of something . . .

March: We'll come to that, July, but first you mustn't forget that when Liverpool became the first and so far only Premier League team to win a Champions League game against Barcelona at the Nou Camp, in 2007, Messi had fewer touches of the ball than Steve Finnan. I know that you're all thinking about Chelsea and Gary Neville and Fernando Torres now, but check the records and you'll see that that game ended 2–2.

January: Ooh, I've thought of one as well. It was 11 January 2015; Messi, against Atlético, concedes his first and so far only penalty in La Liga. A liability of a player, frankly.

November: He's yet to score an own goal, though. That's the real quiz.

July: Can we finally move on to the eternal question. Can Messi be seen as the greatest player of all-time when it looks like he'll never win the World Cup? The 2014 World Cup represented his greatest opportunity, with Argentina making the final across the border in Brazil but losing out to a Germany team who, instead, became the second European country in succession to win a world title outside their home continent.

August: Messi's issue is that there has never been a clearer example of a single player dragging a team to a World Cup victory than Diego Maradona in 1986. He scored five and assisted five more, meaning he was directly involved in 71 per cent of Argentina's goals that year. In comparison, Messi in 2014 scored four and assisted one more, 63 per cent of Argentina's frankly paltry total of eight, a contribution that isn't massively smaller than his skill ancestor 28 years earlier, which suggests instead that it was the sheer spectacle of Maradona that lives on through the ages. The older man took extreme punishment, 152 fouls won in 21 games, whereas playmakers in Messi's era get time and space to conduct their craft. Obviously, I'm going to defend Leo, I'm August [*glances at camera*], but I feel he deserves it.

July: Fair points, my old friend, and I'd add that the chief difference is that in Maradona's era the World Cup was the pinnacle of football, whereas in Messi's it's the Champions

League. So to lambast Messi for not winning the World Cup surely means you have to lay into Maradona for making only as many appearances in the European Cup/Champions League as Titus Bramble. Horses for courses, era by era.

March: I suppose the final question is how much longer Messi can carry on and whether he'll spend his entire career at Barcelona.

June: Thirty years old in June 2017, Messi, less reliant on pace than Ronaldo although no snail, could feasibly contribute for at least another five years at the highest level. Modern sports science is so far advanced and modern superstars so committed to maintaining their performance levels that we have seen Zlatan Ibrahimović move to the Premier League and become the oldest player to ever score 15 or more goals in a single season.

October: Let's do some wholly unreliable maths then. Since the start of the Pep Guardiola era at Barcelona, Messi has averaged 34 appearances per season in La Liga and 35 goals. Let's say that this rate of a goal a game declines to around 0.75 over the next five years, and he makes an average of only 25 appearances, he'll still add another 90-odd goals to his La Liga total, taking him somewhere close to 450.

September: Applying similar parameters to the Champions League, but reducing the number of games per season to eight to take into account being rested in dead rubbers and there being no guarantee Barcelona will continue to reach the latter stages so regularly, we can expect to see Messi add another 20 to 25 goals.

March: Which means Messi could, maybe should, end his career with a total not far shy of 600 goals in domestic league and Champions League football, which is a total that may not be surpassed for a very long time, depending on how the equally astonishing Cristiano Ronaldo pushes the boundaries over the next few seasons.

August: And for all the criticism of Messi as an international, he is still Argentina's top-scoring player of all-time with 58 goals [*a message saying 'Correct at Time of Broadcast' is shown on screen for those watching this clip on an overly elongated documentary version on Netflix*], a total that is higher than Wayne Rooney's and Thierry Henry's, but less than Stern John's. An unlikely but not improbable World Cup win for Argentina in 2018 and Messi can retire comfortably as the greatest player the game has ever produced.

January: Persuasive stuff, pals, but don't forget that players can fade much more quickly, either due to personal decline or a team-wide deterioration. Barcelona's performance in the Champions League in 2016–17 was indicative of the latter and it remains to be seen how Messi will hold up as, one by one, his exalted colleagues fall by the wayside. Barca were fortunate to progress in the last 16 against Paris Saint-Germain and not only failed to score in 180 minutes against Juventus in the quarter-final, but were restricted to just a single shot on target in the second leg. Messi, the precision utensil of the modern game, hit seven shots off target across the two games. A seasonal slump or the end of an era?

May: Loath as I am to raise the eternal and infernal 'could Messi perform on a cold Tuesday night at Stoke?' question, the key thing people have generally ignored in this debate is that it massively depends on who he is playing for. Messi playing for Barcelona in their pomp in the Potteries is unlikely to have many problems, no matter what Charlie Adam pulled from his bag of tricks, but Messi playing for Stoke, or Rotherham, or Slough Town would be a different matter altogether. So much of his game relies on the space created by not-quite-equal-but-reasonably-close team-mates. Look at the latter-day upsurge Messi had as part of the MSN triumvirate he formed with Neymar and Luis Suárez, so planting him into a team of inferior players could be disastrous for his reputation. On a minor scale, this is surely what has happened with Messi and Argentina. A football team is a sum of its parts, even when one of those parts is cast from shimmering platinum.

February: Wait. Does this mean that Maradona really is the greatest player of all-time?

June: Feb, son, there is no answer to this. Comparing players from different eras is impossible, the endless debating of Messi versus Cristiano Ronaldo shows it's the same when the players are almost exact contemporaries. I think we should leave the final word to Pep Guardiola, who said: 'Don't write about him, don't try to describe him, just watch him.'

September: Wise words and we should, perhaps, remember that all football is merely energy condensed to a slow vibration, that we are all one consciousness experiencing itself subjectively, that there is no such thing as death, life is only a dream and we are the imagination of ourselves.

April: In that case, Messi is the greatest creation of modern times.

December: Amen.

June: Guys, wasn't that just a rip-off of Bill Hi—[*Theme music plays.*]

Premier League season No. 19: 2010–11

Is it still called the Premiership? THOSE DAYS ARE LONG GONE, MY FRIEND

Champions: Manchester United

Relegated: West Ham United, Blackpool, Birmingham City

Top scorer: Carlos Tevez/Dimitar Berbatov (20)

Most assists: Nani (14)

Biggest win: Manchester United 7–1 Blackburn (and four 6–0s; see below)

Overview

When your arch-rivals have sat on their perch with 18 league titles for two decades and you've clawed, scrapped and waltzed your way closer and closer and closer to them, a 19th crown will always be special. But Manchester United's 2010–11 title remains a curate's egg of a Premier League triumph. It counts just as much as all the other ones, yet remains somehow forgettable, unless you're a United fan, or Nani. Or both.

If great teams can win at any venue with ease, then Manchester United in 2010–11 were not, as suspected, a great team.

Their total of 25 points away from home is the lowest recorded by a title-winning team in the three-points-for-a-win era (and the lowest, based on that rule, since Liverpool in 1976–77). United won just five of their 19 away games, only as many as Blackpool, who finished 19th, and managed to lose away at Arsenal, Chelsea and Liverpool, yet, and here's the key thing, still won the title.

If great teams score memorable goals, and headed goals are generally the preserve of the meat and drink enthusiasts lower down the pyramid, then, again Manchester United in 2010–11 were not, as suspected, a great team. They scored 18 headed goals that season, which is the most by a Premier League-winning team and the joint third highest total in the competition's history. Look at the sides around them in this category: the Wimbledon team of 1995–96 with 22; Newcastle in 1999–2000 with 19; the likes of Oldham and Crystal Palace in 1992–93, also with 18. These, whatever they were, were not progressive teams that challenged for the title.

Even having the joint top scorer in the league, in the form of Dimitar Berbatov, was less impressive than it looked at first glance. The Bulgarian reached 20 goals for the only time in his eight-year Premier League career, but 16 of those goals came at home, with five coming in one game against Blackburn. Meanwhile, Wayne Rooney's season was overshadowed by news in the autumn that he was interested in following Carlos Tevez to Manchester City, and creative duties duly passed to Nani, who did, it's true, assist 14 goals, but the Cristiano Ronaldo era this was not. Ultimately United were helped by Chelsea being unable to defend their title (eight wins from 10 was a good start, but a spell of two wins in 11 between November and January undid all that) and Manchester City still being a work in progress under Roberto Mancini, albeit one that could land an FA Cup after defeating United in the semi-finals. (Indeed, the fact that United sealed the title on the same day that City won the cup somehow seemed to diminished both achievements a little.)

At the bottom Birmingham, who, as we discovered with delight, scored 38 goals and finished in the top half in 2009–10, scored just one goal fewer a season later and went down. They were joined by West Ham and Blackpool, led by faux curmudgeon Ian Holloway, who oversaw a team who entertained by scoring 55 and letting in 78; that combined total of 133 goals is the fifth highest in a 20-team Premier League campaign.

Three Things We May Have Just Learnt About 2010–11

Scoring's not boring

The 2010–11 season was the first in the Premier League without either of José Mourinho and Rafa Benítez since 2003–04 and, possibly coincidentally, the goals started flowing like wine. The 1,053 in 2009–10 had been the highest number since 1999–2000 but, a year on, the league added an additional 10, as it moved into the first of the three highest-scoring seasons (based on goals per game) in the modern era. It was helped by a supernova of strikes in the first month of the season, with champions Chelsea continuing their goal streak from the end of the previous campaign with a pair of 6–0 wins (yes, Wigan were involved). Over the heady weekend of 21–22 August three teams – Arsenal, Newcastle and Chelsea – all won 6–0, meaning that August 2010 was the first month to have four games in which teams scored six or more goals since May 1967.

It's Raining Men (who are scoring goals)

If 2010-11 creaked under the heavy load of goals it was carrying, then Saturday February 5 was the day that its knees shook and very nearly buckled under the vast pressure. The history of the Premier League has seen so many carefully planned and curated days and yet a regulation Saturday afternoon in late winter came up with all the goods. Eight games, 41 goals, a rate of 5.1 per game a record for a single (busy) day in the 20-team Premier League era. Applaud the art-house stylings of West Brom, the only one of the 16 sides not to score that day, marvel at Newcastle's pulsating comeback from four down against Arsenal to draw 4–4 and chuckle as Everton beat Blackpool 5–3 in a fixture/result combo like something from a book about Stanley Matthews. Or gasp as you recall bottom club Wolves defeat league leaders Manchester United (hitherto undefeated), one of only four instances where the table proppers have bested the table toppers (50 per cent of which, strangely, have been Wolves v Manchester United fixtures). February 5 2011: the day the goal nets wept.

Red Alert

It was not a classic campaign in Liverpool's history books, with Roy Hodgson, Northampton Town and the Andy Carroll purchase just three of quite a few low points, but the Reds did at least register the earliest and latest goals of the season. The earliest came via Maxi Rodríguez after 32 seconds in the 5–2 late-season win at Fulham. The latest, and it remains the latest Premier League goal in Opta's entire database, was after 101 minutes and 48 seconds, from Dirk Kuyt, in the match at Arsenal in April. The match had already seen Robin van Persie score from the spot after 97min 10sec, only for Kuyt to despatch a spot-kick of his own four and a half minutes later.

Verdict

Manchester United's 19th league title gave them, finally, the lead over Liverpool and will be cherished by their fans for ever more for that aspect alone. It wasn't a classic title race or a dominant procession, instead there was a sense that this campaign was the quiet before the storm as Manchester City prepared to finally mount a credible title challenge. Could the veteran Ferguson hold the noisy neighbours at bay?

Premier League season No. 20: 2011–12

Is it still called the Premiership? ONLY YOUR DAD STILL USES PREMIERSHIP

Champions: Manchester City

Relegated: Wolverhampton Wanderers, Blackburn Rovers, Bolton Wanderers

Top scorer: Robin van Persie (30)

Most assists: David Silva (15)

Biggest win: Manchester 8–2 Arsenal/Arsenal 7–1 Blackburn

Overview

The number of seasons that go down to the final day is relatively small (only six in Premier League history), the number of seasons that go down to goal difference is even smaller (only six in top-flight history) and the number of seasons that go down to the last meaningful kick of the season is tiny (only 1989, Arsenal, and 2012, Manchester City, in the modern era). If you ever doubt whether you enjoy football or not, watch one of the many YouTube clips of Sergio Agüero's winner against Queens Park Rangers in May 2012 and monitor your pulse at the same time. If it remains steady then I'm afraid it's time to walk away from the game for good.

One of the reasons Manchester City's title triumph in 2011–12, their first since 1968, was so compelling was that it looked completely squandered on more than one occasion. The team, guided by the brooding Roberto Mancini and containing talents as varied as Yaya Touré, David Silva, Agüero and Mario Balotelli, started the season like a train delivering cashmere scarves to north-west England. Eleven wins and a draw from their first 12 games was a start that has been matched only three times in top-flight history (Spurs, 1960–61; Man United, 1985–86; and Liverpool, 1990–91). The keen-eyed will note that of those three other sides, the latter two failed to land the title in those seasons. City's start was incredibly good, but it meant nothing.

This was largely because Manchester United had almost kept pace with their city rivals. Sir Alex Ferguson's team ended 2011 with a home defeat to Blackburn, but City started 2012 with a defeat at Sunderland (the Black Cats were also the only away team to prevent City winning a league game at the Etihad in 2011–12), meaning both teams were level on 45 points with half the season remaining. United had won seven away games by this point, already two more than in their title-winning campaign a year earlier, although the home crowd at Old Trafford was still reeling from the 6–1 schooling City had handed out in October. That winning margin of five goals was City's biggest league win against United since 1955 and only the second time they'd hit six against them. The swing in goal difference was to prove reasonably important seven months later.

Between 11 March and 8 April, City took just five points from five games, leaving them eight points behind with eight games to go; Balotelli's red card away at Arsenal proving a delicious and tempting honeypot for British ex-pros bemoaning attitudes in modern players. It was over, barring the sort of slump that Ferguson had rarely encountered in the Premier League era. But then, exactly that, the unthinkable, occurred. A 1–0 loss away at Wigan and an inexplicable 4–4 draw at home to Everton meant that United headed to the Etihad knowing that defeat would allow their old, and new, rivals to replace them at the top, something they duly did.

And lo, it came to the final day. City just needed to match United's result and, with a record of P18, W17, D1, L0 at home, and relegation-haunted QPR to come, it all looked a formality. Less so after 90 minutes, when the Londoners led 2–1. Everyone knows what happened next (Dzeko 91.15, Agüero 93.20) but possibly less well known is that City's total of 44 shots in that match remains a Premier League record for a single game (for matches Opta has recorded in the past 14 years) and that Balotelli's calm pass for Agüero's winner was the only assist he recorded in 70 Premier League appearances for either City or Liverpool. United, meanwhile, ended with 89 points (nine more than they had collected in winning the title 12 months earlier) and nothing to show for it. In fact, 14 of the club's 20 league titles have been collected with an inferior record to 2011–12. Some seasons are just different.

Three Things We May Have Just Learnt About 2011–12

Unknown Pleasures

Arsène Wenger's Arsenal teams have always been susceptible to the occasional shellacking down the years but their 8–2 loss to Manchester United in the dog days of summer 2011 echoed down the ages. It was one of only two games in the Alex Ferguson era to contain 10 goals (along with his final match, the equally barmy 5–5 draw at West Brom), and remains the highest number of goals Arsenal have conceded in a top-flight game. It also served as one of the first football Twitter memes, with increasingly strained variations on 'I'd 8–2 be an Arsenal fan' still in service six long years later.

Askew Downing

Liverpool's experimentation with 'Moneyball' signings in 2011 (NB, this actually bears little relation to the popular book *Moneyball*) brought the likes of Stewart Downing, Charlie Adam and Jordan Henderson to Anfield. Henderson (eventually) thrived, but Downing and particularly Adam struggled to adapt. Downing was particularly unlucky in his first season at the club, ending 2011–12 as not only the player with the most shots (72) without scoring, but the most chances created (55) without an assist. Even Billy Beane couldn't figure that one out.

The humble English swan

In 2012 London hosted the Olympics and the word 'Brexit' was coined (not at the same time), but the Premier League was still a melting pot of nationalities and cultures. Even on a local level, teams were mixing it up, with the first non-English club to appear in the competition, Swansea City, recording a higher percentage of goals from Englishmen (71 per cent) than any other team.

Verdict

I swear you'll never see anything like this ever again. So watch it; drink it in.

Premier League season No. 21: 2012–13

Is it still called the Premiership? THIS ISN'T RUGBY, PAL

Champions: Manchester United

Relegated: Queens Park Rangers, Reading, Wigan Athletic

Top scorer: Robin van Persie (26)

Most assists: Juan Mata (12)

Biggest win: Chelsea 8–0 Aston Villa

Overview

The final flourish. That horror film cliché, the dead zombie who springs back to life as the heroes relax at what had seemed like the end of their ordeal, is perhaps a little strong for what remains Manchester United's most recent title win, but there is some element of truth there. Bested (psychologically, if not on points) by Manchester City in 2011–12, the true measure of Sir Alex Ferguson's genius was his 13th Premier League crown, given the apparent quality of the squad he did it with, and the club's subsequent decline immediately after he retired.

By all accounts, in 2012, United's greatest manager decided

Outside the Box

to continue for one more season to try to wrest the title back from the club's cross-town rivals. And, thanks to the deadly efficiency of summer signing Robin van Persie and Ferguson's unrivalled ability to coax performances and wins from some ordinary players, he achieved his aim.

The key to the season was the autumn, when United rarely looked in control yet still managed to collect wins like conkers. They lost their opening game of the season, at Goodison Park (2012–13 would be the third time United lost their first match but still won the title, after 1992–93 and 1995–96) and by October they had conceded the opening goal in eight of their 12 games in all competitions. Yet fast forward a few months and they remain the only team in English top-flight history to have won 25 of their opening 30 games.

The spirit, the sheer resilience, in the side was awesome, with their total of 29 points from comebacks the second highest total recorded in the Premier League era. Ferguson's team trailed in 16 league games in 2012–13, only four fewer than 13th-place Stoke, yet came back to win nine of them. They also shared the goals among 20 players, a Premier League record, with the likes of Alexander Büttner (2) and Nick Powell (1) contributing, albeit not as often as van Persie, whose 26 goals, including a hat-trick against Aston Villa in the title-clinching fixture in April, was the culmination of his three-season holy period (two at Arsenal, one and a title at United). Neither the Dutchman, nor his new club, would quite be the same again.

Such was United's will to win in 2012–13 that there were only four leadership changes at the top of the table all season, with the champions-elect immovable from November through until May. After sealing the title in April, a new top-flight points record of 96 was on the cards had they won their final four games. Instead they collected just five more, drawing

252

with Arsenal, losing to Chelsea, winning their manager's final home game against Swansea and then completing Ferguson's time in management with the first 5–5 draw in the English top flight since 1984.

At the bottom, in a gloomy but niche world dominated by your Sunderlands and your Derbys, QPR 2012–13 generally escape much focus when people examine the worst performances in the Premier League, but Rangers' wait until their 17th game of the season for a win was the longest winless start in the top flight since Sheffield United in 1990–91. The Londoners filled 20th place and were joined in demotion by Reading, despite Adam Le Fondre's best efforts (see below), and, finally, Wigan. Having stayed up three years later with a goal difference of minus 42, the Latics succumbed, although did so accompanied by the joy of winning the FA Cup, the only team to suffer those extremes in the same season.

Three Things We May Have Just Learnt About 2012–13

Melt in the south

Reading's third (was it their third? Yes, I just checked and it was their third) season in the Premier League ended like the second, with relegation, but one man tried his best to keep the Royals in the top flight: Adam Le Fondre. Le Fondre, 'the melt' in French, was in fact one of the few players at the Madejski Stadium who could be relied on to keep his cool. His total of eight goals from the bench in 2012–13 is a Premier League record, with five of them coming in three heady games in January. Le Fondre was less successful when he started games, scoring just four, but that combined haul of 12 was as many as

Sergio Agüero and Wayne Rooney managed, and one more than Carlos Tevez.

BB-9

The 2012–13 season was the first in the top flight since 1991–92 without any clubs beginning with the letter B, but making amends for the alphabet's No. 2 was Gareth Bale, with this being the campaign that elevated him from 'that Tottenham player who seems to be playing well' to 'I think Gareth Bale might be one of the best players in Europe.' His total of nine long-range goals was more than any other player in Europe's big five leagues in 2012–13, and his nine winning goals, a Premier League high, almost dragged Spurs to fourth place in the spring. The first Spurs player to break the 20-goal mark since the 1990s, Bale's dominance earned him a (then) world record transfer to Real Madrid. B-bye.

Pleased to Michu

With two goals and an assist on his Premier League debut, Spanish curiosity Michu started his career as he meant to go on. Eighteen league goals in his first season in England led to a) many bigger clubs coveting the Swansea man and b) an endless list of comparisons with other players, given Michu had cost the Welsh side only £2 million. Yet owing to a combination of injuries and form, he scored only two more goals in the Premier League, but can console himself with being one of only nine players to score 20 or more goals in the division despite playing only two seasons (along with Klins-mann, Ravanelli, Crespo, Pellè, Josh King, Firmino, Deeney and Dele Alli).

Verdict

No man has dominated the Premier League in its 25-year his-tory as much as Alex Ferguson. He started English football's new era in 1992 as a man who knew time was running out if he was to win the league title for his championship-starved club; he ended his spell with a preposterous 13 of them in the trophy cabinet. The 2012–13 team gets credit, and rightly so, for pulling a rabbit out of a hat, but the sheer succession of wins for the first three-quarters of the season marks this team out as, statistically at least, one of the most impressive outfits in the modern era.

8.

The Red and the Black: Finding Perspective on Arsène Wenger

'The only moment of possible happiness is the present. The past gives regrets; and future uncertainties. Man quickly realised this and created religion. It forgives him what he has done wrong in the past and tells him not to worry about the future, as you will go to paradise'

— Arsène Wenger, 2015

Like life in the mafia, there are generally only two ways for a football manager to leave a club. A chosen few, like Sir Alex Ferguson or the French Sir Alex Ferguson, Guy Roux, leave a legacy so rich that subsequent managers can do little more than go through the motions, haunted by what came before and broken by the heft of expectation. The majority of coaches, though, do a bad/reasonable/good job for a period of time between six months and three years and then move on, or are summarily removed, depending on their performance, carving a slice out of a club's history, rather than a vast slab.

Arsène Wenger seems to occupy a curious witchspace between these two eventualities, with the longevity of a Ferguson but an increasingly battered legacy that has sapped the enthusiasm of many, perhaps even most, Arsenal fans. The 2016–17 season even featured a replay of the Battle of Britain in the southern English skies, albeit one that showed a level of self-absorption that would have been a confidence boost for the Luftwaffe, as both pro-Wenger and anti-Wenger cabals hired light aircraft to support/attack the manager via the medium of banners. This sense of pantomime ennui was illustrated in the penultimate home game of the season, against Sunderland, a must-win match for Arsenal's ambitions of finishing in the top four, but one where empty seats littered the Emirates Stadium. Questioned on this visual critique of his modern regime, Wenger could offer only 'it is Tuesday night'; factually correct but not the most inspiring quote from one of the Premier League's more loquacious managers.

A rash of Wenger anniversaries in the mid-2010s (1,000 games, 20 years since he was appointed, the 10th anniversary of Sol Campbell scoring in a Champions League final) focused attention on the Frenchman's achievements at Arsenal but also highlighted the almost binary nature of his spell at the club. In the stirring words of Sven-Göran Eriksson, 'first half good, second half not so good', and it's true that 11 of the 15 trophies Wenger has won at the club came in his first 10 years. But you can't just abandon the second half of his career as tedious sludge. For starters it contains three times as many FA Cup wins than, say, Leeds United have won in their entire history. Overall Wenger has won 3.9 per cent of all the league titles and FA Cups ever competed for in England, so for him to be almost relentlessly harangued in 2017 about a lack of trophies (until another FA Cup final win at least) suggests that Arsenal fans may have been spoilt over the past two decades.

I thought about dividing this chapter into three sections called The Good, the Bad and the Ugly (apologies) but first, there haven't been too many ugly things about Wenger's Premier League career (unless you are offended by a steady conveyor belt of red cards and/or Martin Keown landing on

Ruud van Nistelrooy like an eagle), and, second, there are so many other facets to the man who has managed Arsenal for 16 per cent of their entire existence. This, then, is a deep dive into Wenger's time at London's most successful club, and his part in it.

The record breaker

In the final week of the 2016–17 Premier League season, Arsenal hit 36 shots against Sunderland in what, despite the shot-every-two-and-a-bit-minutes pace, felt like a low-key 2–0 home win. Other than securing the three points they needed to maintain their hopes of qualifying for the Champions League yet again, the game was relatively uneventful – to the naked eye at least. In fact, Arsenal's shot total was a record for a Wenger team in a Premier League game, a small but illustrative example of how his sides can innocuously carve out little bits of footballing history, even during the bad times.

Of course, some of Wenger's entries in the big book of things that have happened in football are considerably more dramatic than putting David Moyes's Sunderland under concerted pressure. Go back to the 2000s and a new marker, a glamorous benchmark, a steely resolve was evident as Arsenal closed out the 2001–02 season with 13 consecutive wins and the Premiership title. A win against Birmingham in the first game of 2002–03 extended the hottest of hot streaks to 14 games, taking them past a trio of clubs on 13 wins in a row (Preston and Sunderland in 1892 and Tottenham in 1960).

In that 2001–02 season, Arsenal scored in every game, something that hadn't been done since the 19th century, while they also ended the season unbeaten away from home (W14

D5), after which Wenger boldly predicted his team could go an entire campaign without defeat. 'It's not impossible as AC Milan once did it, but I can't see why it's so shocking to say it. Do you think Manchester United, Liverpool or Chelsea don't dream that as well? They're exactly the same. They just don't say it because they're scared to look ridiculous, but nobody is ridiculous in this job as we know anything can happen.'

When Arsenal eventually suffered defeat in 2002–03, via Wayne Rooney's first Premier League goal for Everton, Wenger did indeed receive some stiff servings of ridicule for his notion that a modern team could go a whole season without defeat. And when Manchester United defeated the Gunners 2–0 in November (ending the London side's run of scoring in consecutive top-flight league games at 55, which is, as you might have already guessed, another record) it looked as though this team was too brittle to establish a dynasty to rival United, which, to be fair, was true, but it didn't stop them setting another stunning, epochal record in 2003–04, by doing the impossible; 38 games, zero defeats.

Sir Alex Ferguson was not impressed (see 2003–04 season review for more) but he was in the minority. It remains Wenger's masterpiece, as well as his third and very likely final Premier League title. The arrival of José Mourinho in 2004 meant that Arsenal's manager was now fighting mind-game battles on two fronts, and his team have never really come close to adding a fourth crown. It was not, though, the end of the records and landmarks, even as Chelsea and others marauded over their territory on the domestic front.

The unbeaten run continued into 2004–05, the fixture computer making a small but significant adjustment so that the Gunners played Blackburn at home instead of Chelsea in the 43rd game of the run. Eventually the all-time great domino run of losslessness came to an end at Old Trafford after 49 games, the team exiting the Theatre of Dreams by launching a range of pizzas at their arch-enemies.

In the 'Invincibles' season a sprightly pre-Mourinho Chelsea knocked Arsenal out of the Champions League, in what was surely their best chance to win the competition, but two years later Wenger's team found defensive nirvana as they kept an all-time European Cup record of 10 clean sheets in a row to reach the final in Paris. Goalkeeper Jens Lehmann, possibly the most underrated or under-remembered player at the club in this period, was the rock this run was built on, but his red card in the final, after only 18 minutes, was a breach in the hitherto impregnable wall of Arsenal's Château Gaillard defence and Barcelona's tiny, technical foot soldiers swarmed gleefully into the gap.

The records continued to arrive in the 2010s, but they were of a bleaker hue. Heading to Old Trafford in late August 2011 in the unfamiliar position of 16th, Arsenal subsequently lost 8–2, only the second time they had let in eight goals in a league game after an 8–0 defeat to Loughborough in 1896 (when they had the above-average excuse of having an FA Cup tie *on the same day*). At least Ferguson came out in support of Wenger that day; in 2014 the Frenchman suffered one of the most unpleasant scenarios imaginable when he lost his 1,000th game in charge of the Gunners 6–0 away at Chelsea, with the home fans lustily singing 'Arsène Wenger, we want you to stay'.

Just as he had been when Chelsea had beaten Arsenal in Wenger's 500th match, José Mourinho was managing the west Londoners and, far from commiserating with Wenger, he left his dugout early, claiming in a post-match interview that he wanted to call his wife to tell her the score. Wenger might have once claimed that 'everyone thinks they have the prettiest wife at home' but if nothing else this game proved that judging whether wives have a BT Sport subscription is harder to ascertain.

European competition also dished out its own punishment, both slow torture (exits from the Champions League last 16 in seven consecutive years) and rapid punches to the ear, in the form of a 10–2 evisceration by Bayern in spring 2017. A 5–1 defeat in Bavaria was bad enough but then the German perma-champions decided to produce the same scoreline in north London, the result of which was the second biggest aggregate defeat in Champions League history and the biggest ever suffered by an English club.

Outside the stadium, bands of discontented fans roamed, YouTube channels prodding them for angry quotes that could go viral. The sun's reflection glinting gloriously off the Premier League trophy on a happy afternoon at Highbury had never seemed longer ago.

Alsatian cousin

Taking charge of basic Arsenal in the dying days of John Major's back to basics government, Wenger can be seen as epitomising the changing face of England in the late 1990s (even though Cool Britannia is also Wenger's least favourite weather/stadium combination). His first title-winning team was a Euro-fusion of George Graham's British defensive unit and an influx of continental nous, in the form of Patrick Vieira, Nicolas Anelka, Remi Garde et al, but, by the time the Premier League was recaptured in 2002, the English involvement had slipped, and when the Invincibles rolled into town, only a fifth of the minutes played were by English players. Wenger revolutionised English football and, like many radical leaders, as his cause progressed he had to muster troops from foreign lands.

Season	% of mins played by English players at Arsenal
1997–98	56.9%
2001–02	39.9%
2003–04	20.8%

Wenger is also the key figure in the rise of what must be called 'the fully foreign starting XI', even with the slightly tiresome connotations that brings. Based on players hailing from outside the UK or Ireland (the latter included as it has been a key talent pool for the English top flight for more than a century), Wenger has named 123 entirely foreign teams in the Premier League, 112 more than any other club. In fact, add all the other teams to do it at least once together and they reach only 30.

Premier League since 12 Oct 1996	Fully foreign starting XIs
Arsenal	123
Manchester City	11
Newcastle United	6
Bolton Wanderers	6
Chelsea	3
Fulham	3
Watford	1

A further illustration of the contrasting fortunes of local players and the others in the Wenger era is the difference between English and French players under him. He has used 46 Englishmen for Arsenal in the Premier League and only 25 Frenchmen, yet the English players have a combined appearances total of 2,478, compared to 2,651 for their Gallic pals. Essentially the Frenchmen, with a few exceptions (hello, David Grondin), have been key personnel whereas a lot of the English have been subjected to try and goodbye policy, with nine of them playing just one league game under Wenger (step forward Lee Harper, Ryan Garry, Matthew Rose, David Bentley, Nico Yennaris, Julian Gray, Jay Emmanuel-Thomas, Ian Selley and Isaiah Rankin).

At the other end of the involvement scale, the Frenchman used most often by Wenger in the Premier League is Patrick Vieira, with 276 appearances, whereas Theo Walcott occupies the same role for the English contingent with 264. Different players, different eras, same manager.

Le Sportif du Mind

Although in recent seasons Arsène Wenger's chief battles seem to have been with his own legacy and some of Arsenal's more vocal supporters, his early period saw him engage in managerial skirmishes on an epic scale. The first manager in the Premier League era to successfully rattle Alex Ferguson, Wenger spent much of the 2000s fighting a culture war against rudimentary battle-masters like Sam Allardyce, Tony Pulis and Mark Hughes, most of whom enjoyed cold war support from the Old Trafford superpower.

Ferguson's antipathy to Wenger was powered by the sores of defeat, with the Frenchman recording a highly respectable record of W11 D7 L7 against United in his first 25 games against them. In the subsequent 33 matches (a period that includes Ferguson's less than stellar successors) Arsenal have won just seven times (D8 L18, including the 8–2 demolition at Old Trafford). The decline in Wenger's ability to beat United was exactly in step with a change in Ferguson's stance towards his rival, from loathing to mild fondness. By the early 2010s, nearly all the poison had disappeared from the fixture, along with much of the excitement.

Such was United's strength, they could threaten Wenger's team in any stadium. With most of his other keen rivalries, though, it was only once you could prise Arsenal away from their comfortable home in trendy Islington that you could start to undermine them. The Britannia (now bet365) Stadium and the Reebok (now Macron) Stadium were opened within days of each other in 1997 and both turned into cauldrons of doom for Wenger, with his teams invariably unable to cope with a long-ball barrage from the Trotters and long-throw flak from the Potters. Arsenal's 4–1 win at Stoke at the tail end of 2016–17 was only the second time they'd won there in 10 Premier League trips, and it is still the stadium where they have the lowest win percentage under Wenger, lower than Stamford Bridge, Anfield and Old Trafford (if you include cup semi-finals for the latter).

The manager Wenger has found hardest to cope with, though, is José Mourinho. Clashes between them have often sunk below the already fairly modest accepted-nature-of-behaviour standards, with Mourinho calling Wenger a 'voyeur' and a 'specialist in failure' at different points, and Wenger saying that 'when you give success to stupid people, it makes them more stupid sometimes and not more intelligent' in response to the Portuguese's barbs.

One of Mourinho's more memorable statements about the Arsenal manager came in 2008. 'The English like statistics a lot,' he said. 'Do they know that Arsène Wenger has only 50 per cent of wins in the English league?' I think we can join hands and hope that the first part of that is true, but it's certain that the second part is not. Even in 2017, with Arsenal having finished in the top two only once in a decade, Wenger's win percentage was still 58 per cent; lower than Mourinho's (63 per cent) but the fifth best of any manager to have taken charge of more than 100 Premier League games. With Wenger rapidly approaching 800 matches, that is no mean feat.

A rivalry on a much less poisonous scale is the one with Liverpool, which generally has been conducted entirely on the field of play. Games between the sides in the Premier League era, particularly when compared to the late 1980s and early 1990s when they did have an edge to them, have been notable for nothing more sinister than excitement and drama, with the fixture having more 90th-minute goals than any other, as well as the most hat-tricks and the most missed penalties.

The master of the FA Cup

If there is one competition that has treated Arsène Wenger with an almost unfailing kindness it's the FA Cup. In the 2010s, when Arsenal were engaged in an endless circular season of crashing out of the Champions League and then skulking back in by finishing in the Premier League's top four, a pair of FA Cup wins in 2014 and 2015 gave Wenger some breathing space. Failure to win the cup for a third season in a row in 2016 was lessened by a rare second-place finish in the league, and just as the howls of derision reached fever pitch in 2017, Arsenal and Wenger went and landed the cup once more. Seven FA Cup wins – 1998, 2002, 2003, 2005, 2014, 2015, 2017 – makes Wenger the most successful FA Cup manager in the game's history and puts him level with Liverpool, Chelsea and Aston Villa, while 5.1 per cent of FA Cups, first held in 1872, have had Wenger in charge of the winning team.

Stick a pin in most major FA Cup events of the past 20 years and you'll find Wenger lurking. The last semi-final that went to a replay? Wenger's Arsenal falling to Ryan Giggs's hirsute wonder goal at Villa Park in 1999. The first final to go to a penalty shoot-out? Arsenal against Manchester United in 2005, a match in which the Invincibles adopted a very un-Wenger like defensive posture to secure what would be their last trophy for nine years.

Wenger's karma in the FA Cup seems to be stronger than in any other competition, possibly stemming from his decision in 1999 to offer Sheffield United a replay after Kanu and Overmars combined to score after the Blades had put the ball out of play because of an injury to their own player. Arsenal won the replayed fifth-round tie 2–1 and Wenger's ultimate reward was seemingly to be forever spared that most painful of experiences for a manager of a big club; a third-round FA Cup exit. The 2016–17 campaign was Wenger's 21st in the FA Cup and he has successfully reached the fourth round in every one. For a long time he enjoyed the same luck against teams from a lower division, progressing in 28 consecutive ties before Blackburn won 1–0 at the Emirates in 2013. Since then, though, the business of domination has resumed, with 10 successive wins against teams from lower in the pyramid, including two non-league sides, Sutton and Lincoln, en route to the 2017 win.

Perhaps the one negative about Wenger's placid mastery of the FA Cup is that it has gone hand-in-hand with the decline of the FA Cup song. Before the 1998 final, the team recorded the seminal 'Hot Stuff', which was one of the last football songs to break into the top 10 in the charts (reaching No. 9), but no subsequent Arsenal cup final appearance has been accompanied by an official recording, an increasingly archaic practice that now seems to belong to lower division clubs who reach the final and enjoy their brief moment in the spotlight with all the traditional trimmings. What the world would give for a late-era Wenger singing with gusto on a song.

Style Council

Arsenal and non-Arsenal fans alike can see that the way the team played in, say, 2003–04, is different to how they did in 2016–17. Performance data 13 years ago was more limited than it is now but there are certain metrics that you can compare across the whole period.

Generally, the impression is of a team functioning in a fairly consistent fashion going forward across the period, particularly when it comes to shots. An average of 5.8 shots on target per game in 2003–04 is similar to 5.6 in 2015–16, just with a big zero in the league defeats column. Where there is a change it is either mirroring the Premier League generally (increased number of passes, fewer fouls) or defensively. It's notable that the last time Arsenal conceded fewer than 30 goals in a season, they won the title. Defences win you honours, something that Wenger seemed to forget for a long while, barely adjusting his approach until Arsenal's Champions League qualification looked in jeopardy in the second half of 2016–17.

PL season	Shots on	Total shots	Passes	Fouls	Fouls won	Goals conceded
2003/2004	5.8	14.2	483	14.2	14.4	26
2004/2005	6.1	14.9	513	12.4	14.4	36
2005/2006	5.7	14.6	488	13.6	15.7	31
2006/2007	5.9	16.8	486	10.6	13.8	35
2007/2008	5.5	16.5	496	10.7	12.2	31
2008/2009	5.8	17.4	500	12.2	12.9	37
2009/2010	6.1	17.4	508	12.4	14	41
2010/2011	6.3	17.2	530	11.9	11.1	43
2011/2012	6.2	16.8	542	10.7	10.8	49
2012/2013	5.4	15.7	556	10.1	10.8	37
2013/2014	5.6	13.8	569	9.2	10.6	41
2014/2015	6.0	16.1	540	9.9	11	36
2015/2016	5.6	15.0	559	9.2	11.4	36
2016/2017	5.3	14.9	563	10.5	10.2	44

In the final few weeks of the season the manager switched to a back three (coincidentally or not, in the same season a team playing with a back three won the Premier League title), his biggest tactical shift for a decade. Whether it was a sticking plaster in a difficult moment (Arsenal won seven of their eight Premier League games in this set-up and defeated Chelsea in a rare FA Cup final battle of two teams playing with a back three) or a permanent change, is something we will discover in 2017–18.

Nine nine nein

Wenger is too urbane a man to believe in curses and hocus-pocus (he seemed to lose faith in Manuel Almunia only after the Spanish goalkeeper claimed his house was haunted), but there is something deeply unsettling about the No. 9 shirt in his time at Arsenal. The incumbent when Wenger arrived was Paul Merson, whose best days at the Gunners were behind him. A season later the shirt was inherited by Nicolas Anelka, who scored 23 goals in 61 games across 1997–98 and 1998–99. The No. 9 was being honoured in the correct manner, Arsenal had a new hero, the Premier League had a deadly new predator in its midst.

Except . . . Anelka agitated for and got a big move to Real Madrid in 1999, the start of a series of summers in which La Liga giants would sift through Arsenal's collection of well-regarded players, nodding imperceptibly at the ones they favoured, like a farmer buying livestock at an auction. With Anelka gone, the shirt was inherited by Davor Šuker, an unusual signing for Wenger given that the Croatian was at the tail-end of his career. Eight goals in 22 games wasn't a terrible return from Šuker, but he won only 10 of his games, emblematic of a spell when Arsenal were inconsistent and thus unable to challenge peak-ScholesGiggsKeaneBeckham Manchester United.

It was after Šuker's departure that the No. 9 shirt really hit problems, though, with Wenger handing it to Francis Jeffers in a summer of ostentatious reconstruction in 2001. 'He is obsessed with scoring goals,' Wenger proclaimed, which might have been true at that point (18 in 49 as a youngster at Everton) but obsession turned into obstruction in Jeffers' laborious Arsenal career, with the forward scoring only four goals in two seasons with the Gunners, and only a paltry three after that in the remainder of his Premier League career with Everton, Charlton and Blackburn. To make stark matters even starker, Arsenal sealed the Jeffers deal on the same day Chelsea signed Frank Lampard.

As Jeffers was ushered on, the Arsenal No. 9 needed a strong reboot and it looked like it had one when Wenger gave it to quick Andalusian José Antonio Reyes, who not only joined Arsenal midway through the glorious 2003–04 season but didn't do a Faustino Asprilla and torpedo their title bid. Reyes's subsequent time at Arsenal was a curious mix of excellent (16 goals, 21 assists and 42 wins in 69 Premier League appearances) and not-so-excellent, with stories of homesickness and a lack of understanding with certain team-mates apparently behind his departure to Real Madrid in 2006. In return Arsenal received, on loan, Júlio Bapista, a man who, a four-goal League Cup burst at Anfield aside, did not honour the No. 9 shirt adequately. In fact, those four goals at Liverpool were more than he managed in 24 league appearances for the Gunners.

Eduardo was the next recipient of the No. 9 and, though blameless for his career-threatening injury at the hands of Martin 'Tiny' Taylor at Birmingham, it was nonetheless more petrol on the fire of conspiracy about this particular squad number. Wenger's next move was to give it to South Korean Park Chu-young, whose entire Premier League career consisted of six minutes in a 2–1 home defeat to Manchester United.

The first post-Park occupant of the shirt was an improvement (it's difficult to see how he could have done any worse), with zany German Lukas Podolski providing 19 goals and

11 assists in 60 Premier League games but never really gaining the trust of his manager, something that also seems to be the case with the current No. 9, Lucas Pérez, who scored just once in 11 league games in 2016–17, although he did make pesto out of Basel with a hat-trick against the Swiss in the Champions League.

Overall, it seems vaguely appropriate that a manager as determined as Wenger has been to tear up certain traditions, has turned the No. 9 shirt, possibly the most traditional garment in the English game, into a carousel of bit-partism. Far from locating a fox in the box, Wenger instead found a series of lone wolves who struggled to fit into his vision for the club.

We also shouldn't forget a darker side to Wenger's character – a willingness to hand out inappropriate squad numbers: from midfielder Abou Diaby emerging from the medical centre to play in the No. 2 shirt, right-back Bacary Sagna wearing No. 3; from Nicklas Bendtner in the appropriately outlandish 52 (rumoured to reference his £52k a week wage) to, worst of all, centre-half William Gallas wearing No. 10 (echoing Steve Bould wearing the no. 10 shirt in Arsenal's title winning game at Anfield in May 1989.) A No. 10 should be wily and creative rather than sitting furiously in the centre circle at St Andrew's.

The European question

If the FA Cup makes Wenger feel like Superman, then ventures overseas in the continental cups are the kryptonite that turns the grandiose Frenchman into an ordinary citizen. It's realistic to suggest that Arsenal should, or could, have at least three European honours under their long-serving manager (defeat in the UEFA Cup final in 2000, the Champions League final in 2006 and the missed opportunity in the 2003–04 edition), and yet the Gunners' last international honour was the 1994 Cup Winners' Cup.

Astoundingly, or perhaps not, Wenger's total of 86 wins in the Champions League is the second highest number in the competition's history (1992–present), behind only Alex Ferguson and ahead of numerous men who have led teams to the ultimate prize. The next highest number of wins by a manager not to have won the Champions League is 36, by Mircea Lucescu, a full 50 fewer than Wenger, while, as the sun set on the 2016–17 season, Wenger had two more Champions League match wins than Pep Guardiola and Diego Simeone combined.

With time running out to land a European pot, Wenger's entry into the Europa League in 2017–18 might be the slice of variety that he has been looking for after years of drudge in the Champions League. As it stands, he remains the only manager to lose in the final of all three major UEFA competitions (Champions League and UEFA Cup with Arsenal, Cup Winners' Cup with Monaco); a unique if unwanted record.

The comebacks

Let's not get hysterical, all football teams record both comebacks and see opponents come back against them. That said, Wenger's Arsenal have extreme form in both, going from the sublime (4–0 down to Reading in the League Cup and winning 7–5) to the ridiculous (4–0 up against Newcastle in 2011 but drawing the game 4–4, the only time a team has failed to win from a four-goal lead in the Premier League).

Les cartes rouge

The classic Anglo-Saxon boo has become more prevalent at the Emirates in recent seasons, even though Wenger's teams of the 2010s seem increasingly unlikely to do the same to geese or other waterfowl. A lot has changed, then, since the late 1990s and early 2000s when Arsenal and red cards went hand in hand. It seemed as if the Gunners were reduced to 10 men almost every week, their aggressive players excused by their professorial leader, much to the manufactured outrage of the ex-professionals sitting in television studios, many of whom regularly launched their own legs into far worse situations than any created by the Arsenal men.

Even now Arsenal's lead, in the Wenger era, in the number of games won when having a man (or men) sent off is striking; more than twice as many as Manchester United and 14 clear of their nearest rivals in this arena, Chelsea. There's a reasonable argument that the modern game's advanced fitness and modern humans' increased physical size means that the 11 versus 11 blueprint, decided upon nearly 200 years ago, is outmoded and that a football game involving 20 players would be a better spectacle than one with 22. Either way, there has rarely been a better example of a team functioning well with 10 players than Arsenal under Arsène Wenger. The move from Highbury to the lush pastures of the Emirates seemed to reduce this capability a little, but even so Arsenal still managed three red-card wins in 2016–17, including on the final day against Everton. The force is strong in these ones.

1996–present	Wins after recieving a red card
Arsenal	31
Chelsea	17
Everton	15
Liverpool	15
Manchester City	14
Manchester United	14

The broken legacy?

The number of Premier League players born after Wenger's first game as Arsenal manager currently stands at 59. His reign pre-dates the invention of Wi-Fi by a year and Google by two. Wenger has managed Arsenal for 16 per cent of their existence and has won seven of their record 13 FA Cups. He revolutionised not only his own club but the English game in terms of recruitment, style and ambition, and he even has an asteroid – (33179) Arsènewenger – named after him.

Yet Wenger will begin the 2017–18 season as a man who knows that a sizeable proportion of the Arsenal fan-base are itching to see him move on, despite a haul of three FA Cups in four years. Myriad disappointments and various perceived slights over the past decade have produced a crescendo of anger, although at least some of the opprobrium has now been redirected towards the club's board.

It's hard to work out whether this is unfair with numbers alone but I think Wenger's time at Arsenal, the nature of modern football fans and the FA Cup's decline in prestige can be glimpsed in the table below. The manager's win percentage in the second half of his career is almost *exactly the same* as it was in the first half. The difference is the number of trophies won. A few miles up the road, Tottenham continue to profess that the game is about glory but ultimately, whether you support Arsenal, Barcelona or Sittingbourne, the game is about trophies. Wenger has won a lot of them but the sense that he is unlikely to win another Premier League is overpoweringly infuriating to too many people. Sir Alex Ferguson departed with a fresh league title on the table; does Arsenal's record-breaking manager have it in him to do the same?

Arsène Wenger	Major trophies	PL finishes in top two	European finals	Win %
1996–97 to 2005–06	7	8	2	57.6%
2006–07 to present	3	1	0	57.5%

Premier League season No. 22: 2013–14

Is it still called the Premiership? I STILL HEAR THE
NAME BUT I DON'T PLAY THE GAME

Champions: Manchester City

Relegated: Cardiff City, Fulham, Norwich City

Top scorer: Luis Suárez (31)

Most assists: Steven Gerrard (13)

Biggest win: Manchester City 7–0 Norwich

Overview

Welcome to the goal frenzy. For the first time since 1986–87,
an English league season kicked off without Alex Ferguson
and everyone went potty. No one outside the most ardent of
Liverpool fan websites and the brain of Brendan Rodgers predicted that Brendan Rodgers' Liverpool would challenge for
the title, let alone still stand a chance of landing it in May. José
Mourinho had returned to Chelsea, Arsenal were hoping to
mark the 10th anniversary of getting a golden Premier League
trophy by winning a silver one and Manchester City were
determined to make amends for their weak defence of the

title in 2012–13 and could also boast a new manager, the jovially taciturn Manuel Pellegrini.

And then there was Manchester United. David Moyes's Manchester United. 'Your job now is to stand by the new manager,' Ferguson had asked/pleaded/demanded at the end of the previous campaign, forgetting that football fans, like chairmen, judge managers on performance rather than recommendations from a legend. Moyes began his Premier League adventure with United by winning 4–1 at Swansea to go top of the table, but four points from the next five games batted the bewildered champions down into 12th; they would not trouble the top four for the rest of the season.

Old Trafford, that ancient cathedral of dominance, staged seven home defeats in the league (six under Moyes, one under caretaker Ryan Giggs), the highest number since 1973–74, while their final position of seventh was the lowest Premier League champions had finished since Blackburn in 1995–96 (unwittingly, United were starting a trend for reigning title holders to implode, a blueprint followed faithfully by Chelsea in 2015–16 and Leicester in 2016–17).

In place of a dominant Manchester United was a thrilling title race, one featuring 25 leadership changes, 21 more than there had been in the previous campaign. The contenders were Arsenal, who led for all but a few days from September through until February, Liverpool and Manchester City, whose prospects looked turgid both in the autumn, before a run of 11 wins from 12 over the festive period and into the new year, and again when they lost a pulsating, era-defining game at Anfield in April. But five successive wins at the campaign's conclusion edged City to their second crown in three seasons, the starkest illustration of their improvement being the fact that, after taking four points from their first six away games, they then picked up 30 from the remaining 13.

Mourinho's Chelsea, meanwhile, acted as brooding king-makers, winning home and away against both Manchester City and Liverpool, their win at Anfield a psychological mis-ericord through Liverpool's (title-yearning) heart. Steven Gerrard's slip is the everlasting image from the match, but his team's ferocious approach to the game (understandable, given that their total of 59 first-half goals was not only a Premier League record but also more than 14 clubs managed in total) was unnecessary, given that a draw against the Londoners would have maintained Liverpool's advantage with two games to go. The sheer goalscoring muscle of the top two defined the season, though, with City scoring 102 goals and Liverpool just one fewer. It was the first time that two or more sides had reached three figures since 1960–61, and Luis Suárez equalled the Premier League record of 31 goals in a 38-game season (10 of them in December alone, and five against Norwich; 2.4 per cent of all the goals Norwich have conceded in the Premier League have been to Suárez) held by Alan Shearer and Cristiano Ronaldo, but without any penal-ties. Over at the Etihad, Yaya Touré became only the second central midfielder to score 20 or more goals in a single cam-paign. It really was that sort of season.

At the bottom, Cardiff's first season in the top flight since 1962 ended with the Welsh side finishing bottom (certain peo-ple's dreams of a top flight containing only 18 English teams sort of came true in 2013–14). Owner Vincent Tan had caused outrage in the principality's capital by changing the club's home colours from blue to red, on the basis that the latter was seen as a more dynamic tint, yet, not only did his club finish bottom, no team clad in red has become champions of England since Cardiff reached the Premier League.

Three Things We May Have Just Learnt About 2013–14

Martin O'Wngoal

Liverpool maintained a title challenge despite conceding 50 goals (had they succeeded they'd have been the first champions to concede that many since Ipswich in 1962), and one of their own, Martin Skrtel, was responsible for four of them, a number that remains a Premier League record for a single season. The Slovakian countered his reverse prowess by scoring seven times at the right end, meaning that he ended with a Premier League career-best personal goal difference of plus 3.

Play like Fergie's boys

Two numbers hover hauntingly above David Moyes's (almost full) season at Manchester United. The first is the 81 crosses the team mechanically delivered against Fulham at Old Trafford in February, to no avail. A record for any Premier League game Opta has analysed, Fulham defender Dan Burn's dismissal of United's tactics as reminiscent of the Conference was one of the thousand (and 81) cuts that slowly drained Moyes's footballing lifeblood. Another was the fact that he named a unique starting XI in all 51 games he took charge of. There are impromptu holiday five-a-side teams with more consistency than that.

13 seconds

Not only were there three goals scored after just 13 seconds in 2013–14, but one of them came from Stoke goalkeeper Asmir Begović, the fifth and so far last goalkeeper to register a goal in the Premier League. In what was a landmark season for the No. 13, Steven Gerrard became the only player in the competition's history to score exactly 13 goals and provide 13 assists in the same season. Thirteen, viewed as unlucky in many countries and cultures, seemed to have no ill effect at all on Gerrard's season. Definitely not.

Verdict

With more (hashtag) narrative and intrigue than many other league campaigns combined, 2013–14 rides high as one of the very best seasons the Premier League has produced. Manchester United's rapid decline post-Ferguson made it seem very different but, with Arsenal imploding in the spring and Liverpool failing to end their title drought, deep down it was reassuringly familiar.

Premier League season No. 23: 2014–15

Is it still called the Premiership? IN SCOTLAND, YEAH

Champions: Chelsea

Relegated: Queens Park Rangers, Burnley, Hull City

Top scorer: Sergio Agüero (26)

Most assists: Cesc Fàbregas (18)

Biggest win: Southampton 8–0 Sunderland

Overview

The charm before the storm. After the twists and turns of 2013–14, Chelsea, led by José Mourinho, the man who they have sacked twice, went hard and went early, remaining top from the end of August all the way through to the season's end nine months later. In total, the Blues topped the table for a Premier League record 274 days and, while defending champions Manchester City kept pace until Christmas, they slowly fell behind during the new year, leaving Chelsea to complete a functional and somewhat grey run-in.

There was an (accurate) sense that Chelsea were fading by the season's conclusion (they scored only 19 goals in their final

14 games after rattling home the same amount in their first six matches), but they still lost only three times all campaign (only twice before the confirmation of the title). New signings Diego Costa and Cesc Fàbregas were star performers, with Fàbregas recording 18 assists, more than he ever had in a single season for Arsenal, although he did end the season with a wondrously niche red card for pinging the ball at Chris Brunt's head during a penalty box melee at the Hawthorns.

Mourinho also managed to get one last productive season out of his pugnacious muse John Terry, who became the top-scoring defender in Premier League history and also played every minute of every game, becoming only the second out-field player to do so for a championship-winning team after Gary Pallister in 1992–93 (Leicester's Wes Morgan would match this achievement a year later).

Of the other contributors to the drama the previous season, Liverpool, shorn of Luis Suárez, looked dysfunctional. After the Boxing Day fixtures, the Reds were down in ninth with a W-D-L record of 7-4-7 but the only jets were coming from Steven Gerrard's ears as he realised his final opportunity of winning a Premier League title was evaporating. By the end of the campaign, Liverpool had mustered only 52 goals, the total Suárez and Daniel Sturridge had plundered between them a year earlier, while in Gerrard's final game he, fittingly, scored the team's only goal in a 6–1 debunking at Stoke, the first time the Reds had let in six or more goals in a league game since 1963.

Meanwhile Arsenal, with Alexis Sánchez the first player since Thierry Henry to score 20 or more goals in his debut season with the club, started underwhelmingly but won 13 of their last 18 games to once again finish comfortably in the Champi-ons-League-last-16-inevitable-defeat qualifying positions.

At the bottom, the mundanity was provided by QPR, who became the first team since Liverpool in 1953–54 to lose each of their first 11 away games, while the sensationalism was provided by Leicester, who spent a record 140 days on the bottom of the table without going down, while also becoming the first and so far only Premier League team to come from two goals behind against Manchester United and win. Was there hidden potential in this rag-tag bunch of Midlanders? (Incidentally, the game between QPR and Leicester in November contained a record 52 shots but a combined passing accuracy of only 72 per cent. Is this good? Bad? No one can say.) Hull and Burnley joined QPR in demotion, the Clarets' strange influence on Chelsea's title hopes (in their three seasons in the Premier League, the Londoners have won the title) continuing.

Three Things We May Have Just Learnt About 2014–15

Three-minute warning

Even though there were no friendly data companies to record the exact timing of Robbie Fowler's hat-trick against Arsenal in 1994, rudimentary digital watches did exist and it was generally agreed to have taken four minutes and 33 seconds. Fewer than five minutes to score three goals in one of the toughest leagues; surely this would never be beaten. But it was, by Sadio Mané in May 2015, when he slammed (and if you score three goals in fewer than three minutes you definitely slammed) home three goals for Southampton against Tim Sherwood's Aston Villa. It came barely more than a month after Yannick Bolasie had scored an 11-minute hat-trick against Sunderland, although compared to Mané's efforts, that looks sickeningly pedestrian. Liverpool, reeling from the loss of their precious fastest hat-trick record, waited 12 months (31,536,000 seconds) and then signed Mané for themselves.

The beginning of the twist

In the 20th century, Sunderland won three league titles and two FA Cups but the 21st has been less kind to the north-east side, instead condemning them to some of the most repetitive relegation battles ever seen (and re-seen). They did at least achieve something in 2014–15, other than a late recovery to escape demotion, and that was the Premier League record for the number of yellow cards in a single season: 94. No one could provoke bookings like the Black Cats in this campaign, with Lee Cattermole leading the way, equalling the individual record of 14 in a solitary season and making sure that all 14 of those cautions were for good, honest, English fouls. No dissent, abusive language or continental shirt removal here.

Jump start

As this book has hopefully illustrated, there are many elements of football that are surprising, but there are many things that are just as they should be, and that includes the fact that Peter Crouch has scored more headed goals than any other player in Premier League history. The lofty forward overtook Alan Shearer's previous record of 46 in May 2015, although he then celebrated his unmatched aerial prowess by failing to register a single goal (headed or otherwise) in 2015–16.

Verdict

While Chelsea's play in the autumn was occasionally thrilling, and their fans certainly celebrated their fourth Premier League title with the reverence a championship deserves, compared to the unpredictable events of the previous campaign, and given what was to unfold in 2015–16, this remains one of the dourer Premier League terms. Ultimately, this was the season that José Mourinho matched Arsène Wenger's total of three English titles but neither of them looked particularly happy about it.

Premier League season No. 24: 2015–16

Is it still called the Premiership? LEICESTER HAVE NEVER WON THE PREMIERSHIP

Champions: Leicester City

Relegated: Aston Villa, Norwich City, Newcastle United

Top scorer: Harry Kane (25)

Most assists: Mesut Özil (19)

Biggest win: Aston Villa 0–6 Liverpool

Overview

Well now. So many aspects of 2015–16 have been nostalgically hardwired into the nation's consciousness that it's hard to know where to start or finish, but let's at least try to sum up possibly the most radical football campaign in the sport's entire history (NB, excluding some unusual Scandinavian second-tier season you have bookmarked on rsssf.com). Leicester City, the escapees of 2014–15 and tipped to struggle once more a season on, especially after replacing the corporal tactician Nigel Pearson with line-up rotation aide Claudio Ranieri, went and won the Premier League title.

Before 2015–16 Leicester had topped the division for a mere 13 days, the result of a brief flowering in the autumn of 2000. By the end of 2015–16 that number had increased to 162 and Wes Morgan had done in two seasons what Steven Gerrard had failed to do in 17.

The bare facts of the Foxes' glorious campaign are this: they had the second lowest pass completion (70.5 per cent), the third lowest average possession figure (42.4 per cent), the greatest points-per-game increase from one top-flight season to another in the English game's history (1.05) until Chelsea did even better in 2016–17 (1.13), the second lowest number of starting XI changes by a Premier League champion (33, second only to Manchester United in 1992–93 when rotation was something only the earth did), the fewest number of players used in 2015–16 (23), the longest run of goals in successive Premier League games by a single player (11, by Jamie Vardy) and the player with the most tackles and interceptions (N'Golo Kanté). They became the first new champions since Nottingham Forest in 1978 and won a joint Premier League record 13 penalties. Add these things together and bake and you'll have a fruity title success to enjoy.

Elsewhere (there were, in fact, 19 other teams taking part in the Premier League in 2015–16), Chelsea posted a title defence that was as bad as Leicester's title challenge was surprising, ending the season in 10th. The Blues, who had conceded as many goals after five games as they had after 32 matches in 2004–05, were in 16th after they succumbed to the Foxes' New Power Generation in mid-December, a game that meant José Mourinho's second spell ended like his first, with the bullet. The Stamford Bridge players then reacted by going on a 15-game unbeaten run, the longest by any club that season.

Manchester United continued their post-Ferguson malaise

under Louis van Gaal by scoring only 49 league goals, the first time they'd dipped under 50 since 1989–90. By way of comparison, in their treble season of 1998–99, United scored 48 goals in the cups alone. Although they came second, Arsenal were possibly the biggest losers of 2015–16. In a campaign when nearly all of the big clubs were taking a fallow year, the Gunners should have mopped up a long-awaited fourth title under Arsène Wenger, but instead of surging onwards after beating Leicester at home on a selfie-soaked Valentine's Day, they proceeded to lose two games in a row and leave Tottenham alone to unsuccessfully pursue the Foxes.

Three Things We May Have Just Learnt About 2015–16

Exit means exit

Aston Villa's relegation in 2015–16 reduced the number of ever-presents in the Premier League to six but whereas once it would have been a real surprise to see the 1982 European Cup winners drop into the second tier, by 2016 it looked an act of mercy. In 2014–15 Villa scored only 31 league goals, at the time a record low, but a season on they could manage only a gruel-thin 27, a total that they cashed in for a paltry 17 points, fewer than they had ever recorded in a single season (even in the two-points-for-a-win days). While six points higher than Derby in 2007–08, and two higher than Sunderland in 2005–06, Villa's abjectness was demonstrated by the fact that they lost 11 successive games between February and April and led for just 243 minutes all season, a record low. They even went two games without a corner in February.

Finest worksong

The 2015–16 campaign began with many people convinced that Tottenham's Harry Kane was a one-season wonder. He ended it at the very least as a two-season wonder (then transformed into a three-season wonder in 2016–17) and the first Englishman to end the season as top scorer (Kane scored 25 goals, 15 of which came away from home) in England since Kevin Phillips in 2000. He also became the fifth Englishman to score 20 or more goals in consecutive Premier League campaigns (after Alan Shearer, Andy Cole, Les Ferdinand and Robbie Fowler), started and finished all 38 games for his club yet ended the campaign taking corners for England at Euro 2016, possibly not the best use of him by erstwhile national manager Roy Hodgson.

Treble trouble

'Get Victor' was the whispered instruction at the referees' secret lair deep inside Discipline Mountain in summer 2015. We don't have actual evidence for this but we do know that Victor Wanyama became only the seventh player in Premier League history to receive three red cards in a single season, alongside such aggro luminaries as Vinnie Jones, Slaven Bilić, David Batty and Franck Queudrue. Confused moralists who maintain that crime doesn't pay should note that Wanyama then sealed a lucrative transfer to Tottenham Hotspur in June 2016. The crazed agitators holed up in Discipline Mountain, meanwhile, were forced back to the drawing board.

Verdict

Leicester City won the Premier League and no one could believe it or logically explain it. But every now and then people across the UK would come to a halt in the street, stop quietly and try to come to terms with the fact that the Foxes were champions of England. As an advert for the majestic appeal of sport, it was certainly a good one.

Premier League season No. 25: 2016–17

Is it still called the Premiership? COME ON, IT DOESN'T EVEN HAVE A TITLE SPONSOR NOW

Champions: Chelsea

Relegated: Sunderland, Middlesbrough, Hull City

Top scorer: Harry Kane (29)

Most assists: Kevin De Bruyne (18)

Biggest win: Hull City 1–7 Tottenham Hotspur

Overview

London, can you wait? All the talk as 2016–17 approached was about how Manchester was the new capital of English football, with José Mourinho and Pep Guardiola, the Morrissey and Marr of the 21st-century European coaching community, now jamming in the same city. What difference would it make? The answer was: not much. Instead, the nation's capital provided the top two for just the third time in top-flight history, after Arsenal and Chelsea exchanged first and second places in 2003–04 and 2004–05.

This time it was Chelsea in first, seven points clear of

Tottenham, who were eight points clear of the rest. Don't worry about minding the gap, but do watch out for the chasm. Chelsea's triumph wasn't predicted by many at the start of the season but, under new manager Antonio Conte, they exerted a firm grip on the division with 13 successive wins between 1 October and New Year's Eve. It equalled the record run of consecutive top-flight wins in a single season, before defeat to Tottenham on 4 January prevented them matching Arsenal's all-time record of 14. It was the fourth successive season that Conte had led a team to a league title.

It became apparent in the spring that Spurs, Leicester's closest challengers a year earlier (despite finishing third), were the only team able to live with Conte's title hunt. After losing away at Liverpool in February, Tottenham won 12 of their final 13 Premier League games, yet still came a decent distance behind the new champions. A run of four successive draws in October and early November was what ultimately hamstrung Spurs, although their total of 86 points would have been enough to win the Premier League in 11 previous campaigns and their final goal difference of plus 60 (boosted by plus 11 in the final two games) is the biggest recorded by a Premier League team who didn't win the title. It's even more impressive when you consider that their overall goal difference for the previous 24 Premier League seasons combined is only plus 110.

They also remained unbeaten at White Hart Lane for the first time in a league season since 1964–65. The old ground must have smiled quietly to itself at the wondrous scenes unfolding, the wan grin turning to fear as the first bulldozers shattered both the peace and the foundations. Whether Tottenham can remain as strong while having to play 38 away games in 2017–18 (their 19 'home' games will take place at Wembley, where they struggled in Champions League matches in 2016–17) remains to be seen. Cruelly, despite being the second-best team of the season and arguably the most attractive to watch, Tottenham did not spend a single day on top of the table, something enjoyed by lowly Hull City among others, and they also had to watch Chelsea and Arsenal pick up the two major domestic honours. After third place in 2015–16, and then second in 2016–17, Spurs will aim to become only the third team in English top-flight history to pay tribute to Ted Rogers (Google it) by finishing 3–2–1 in successive seasons, after Sunderland between 1900–1902 and Manchester United between 2005–2007.

Chelsea's consistency was as stark as their decline had been a season earlier, the team recording a 100 per cent win record in the league in August, October, November, December, March and May. The key gap in that run of months is September when, after taking one point from three games against Swansea, Liverpool and Arsenal, Chelsea sat in eighth place and looked to be suffering from the same mysterious malaise that did for Mourinho 12 months earlier. Conte's decision to switch to a back three during the Arsenal game not only stemmed the swarming Gunners, who had galloped to an early 3–0 lead, but crystallised his approach for the remainder of the campaign. Chelsea started in their new shape for the next match and proceeded to win 27 of their remaining 32 league games. (Arsenal experienced a similar improvement when Arsène Wenger cast off decades of his own traditions by switching to a back three for the final eight games, of which they won seven, before beating Chelsea at their own game in the FA Cup final.)

Scattered defeats throughout the season to Liverpool, Arsenal, Tottenham and Manchester United do not matter when you win virtually every other match. Chelsea ended the campaign with 30 wins from 38 games, the first time any team has recorded this many in a 20-team top-flight season, and something done in the 42-game era only twice, by Tottenham in 1960–61 and Liverpool in 1978–79.

The Blues now have the top two points totals in English top-flight history (95 in 2004–05 and 93 in 2016–17) and remain the top-scoring team in a Premier League campaign (103 in 2009–10). For a club accused by some fans of rival teams as having no history, Chelsea sure are racking up a lot of . . . history. Winners of the league title in each of the last four years in which the UK has held a general election, Chelsea's defeat in the cup final removed a modicum of shine from a strong and stable season, but only a little.

For the glamour twins, Mourinho and Guardiola, Premier League ambitions were abandoned fairly early, although anyone, myself included, who had tipped City for the title were feeling comfortable when Guardiola nudged them into winning their opening 10 games of the season across all competitions, just one short of Tottenham's record of 11 set in 1960. But in the global super-manager showdown that the Premier League resembled in 2016–17, Guardiola, hitherto a domestic god in Spain and Germany, was about to be bested by Antonio Conte and others. The Chelsea manager became the first manager to engineer home and away league victories against a Guardiola team in the same campaign, while Everton's Ronald Koeman saw his team hand out Pep's worst ever league reverse when they humbled City 4–0 in January.

A third-place finish was the first time Guardiola had ended up outside the top two in his managerial career, but it was three places higher than Mourinho managed, Manchester United's sixth place being the first time he had completed a season as a manager outside the top three. With Bolton securing promotion from League One in second place, neither Guardiola nor Mourinho secured the highest finish in a professional league by a team in Greater Manchester, let alone in the nation they were supposedly about to dominate.

At the bottom of the table, the relegation battle was a mixture of the usual suspects and some fresh blood. Sunderland finally succumbed to the sweet embrace of the Championship in their 10th season since promotion; it had been a long time coming. Of the eight ever-present teams in that decade since they came up, the Black Cats had lost 76 more games than any other (181 compared to Everton's 105). Each year a selection from a seemingly random pool of managers had kept Sunderland's heads above the oily relegation waters but David Moyes, reeling from his torrid spells at Manchester United and Real Sociedad, rarely looked capable of pulling off what those in the game term a Ricky Sbragia, and resigned 24 hours after the season had concluded. Just four years after signing a six-year contract at Manchester United, Moyes has now been dispensed with by three clubs.

A 4–0 win for Sunderland at former manager Sam Allardyce's Crystal Palace in early February looked briefly like a beacon of hope, but it was merely a lighthouse built on blancmange. The Black Cats failed to score in the next seven games, and those four strikes at Selhurst Park represented a third of the team's goals in the second half of the season. In the end, Sunderland spent 189 days at the bottom of the table and joined Nottingham Forest as the only team to end three Premier League seasons there. If you adjust all seasons for the three-points-for-a-win rule, Sunderland have three of the 11 lowest points hauls in the top flight since the Second World War. They still have six league titles in their history, though, as many as Chelsea – for 12 months at least.

In a bleak season for Yorkshire and the north-east, Middlesbrough and Hull City joined Sunderland as the most northerly trio to go down in English top-flight history. With Brighton coming up, and Bournemouth and Southampton already in situ, the division is in danger of resembling an unambitious UCAS form, with a dwindling band of representatives from some of English football's traditional heartlands. Boro's issue all season long was scoring goals. They ended the season with a paltry 27, two fewer than Golden Boot winner Harry Kane – only the fifth time a team has scored fewer than a player in the competition's history.

Hull's problem was winning their opening two games, which not only provided them with 18 per cent of their points for the season, but also persuaded the club to appoint Mike Phelan as their permanent manager, a decision they reversed in January after he picked up a mere seven points in the next 18 matches. His Portuguese replacement, Marco Silva, was maligned by elements of the UK media, largely it seemed because he had never seen Trooping the Colour or eaten a Kellogg's Variety Pack, but he nonetheless collected 21 points in 18 matches, and had his pick of job opportunities in the summer.

12 *Things We May Have Just Learnt About 2016–17*

Youth club

The proximity of their final league game to the Europa League final meant that José Mourinho was always likely to make drastic changes as Manchester United's season of seemingly always being in sixth place did end up with them in sixth. Players such as Scott McTominay and Josh Harrop being in the starting XI against Crystal Palace helped lower the average age of the team to 22 years and 284 days, United's youngest ever side in the competition (despite the brooding presence of club record scorer Wayne Rooney in the side) and the third youngest of any club. Even better, in the closing few minutes Angel Gomes came on and became the first player born in 2000 to appear in the Premier League. Two weeks younger than *Dora the Explorer*, Gomes made 13 passes in his cameo, only six fewer than relative veteran Anthony Martial had made in the entirety of the second half.

Sixth for ever

As mentioned, much of Manchester United's season was spent in sixth place, including a run of 104 consecutive days between December and March, a period in which they did not lose a game. In truth, their unbeaten run of 25 games was one of the least inspiring periods of infallibility in top-flight history, with 12 of the games ending level and United scoring more than twice in only four of the matches. The club whose manager at the time claimed that Arsenal's 12 draws devalued their unbeaten season in 2003–04 drew 10 matches at Old Trafford in 2016–17, a joint record in the competition. The Theatre of Dreams had turned into the Theatre of Dra . . . (you do the rest).

One of thine own

It's official: Harry Kane is a top, top player and the numbers more than back this up. The Golden Boot winner in 2015–16,

Kane went into the final week of the 2016–17 season two goals behind Romelu Lukaku but somehow plundered seven goals in his final two matches to take his season's tally to 29 in just 30 appearances. He was the first player to score hat-tricks in successive Premier League games since Wayne Rooney in 2011, the second player after Alan Shearer (who registered five in 1995–96) to score four hat-tricks in a Premier League season and now has as many Premier League hat-tricks as Cristiano Ronaldo, Gianfranco Zola, Dennis Bergkamp, Éric Cantona, Diego Costa and Gareth Bale combined. With 78 goals in just 116 matches, he just needs one in August (10 appearances, zero goals) to complete football. Oh, and possibly some sort of trophy.

Flaming June

He could finish only joint fourth in the Golden Boot rankings, the official main competition of the last week of the 2016–17 season, but Chelsea's Diego Costa did win his second league title in three years at the club, as well as also managing to score in every single month of the season, only the 16th player to do this in the Premier League era and the first since Charlie Austin in 2014–15. August to May, then, was peachy, only for June to bring Costa a text from his manager saying he was no longer in his plans. Spurned.

Snakes on a Midlands plain

Leicester's decision to sack manager Claudio Ranieri in February led to a severe outbreak of moral panic. The same people who had said that the key to the Italian's shock success in 2015–16 was that he hadn't changed anything were now claiming that sacking him was proof that Leicester were doomed. Predictions that the cruel Foxes were now certain to become only the second reigning champions of England to be relegated were rife, but instead caretaker manager Craig Shakespeare won his first five Premier League games, the first British manager to do this. Such was the turnaround in form that Leicester became only the second team in Premier League history to record five wins straight after five successive losses. As the champions eased themselves back into mid-table, Shakespeare could reflect that all's well that ends well, as, measure for measure, he had shown himself to be at least Ranieri's equal. The only disappointment came with the team's exit from the Champions League at the quarter-final stage, denying them an 11th and 12th night in the competition.

Be more etc

Zlatan Ibrahimović's debut season in English football started with rapture and ended in rupture but in between he carved out enough headlines to justify his admittedly hefty wage. A goal on his Premier League debut at what used to be Dean Court continued a run of scoring on his first appearance in Serie A, La Liga, Ligue 1 and the Champions League, while he also became the oldest player (at 35 years and 125 days) to reach 15 goals in a Premier League campaign. Fittingly, in the 25th Premier League season, he was the man who scored the 25,000th goal in the competition, the landmark strike coming at Swansea in November.

The only stat that matters

There was an officially recognised glut of goals in 2016–17, the final total coming in at 1,064, just two short of the record in a 20-team Premier League. Even the bottom side, Sunderland, had a player with 15 goals (Jermain Defoe, the second highest total for someone playing for a team finishing bottom), while five teams scored more than 70 goals (although not the team with the most expensive player in football history), the first time this had happened since 1967–68.

JT26–28

The 2015–16 campaign was John Terry's practice final season for Chelsea, but 2016–17 was the real deal, although he was rarely more than a heritage attraction on the touchline, making just nine appearances in the Premier League, the first time he'd failed to make double figures since 1999–2000. Naturally, with the title won, Terry featured in Chelsea's final game of the season, at home to bottom side Sunderland. Midway through the first half a generic commotion on the touchline was an indication that a substitution was about to be made, but this was to be no ordinary switch. Instead, the aim was to substitute Chelsea's captain and leader in the 26th minute (his eternal shirt number), and yet, in a continuation of a trend in modern football, the fourth official pointedly waited until the clock reached 26:00, the beginning of the 27th minute in other words. Subsequent modernist faffing and glad-handing meant that by the time Terry left the field of play, the game had reached its 28th minute. Much like his departure from Stamford Bridge, it was all much later than expected.

Concertina

Everton were a marooned team in 2016–17. Ronald Koeman's team finished eight points behind sixth-placed Manchester United and a gigantic 15 ahead of coastal giants Southampton and Bournemouth in eighth and ninth. In fact, the gap between Saints in eighth and Watford in 17th was just six points, meaning that the Premier League was made up of the Big Six, lonely Everton, a thin spread of 10 scrappers and then the three relegated sides. Arsenal's total of 75 points was only enough for fifth place but, in 1996–97, was the total that champions Manchester United recorded. It seems that the league within a league now has additional leagues within its leagues.

Crouch/soar

If anyone other than Peter Crouch had the Premier League record for headed goals then it would be time to give up entirely on the sport, but thankfully he does. Furthermore, on the final day of the season, his goal for Stoke at Southampton meant he had reached the blessed landmark of 50 with his famous skull, drawing him level in the competition with both Ipswich and Wigan.

Hail César

For many years Gary Pallister would entertain family and friends by explaining that he was the only outfield player to play every minute of a season for a team who had won the Premier League. People would take a few moments to work out what he meant and then applaud him heartily. But Gary Pallister is sad now. He is sad because his unique record keeps getting diluted. First, John Terry matched him in 2014–15, then Leicester's Wes Morgan in 2015–16 and now César Azpilicueta in 2016–17. Gary Pallister is impressed by what these three players did but no one applauds him now, not even when he patiently explains he had to play 42 games rather than 38.

Final roll call

Special mention must go to: Alexis Sánchez for scoring 15 away goals, the most by an Arsenal player since Ted Drake in 1934–35; to West Brom's Salomón Rondón for becoming only the second player after theft prevention's Duncan Ferguson to score a hat-trick of headers in the Premier League; to Dimitri Payet for being West Ham's most creative player of the season despite leaving the club in January; to Leighton Baines for becoming the first defender to assist 50 Premier League goals; and to Michy Batshuayi for winning the title with his third shot on target of the season and before he had started a Premier League game for Chelsea.

Verdict

The 25th top-flight season was 1912–13, a campaign that ended with Sunderland finishing top, and Chelsea and Tottenham in the bottom four (with Arsenal rock bottom, #WengerOut). Fortunes 104 years later in the 25th Premier League season were a little different but the basic building blocks were the same – 20 teams, 380 games and a whole lot of goals (an extra 89 in 1912–13, though). Maybe the 2016–17 edition wasn't the greatest of the quarter-century of campaigns since the great schism in 1992, but it nonetheless offered another solid block of great goals, entertaining matches and intriguing sub-plots. With 9,746 games and 25,769 goals, the Premier League has, after all, been a whole new ball game. Here's to the next 25 years.

10.

The Premier League Glossary

'Thou whoreson zed, thou unnecessary letter!'

– *William Shakespeare*, King Lear

Letters and numbers, the eternal battle. But what if you combined them in the cause of the Premier League? Well, then you'd have the ultimate alphabetical glossary for the competition. And now you do.

A is for assists. After John Barnes's home debut for Liverpool in 1987, his manager Kenny Dalglish said: 'Barnes did what we expected him to do. He made a goal, scored one, and entertained.' Note the choice of words: *made a goal.* It's not as if people before the 1990s didn't recognise the value of the assist, they just didn't use the same terminology. The quantification of assists began in earnest in the 1990s as fans embraced both computer simulations of being a football manager and fantasy football. Even so, it's still hard to find much mention of assists as a specific term when looking through articles about the likes of Ryan Giggs and David Beckham from the turn of the century. Even when Opta recorded Thierry Henry making 20 assists in 2002–03, a seasonal total that still hasn't been beaten, it passed under the radar. Possibly the first player to both exist in and contribute significantly to the milieu of the assist was Cesc Fàbregas. Even though the Spaniard spent three seasons at Barcelona, he still became the first player under 30 to reach 100 Premier League assists, doing so in 2016–17. Some curmudgeons maintain that the assist is a flawed or misleading stat as it evidently relies on another player doing their job well (scoring a goal), but Opta's complete database of Premier League assists is unique not only for its breadth but also for the fact that it applies the collection criteria across 25 years and more than 25,000 goals. Everyone knows Brian Deane scored the first goal in the Premier League but fewer recall that Manchester United's first strike in the competition was assisted by Peter Schmeichel.

B is for bench. Bench is almost an archaic term nowadays, as substitute footballers invariably relax individually in giant ergonomic chairs, but the skill of altering the direction of a game from the sideline remains tantalising. Towards the end of 2016–17 Arsène Wenger became the first Premier League manager to make 2,000 substitutions (not all of them after 70 minutes), while Shola Ameobi remains the most used substitute in the competition with 142 (although Peter Crouch and Jermain Defoe are closing in). Defoe leads the way with goals from the bench, with 23, while the most creative substitutes in Premier League history are Ryan Giggs and Theo Walcott, who have both assisted 14 times. Chelsea, meanwhile, are the club with the most substitute goals, 164, and also used all three replacements in every game in 2016–17. 'Go and get warmed up, son. I'm thinking of making a switch.'

C is for clean sheets. As exciting as goals for purists, the clean sheet is a sign of a job well done. In 2016–17 Petr Čech extended his individual goalkeeper record to 190, while John Terry left

Chelsea with 214 under his belt; he still needs two more to match Frank Lampard. Manchester United lead the team ranking, with 418, while Swindon, poor Swindon, managed only four in their single Premier League campaign in 1993–94. Surely competition newcomers Brighton and Huddersfield will surpass the Robins in 2017–18?

D is for Diving. You can run but you can't dive. From 2017–18 Premier League players will be subject to a merciless roving eye in the form of a new justice panel, set up to retrospectively punish divers. Diving, or simulation to give it its official, slightly dystopian title, has progressed from a barely remarked upon part of the sport (Michael Owen winning a penalty versus Argentina in 2002, for example) to a great moral crime, an insidious trend that is hollowing out the hard-but-fair essence of the English game. The underlying assumption is that the rise of overseas players in the Premier League has resulted in a surge in anti-gravity skulduggery, yet the simulation yellow card numbers from the last 11 seasons shows three British players at the top: Gareth Bale with seven (including four in 2012-13 alone), David Bentley with five and Ashley Young with four. Tottenham fans will no doubt remember that at least a few of Bale's simu-cautions were dubious, and finding and allowing for the grey area in between blatant dive and clear foul will surely be the toughest task for the new panel in 2017–18.

E is for expected. Expect changes in 2017–18. Expected Goals, a predictive model that professional clubs have been utilising for the past five years, has until now been seen in the outside world mainly on the fringes of popular social media networks, but is likely to make the jump to the mainstream soon. If you are still unsure what to expect, it's a predictive model for shooting (or goalkeeping, or chance creation) based on hundreds of thousands of shots in the Opta database; a probability model that will tell you whether a striker is on an unsustainable hot streak or whether Fernando Torres's form at Chelsea was his fault or not (answer: nobody expects the Spanish indecision).

F is for first. It's good to score first, advantageous even. But some teams struggle more than others to hold on to that lead. The all-time chokers in this regard are Barnsley, who scored first and lost four times in 1997–98, their single Premier League season. Of teams to play a significant amount of matches in the division, Wigan (7.9 per cent) and Southampton (7.8 per cent) have seen a high percentage of them start well and end badly, while at the other end of the scale it's no shock to see Manchester United, the 13-time Premier League champions, having lost only 14 games after scoring first.

G is for Gerrard. Steven Gerrard, arguably the best Premier League player never to win it, won virtually every other competition in his Liverpool career (he's still the only player to score in an FA Cup, League Cup, Champions League and Europa League/UEFA Cup final). His record in the Premier League bears study too: his total of five goals at Old Trafford is more than any other visiting player; his nine goals in Merseyside derbies is a record; and he scored a Premier League record of four winning goals in the 90th minute or later. Take. A. Bow. Son.

H is for hat-tricks. Harry Kane single-handedly brought the hat-trick back into fashion in 2016–17, sliding four of them home, taking his top-flight career total to six. Only four men (Shearer 11, Fowler 9, Henry and Owen 8) have scored more Premier League trebles than Kane, who was still only 23 at the end of the season and who will surely threaten Shearer in this arena, even if he doesn't quite catch him for total goals.

What Kane is yet to do in a Premier League game, though, is score a perfect hat-trick (that is one with his left foot, his right foot and his head). It's almost two years since someone did exactly that – Steven Naismith, for Everton against Chelsea in September 2015. Robbie Fowler, meanwhile, remains the master of the perfect hat-trick with three.

I is for injury-time. 'The fourth official has indicated there will be a minimum of . . .' Injury-time, that vague blob of time added on to the end of halves. No one cares about first-half injury-time, unless there has been some sort of ostentatious two-digit delay, but the amount added at the end of second halves is awaited like news of sighted land by a scurvy-ridden sailor. Three minutes is par, with anything less generally leading to a totting up of substitutions made and goals scored by pedantic conspiracy theorists. Conversely, five or more will seem like a cruel punishment to any team leading by a single goal. The actual, real numbers from 2016–17 show that the average Premier League first half had 2min 11sec of additional time, while the second half had 4min 26sec. West Ham had the most combined injury time on average (7min 27sec) while Bournemouth had the least (6min 13sec). The other 18 teams were distributed somewhere along that 1min 14sec spread. There's no conspiracy. Your team isn't missing out. It's just epilogue.

J is for justice. Referees have gone from minor figures at the start of the Premier League era to fully-fledged stars of the modern game. Mark Clattenburg's decision to leave England in 2017 and move to Saudi Arabia was covered in a manner akin to transfer deadline day. While the nation reels from the loss of its one true sweetheart, we can comfort ourselves by looking at data showing which refs have been strictest in 25 years of the Premier League. In terms of pointing to the spot,

Bobby Madley (Wakefield) leads with 26 penalties handed out in 73 games, a rate of 0.36 per match, just ahead of Mike Dean (Wirral) on 0.34 (147 in 428 games). When it comes to cards, late 90s gaffe-magnet Rob Harris (Oxford) is the man, with 203 in only 50 games, making him the only referee to average more than four per game. The second and third most card-happy officials are Graham Barber (Tring) and Kevin Friend (Leicester) with 3.89 and 3.84 respectively.

K is for Keegan. Kevin Keegan, the great entertainer. Of all the enduring Premier League myths, this is one of the most bulletproof. Yet in 1995–96, the season when Newcastle came closest to winning the title under Keegan, they scored only 66 goals, two fewer than Leicester managed when they won the title in 2016–17 (with what seemed like a succession of 1–0 wins in the spring). Keegan's overall goals-per-game rate as a Premier League manager is 1.53, marginally ahead of Trevor Francis (1.43) but lower than Rafa Benítez, the man who looks set to guide the Magpies on their return to the top flight in 2017–18 (1.66). For the record, Stuart Pearce has a goals-per-game rate of 1.00, with 94 in 94 matches as a Premier League manager. 'You do things like that about a man like Stuart Pearce? I've kept really quiet, but I'll tell you something, he went down in my estimation when he said that.'

L is for Lampard. Lamps are made to shine and this one certainly did. Frank Lampard, a midfielder, is Chelsea's all-time top scorer with 211 goals. Frank Lampard, a midfielder, scored against a record 39 Premier League teams. Frank Lampard, a midfielder, is one of only four players to score 10 or more goals in 10 seasons (the other players to do this are not midfielders). Frank Lampard, a midfielder, has scored more goals from outside the box (41) than any other Premier League player (actually, it makes sense that this is held by a midfielder, but still). Frank Lampard, a model of consistency, appeared in 164 consecutive Premier League games between 2001 and 2005. Frank Lampard scored against Chelsea in his 11th appearance against them and didn't look happy about it. Frank James Lampard.

M is for Mc. Seventy-eight players whose names start with Mc have featured in the Premier League, with seven McCarthys and six McDonalds. From the majesty of Gary McAllister to the distant memory of Mark McKeever, from the aerial superiority and McFlurry of goals from Brian McBride to the ping-pong trips between east London and Wearside of George McCartney, we celebrate them all. McHeroes.

N is for nil-nil. John Salako made headlines in November 2016 by revealing he would have voted for Donald Trump, yet is possibly the player least suited to an alternative life in America. For Salako is the only player in Premier League history to play 100 or more games and see more than 15 per cent (24 of 151) of them end 0–0. This is fact. This is not fake news. Salako = stalemate. Sad!

O is for own goals. 'Putting through your own net', 'cutting a howler', 'a Flemish pass-back', 'breaking the fifth wall'; there are many terms for scoring an own goal, but what never varies is the sense of shame a player feels when he sees (og) next to his name in a newspaper. Richard Dunne, with 10, remains the only player to reach double figures for own goals in the Premier League, while Martin Skrtel scored four in a season in 2013–14 and sits in second with Jamie Carragher on seven overall. One unlikely own goal specialist is Harry Kane, who, when he isn't busy plundering at the right end of the pitch, has found time to score three own goals, more than any other striker in Premier League history.

P is for possession. The first rule of pundit school is 'don't trust possession'. The second rule of pundit school is 'Don't. Trust. Possession'. Show a commentator a possession figure that doesn't correlate with a healthy goal advantage and he'll boil with rage. 'This just shows . . .' he'll fume, tapping a pen on a desk, 'that the only stat that matters is goals.' It's all Pep Guardiola's fault. His great Barcelona team combined an enormous share of possession with strings of wins and trophies, leading some people to think that possession = success. In reality, all possession data does is tell you who had the ball in the game. What they then did with the ball (or without it) is another story entirely. Don't hate possession, hate the game.

Q is for quality. The eternal quest in football. Managers want to 'add quality to their squad' while players embrace teammates who can provide them with 'quality balls'. Where you definitely want quality is in front of goal, and one way of assessing this is Opta's Clear-Cut Chance Metric, essentially any opportunity where you would expect the player to score (an open goal, a one-on-one with the goalkeeper, a shot from extremely close range). In this context the most wasteful player in the Premier League in 2016–17 was Zlatan Ibrahimović, who had 25 clear-cut chances but scored with only seven of them. Perhaps he had been taking tips from Phil Jones, who, in the past six Premier League seasons, has had six clear-cut chances and failed to score with any of them (although he has scored with two more difficult chances).

R is for red. The fumble in the back pocket, the arm straight in the air, the slight turn of the head from the player. The ancient routine for red cards is canonical. And yet there were far fewer of them to enjoy in 2016–17; the final total of 41 being the lowest recorded in a 20-team Premier League season. A new rule allowing referees to show discretion when a goal-keeper concedes a penalty by bringing down an attacker certainly helped (not a single keeper was sent off in the English top flight in 2016–17), and fans of the classic red may have to switch their attention to dismissal paradise La Liga, which once again delivered, with 79 sendings-off in 2016–17, almost twice as many as the EPL (extremely placid league).

S is for Shearer. Top-scoring player in Premier League history (260 goals in 441 games), best minutes-per-goal rate at a single club (106.1 at Blackburn), worst win percentage of any Premier League manager called Alan (12.5 per cent). Nobody's perfect.

T is for Torres. Has a player ever had two such contrasting periods in the Premier League as Fernando Torres? At Liverpool, *El Niño* scored at a rate of one every 121.3 minutes, the fourth best figure at a single club behind Shearer (at Blackburn), Sergio Agüero and Harry Kane. At Chelsea, with a £50 million price tag dangling from his shorts, Torres scored at a rate of one every 340.4 minutes, behind luminaries such as Danny Cadamarteri at Everton. In reductive financial terms, each of Torres's goals for Liverpool cost about £308,000 while his strikes at Chelsea cost £2.5 million.

U is for unlucky. Getting to half-time with a lead is a solid base for any team. Failing to win after leading at half-time could be bad luck, or it could be your own fault. On the opening day of the FA Premier League, in August 1992, Arsenal were 2–0 up against Norwich at the break and cruising to an apparent win. Norwich then proceeded to score four times in the final 21 minutes and post the new competition's first second period switcheroo (the rampant Canaries then did it again four days later against Chelsea). Overall, the team to have led most often at half-time and then lost in the Premier League is Tottenham (oh no, #Spursy), but West Ham and Southampton's total of 21 each is worse, given the time both clubs have spent outside the top flight in the past 25 years. It's happened to Manchester United only four times in the Premier League era, all of them coming away from home. The last team to win a league game at Old Trafford after trailing at half-time were Ipswich back in May 1984, Alan Sunderland poking home the winner a week before Mark Zuckerberg was born.

V is for van. Like Royal Mail or Ocado, the Premier League always makes sure it has a fleet of quality vans at its disposal. The three premium vans (van der Sar, van Persie and van Nistelrooy) to have made more than 100 Premier League appearances have all won the title. Overall there have been 18 vans, with 15 coming from the Netherlands, two from Belgium and just one representing the UK, Wales's Pat van der Hauwe. From Psycho Pat to Postman Pat, we all need our Bedford Rascals.

W is for woodwork. Clunk, thwack, doink. The sight and sound of an adequately inflated football rebounding off a goal frame is as enjoyable as the smell of cut grass or briskly swept AstroTurf. From Tony Yeboah's pinball wizard to Ronny Rosenthal's gaping mercy, a ball hitting the woodwork (metalwork) is satisfying. Ask Premier League fans which team has hit the post or bar the most and they'll invariably think it's their own side, but in the past 10 years it has, in fact, been

Liverpool, by some distance. The Reds have seen the ball strike the frame 211 times since August 2006, 23 times more than Arsenal in second. Player-wise, Robin van Persie leads with 44, 16 more than second-placed Wayne Rooney, with Luis Suárez and Steven Gerrard in joint third on 26. Either way, if the ball hits the goalframe and does not go in, it's a shot off target. Always and for ever.

X is for Xisco. Four and a half years as a Newcastle United employee, seven appearances, one goal and one assist. Good name, though.

Y is for youngest. It's been a while since any of the flagship youngest records in the Premier League have been broken. On 13 May 2017 it had been 10 years since Matthew Briggs became the youngest player to feature in a game (16 years and 68 days) when he played for Fulham against Middlesbrough; happier memories for a man who, in the crueller world of 2017, had just been released by League Two minnows Colchester. The youngest scorer record is even older, as it's still that James Vaughan goal you vaguely remember for Everton in April 2005 when he was 16 years and 270 days old. That capped off a period of two and half years in which the youngest scorer record changed hands three times (from Rooney to Milner to Vaughan). 'How young can it go?' shrieked the media. Possibly not much younger than James Vaughan was the prosaic but accurate answer. Finally, the oldest youngest (sic) record is the assist, set by Aaron Lennon in November 2003 (aged 16 years and 199 days). West Brom's Jonathan Leko (17 years 21 days) came close towards the end of 2015–16 but, with creative duties frequently handed out to expensive imports, you'd imagine that Lennon's record will stand for some time.

Z is for Zimbabwe. Not a nation with an illustrious history in the Premier League but Zimbabwe not only provided the first two Africans to feature in it (Division One stalwart Bruce Grobbelaar and Peter Ndlovu) but also, in the shape of Ndlovu (an early pronunciation test for many commentators, most of whom failed), the first person hailing from outside Europe to score in the nascent division, three days before Dwight Yorke.

Epilogue
Journey For a Man

*'And what is life? An hour-glass on the run,
A mist retreating from the morning sun'*

— John Clare

Humans take comfort from circles. From crude Neanderthal stalagmite circles constructed 175,000 years ago to the modernist stylings of Stonehenge and Rollright, the circle has a mystical essence that underpins our capacity for symbolic thought. Once you accept the circle as the one true building block of our spiritual existence, you start to see them everywhere. The circle of life? Life is a circle.

Take the career of Trevor Benjamin. The striker, born in the closing months of the 1970s, has become the go-to example of the journeyman footballer. He is reminded of this in every interview he conducts; 29 clubs, 16 of them in the pro ranks. From non-league football in the north-east to the sandpits of the Withdean Stadium in Brighton, Benjamin's career took him the length of England and briefly to Australia, the antithesis of a circle. But look more closely, look at the league clubs he was employed by and discard the myriad loan deals that can dilute and pixelate a player's career. Cambridge, Leicester, Northampton, Coventry, Peterborough. Plot those places on a map and it makes a circle. Not only that, the major town in the centre of the circle is Kettering, birthplace of Trevor Benjamin. Life, you must now accept, is a circle.

Over the winter of 2016–17 I often found myself thinking of the geographical perfection of the Trevor Benjamin circle. As someone who also grew up in Northamptonshire, I had become accustomed to accepting that Midlands football was unfashionable. There were some Coventry and Aston Villa fans at my school but, in a dance as old as death, most people opted for Liverpool or Manchester United or anyone enjoying brief success (hi to all the non-local Blackburn fans who are still hanging in there in League One). Midlands football just carried on in the background, occasionally emerging puffy-faced in vignettes such as Sky's *Big Ron Manager*, only to disappear once more. That particular fly-on-the-wall series had been an act of rank desperation by Peterborough United, the £100,000 fee they received in exchange for making themselves look silly helping to stave off financial meltdown, for a few months at least (in fact it helped significantly more than that, as current club owner Darragh MacAnthony invested in the club a few months after watching the programme). Meanwhile the likes of Leicester, Northampton and Coventry have all suffered financial difficulty of varying seriousness since the turn of the century.

But in 2016 the region experienced a once-in-a-generation event: Leicester City became the champions of England. Suddenly tourists were visiting the city, broadsheet journalists were visiting the city, American television was visiting the city. The club who had signed Trevor Benjamin for around £1 million in 2000 were now preparing to make more than that in a day in the Champions League. For a brief, confusing moment, Leicester and the surrounding area was the centre of the world.

More than embodying some kind of listlessly roaming journeyman, the Trevor Benjamin circle seemed to represent a perfect distillation of Midlands and East Anglian football. What understanding of the human condition could be gained from travelling between those five points in a single day? Has anyone even done it? Barry Fry in a mid-range saloon, perhaps. Perhaps not. Imagine the psychological power you can gain from making a unique expedition in a country where millions of journeys are made every day. Salvation through movement. Hope via the Northampton ring road.

It had taken Trevor a decade to move between them but I wanted to do it in one day. I wanted to experience the journeyman's journey and to connect in some way with the landscape of an overlooked part of the country. Even as someone who had grown up near by, I had visited some of these places only a handful of times, almost exclusively for reasons connected with football. Planning a route between them became a labour of love, for there is little better than looking at a map of England and searching for underused and disregarded lanes. There are thousands of minor roads in the country where you might see only a handful of cars all day. You just have to look for them and they'll kindly transport you to a world wholly different to the pessimistic country portrayed so often in the media. In the 19th century the invention of the bicycle allowed the sort of people who couldn't afford horses to explore their localities and beyond. That sense of exploration and discovery is still there, if you want it.

In an ideal world the route research would have been done on Ordnance Survey maps, that fine example of British functional design. Just unfolding one opens a world of possibilities; hidden tracks, green lanes, archaeological sites, reservoirs, streams, contour lines and football grounds. In 2017, though, it's easier (and cheaper) to do it online. Cambridge, Peterborough, Leicester, Coventry, Northampton; they are the waypoints. The rest is down to the gentle bends and turns of the central belt.

I begin, like Trevor, at Cambridge United's Abbey Stadium, on a humid Saturday at the end of May. A football ground when there is no football on is a wonderful thing. It feels like you're witnessing a sacred place of worship by yourself, with time to think. Memories of previous visits and goals flood back, the flood metaphors helped by the presence of a car-washing service set up in the stadium car park. It's eight o'clock in the morning and already 20 degrees but there's a storm coming. The roiling clouds in the south indicate that the future could be turbulent. Isn't it always?

Trevor Benjamin's reputation was built in Cambridge and slowly disassembled elsewhere. In the mid to late 1990s, he scored almost 50 goals in just under 150 games for United, a team who had almost reached the newly formed Premier League in 1992, merrily utilising the weaponised Reepball of John Beck. Benjamin played the majority of his Cambridge minutes under the gentler regime of Roy McFarland but the agricultural Beck would have enjoyed making the most of the striker's rustic talents.

I set out towards Peterborough on a smooth path that runs alongside the utilitarian route of the Cambridgeshire Guided Busway, proud owner of the coveted title 'the world's longest guided busway'. A £181 million converted train track for buses that hurtle along trenches in straight lines, possibly an oblique tribute to John Beck, it is flat, almost unbending and initially nourishing, before the realisation dawns that flat straight paths are the enemy of enjoyable cycling. Like Trevor, I'm heading away from Cambridge at the start of a long journey, confident of a better future.

Moving west towards Huntingdon before turning north to Peterborough, I can see the storm in the south massing like a cheap grey pillow. The linear roads here traverse the flat Fenlands like an abandoned game of Kerplunk and the strong tailwind is appreciated, but with a sense of foreboding that every cyclist knows. What pushes you forwards will also, inevitably, shove you back twice as hard. Concentrating on progressing north and outmanoeuvring the rain, I note that every village near by seems to have the word Ramsey in it, possibly an omen for the FA Cup final to be played between Arsenal and Chelsea later this day (spoiler: it is, he scores the winning goal. Good work, predictive Fenland village system). The road to Whittlesey is about five miles long, dead straight and punctuated by sweeping farms and gigantic UKIP flags that slap about in the strengthening wind. Large gobs of water are dropping occasionally but it's not really raining. It's just grey, colder and definitely not Cambridge.

Trevor's time at Peterborough came towards the end of his time in the Football League, with the highlight being a goal against David Moyes's Everton in the League Cup in 2006, but, as was so often the case, his time as a permanent employee at one club was spent in the service of others, going out on loan to the likes of Watford, Swindon, Boston and Walsall. By the summer of 2007, less than a year after his goal against Everton, Trevor moved to Hereford; his league career was drawing to an end.

I also know my time in Peterborough, like a pedalling Steve Bleasdale, will be brief but that's OK; I've been here plenty enough. Unlike the Abbey Stadium, there's no sign of life at London Road. Lovers of roofs with good acoustics will know that Peterborough's away end is one of the better ones, but today all you can hear is traffic noise and that wind.

Moving away from the ground and heading west into Leicestershire, the sun returns and morale soars accordingly. Be it a 15-year football career or a long bike ride, there are highs and lows, moments of euphoria and moments when you wonder why you ever chose to head down this path.

I'm joined by my cousin for the section between Peterborough and Leicester, just as the terrain turns from flat marshland to the rolling terroir of pork pies. Without wishing to sound like Jamie Vardy's estate agent, rural Leicestershire is a bucolic wonder. Reservoirs, woods, enormous viaducts, sandstone churches poking out of sleepy villages and empty roads, miles of empty roads. It's unlikely that Trevor Benjamin travelled from Cambridge to Leicester via these lanes but I'm certain he'd have arrived in fine spirits had he done so.

The Foxes signed Benjamin for £1.5 million in 2000 and he remained there for four and a half years, one of the select band of Leicester men who played for the club as they moved from ramshackle Filbert Street to the imposing confines of the (then) Walkers Stadium, a period in which the club also topped the Premier League, briefly, lost to Wycombe at home in the FA Cup quarter-finals, got relegated and came back up, all in the space of a few seasons. They also went into administration, with Benjamin, among others, taking a pay cut. He scored in his fourth Premier League appearance, away at Middlesbrough, but that would prove to be Benjamin's only goal in 36 top-flight games. Peter Taylor's gamble to turn the Cambridge man into a Premiership-quality striker didn't work, but Benjamin's commitment was always appreciated by the Leicester supporters.

I roll into Leicester behind my cousin, who helpfully takes me into the city on a route past the house Claudio Ranieri used to live in. It is smaller than you'd imagine a house containing a Premier League title-winning manager would be, and the fact it's clearly empty and currently for sale feels melancholic. Within 10 minutes we have reached Ranieri's arena of choice, the King Power Stadium, a giant modernist bowl in the centre of town. Signs on the outside of the ground read 'Premier League Champions 2015–16'; not quite as dated as the 'Best Kept Village 1994' sign I'd seen in Elton a couple of hours earlier, but both the deposed league champions and the residents of Elton will have to move on soon. Fortunately for the long-distance stadium cyclist, the site of Filbert Street is within 200 yards of the new stadium. Here, though, the gloom really kicks in. The row of terraced houses you could see on television broadcasts of Leicester home games is there, looking exactly the same, but there is a giant football ground-sized space in front of it, derelict ground strewn with detritus and an empty car park. The turf on which Dennis Bergkamp scored that goal is gone. The turf on which Roy Essandoh briefly jumped is gone. The turf on which 6,092 league goals were scored. Gone. I loop past it and turn south-west towards Coventry. I'm gone.

Trevor Benjamin's spell at Coventry was as brief as one of his loan spells, but it was a permanent deal, sealed less than a month after he had signed for Northampton, also permanently. The world was beginning to understand that the word permanent did not really apply to Trevor. Between February and the end of the 2004–05 season, Benjamin scored one goal in 12 appearances, the Sky Blues' opener in a 3–2 win at Watford, a vital result given that the club avoided relegation from the Championship by just two points. Coventry were impressed enough with Benjamin to offer him a longer-term deal in the summer of 2005 but instead he took up the generous offer of three years at Peterborough, theoretically at least.

Whump. The moment you realise the wind, which you've largely benefited from for most of the day, is now directly in your face. The silent enemy, the gusty foe. England has basked in unseasonal heat all week but this wind has the hallmarks of an early spring strength-sapper; 20mph gusts on the straight road to Coventry. It's now about five o'clock and, whether it's because the cup final is going to start in 30 minutes, or just because sullen impatience is now a hard-wired national characteristic, it's suddenly not very pleasant at all. The winding lanes of Rutland are long gone; this is a traffic-dense wind hell and, after five or so miles, I make the decision Trevor did in early July 2005: I give up on Coventry. Suspiciously quickly, I justify my decision in various ways: Highfield Road is long gone; Coventry have suffered more than possibly any club in the region this century; Trevor was there for only 12 games; I have been going for nearly 10 hours; I still have to get to Oxfordshire via Northampton into this wind; this road is horrible. The human brain can justify anything. I turn south-east, still almost 40 miles from Northampton but I feel like I've scored a winning goal in the 96th minute. Small victories. Marginal gains.

Trevor Benjamin's spell at Northampton in the winter of 2005 started with a 19-day loan period and was followed by a 28-day permanent spell at Sixfields. Two goals in five appearances represented one of his better goals-per-game ratios, but he was soon off to Coventry, a return to the Championship from the depths of League Two proving just too tempting. In his final appearance for the Cobblers he was sent off at Bury for elbowing Colin Woodthorpe. It was another example of the rapid waxing and waning Benjamin could experience in a single season (or even a month). The previous season he had gone from scoring in League Two games for Brighton to playing in Leicester's final Premier League game of the season, away at Highbury, in the match that completed Arsenal's unbeaten campaign.

I'm certainly not unbeaten as I make infernal progress towards Northampton. I'm not on the planned route now so on-the-fly GPS decisions take me further into unknown rural territory. Places with names that seem familiar but probably aren't, like Long Buckby and East Haddon and Althorp and Nobottle (I've got two, mate), tick past as my wind-hampered legs keep churning on. At one point I'm directed through a field and I silently obey (because a six-mile detour is just not happening) and I bounce past sheep and then a field of cows. I think they are all cows, although one has the air of a bull. It can't be a bull, can it? Do farmers now have gender-neutral fields? Could that be a thing? I curse never watching John Craven's *Countryfile*. If it was a bull then it was a placid bull (I think it was a cow). Back on Tarmac, I see the first signpost with Northampton on it, albeit with a large number 11 alongside. The wind . . . seems to have died down a little. The sun . . . is out. I feel . . . OK.

Trevor Benjamin's final season in the Football League was 2007–08, when he played a semi-key role in Hereford's promotion from League Two and reached double figures for league goals for the first time since 1999–2000, his final campaign with Cambridge before joining Leicester. The bulk of his goals for Hereford came in the first half of the season and he was used as a substitute only from January onwards, which, in retrospect, was the highlighter pen on the writing on the wall.

I don't give Hereford a moment's thought as I weave my

way south through Northampton towards the Sixfields lei-
sure complex. Modern football stadiums, situated outside
towns, with their Frankie & Benny's, their Vue cinemas, their
endless car parks. Did Northampton start it all? It's hard to be
sure but it feels like it. Even so, their ground, complete with
its incomplete stand, does at least sit in a bowl, so I get a good
view of it as I hop up the kerb and roll to a stop on the grass.
It feels like the end of the journey, but I still have 30 miles to
go and about 90 minutes of sunlight left. I exit Northampton
via its endless roundabouts and settle into a wearisome final
leg. Low on food and water, and too spent to find somewhere
that's open in a village on a Saturday evening, I continue
south, that wind still blowing, weaving past Silverstone and
finally into lanes I recognise. It's the week before Whitsun but
I pass a couple of wedding reception marquees in kempt fields,
the sound of laughter, shouting and men urinating into
hedges. The sun is almost below the horizon now, another
Saturday on Earth ticked off. A day, a life, a career, a memory.
As I turn on my front light for the final few miles I think about
the Trevor Benjamin circle for the final time and decide that
really we are all journeymen, you just need to make sure you
know where you're headed and how you're going to get there.

Period	**Benjamin** 1995–2008	**Alexander** 27 May 2017
Permanent league clubs	6	4
Distance travelled	n/a	274.2km
Active time	13 years	10h 38m
League goals (all clubs)	80	n/a
Average speed	n/a	26.3 km/h

as detailed above an evil wind put paid to reaching what remains of Highfield Road (ie nothing but memories) and Benjamin's spell at Hereford cannot be part of the circle for geographical/shape reasons. Not this time, anyway.

Acknowledgements

I absolutely loved writing this book. I'm acutely aware that the phrase 'Premier League history' annoys a lot of people, but that neat 25-year spell covers most of the period I have been entranced by the game, so to go back and sift through each campaign individually was a joy. A lot of people helped, though, so some gratitude is due. First, thanks to all at Penguin/ Random House/Century/Arrow for their help, particularly editor Huw Armstrong, who was supportive, constructive and deeply wise throughout the long process of writing this book. Thanks also to Fergus Edmondson and Becky McCarthy for their marketing and publicity efforts respectively.

Thanks to all my colleagues at Perform for their help. I'm particularly grateful to Simon Denyer, Andrew Cox and Stefano Faccendini for their encouragement, to Richard Bartlam and Richard Ewing for their encouragement and their support during the long process of writing this book. Thanks to Rob Bateman for great advice, as always, and some lovely Arsenal pointers and filling in all those assists from the 1990s. Big hugs to the peerless Opta Data Editorial team for ideas, research and cross-checking, especially Matt Furniss, Tom Ede, Jack Supple, Jonny Cooper Chris Mayer, Arash Rezai and Alan Duffy.

Thank you to the Perform data scientists Johannes Harkins, Tom Worville and Sam Gregory, who not only answer my inane questions ('can you go through the database and check which goalkeeper has taken the most throw-ins?') but who are working hard at the same time to improve under-standing of the game for clubs and fans alike. Thanks to old master Simon Farrant and nu-master Peter Deeley for their marketing support and expertise.

I'm grateful to OptaPro's Ben Mackriell for answering questions about the professional club space candidly, while I owe Ryan Keaney a thank you for last year. Better late than never. Thanks to early Opta era icon Paul Fowling for checks on the season reviews and for advising me to remove that bit he did.

I am also indebted to Andrew Beesley and Graeme Riley for a couple of pieces of obscure Liverpool history I needed for that chapter, and recommend Simon Hughes's *Men In White Suits*, his excellent series of interviews with 1990s Liverpool players and managers, which was useful when trying to recall the atmosphere at the club throughout that decade of decline.

Finally, thanks to my family and friends, especially to Matt Alexander for guiding me through Leicestershire, and to Zoe, Arthur and Edie for giving me a squad number in their formi-dable team.